The Garden of Allah

sheilah graham

crown publishers, inc., new york

For Mr. Benchley and his friends

I thank all The Garden of Allah people quoted in this book.
Also my daughter, Wendy Westbrook Fairey,
who helped enormously with the research.

Second Printing Before Publication

Manufactured in the United States of America
Published simultaneously in Canada by
General Publishing Company Limited

contents

a note on this book

When I was asked to write a book about The Garden of Allah, I wondered where I should start. At the beginning, when Alla Nazimova, an exotic dark-haired Russian actress, bought a Spanish mansion on a lot between Hollywood and Beverly Hills? Or when she transformed her home into a bungalow hotel under the delusion it would give her financial security for the rest of her life? Or should I start my account of the legendary Garden in the time that I knew it intimately in the decade between 1935 and 1946?

I could start with Robert Benchley, the genial patron saint of the Garden. Or with Scott Fitzgerald, who lived there during his last attempt to write for the screen. Or with Marc Connelly, or Dorothy Parker, or John O'Hara. But they are not the heroes or antiheroes of this book. Our star is The Garden of Allah. The famed celebrities who lived there are the supporting players although very important to the story.

The main house and the twenty-five bungalows arranged around the pool, and the pool itself were a world within the world of Hollywood. It was an oasis for the talented residents who found sanctuary from the frustration of their work in the studios.

The Garden with its lush landscape and fascinating people was a dream that was sometimes a nightmare. It was a miniature city without walls, but only the initiated could gain entrance. It was a microcosm of its immediate world, a reflection of Hollywood. And what was Hollywood but a city built on a gossamer foundation of fantasy?

This comfortable retreat from reality was a convenient home for the distinguished transients who came and went over the decades, who suffered humiliation and frustration for "a handful of silver." When they could not stomach the indignities, they went back east to forget the guilt and be normal for a while, until they needed money again. The Garden took them back with no questions asked. In this book we

11

will come and go with them in the thirty-two-year life-span of the
Garden, and because of this, I ask the reader's indulgence for some
breaks in the chronology.

When Benchley died in the winter of 1945, part of the Garden
died with him. It was never quite the same. It was as though some of
the blood had drained into the earth. The uninhibited behavior, the
childish pranks, the drinking became self-conscious and halfhearted.
The gaiety was gone, and perhaps this was the start of the downward
spiral into the shabby dreariness of the last years.

In any case, The Garden of Allah was doomed. It could not exist
without the covering blanket of prosperity in the Hollywood studios.
The emergence of television in the very late forties started the decay
that led almost to the disappearance of feature-film production in the
major studios. To compete with the small screen in the living room,
millions of dollars were spent on unwieldy epics; bigger and bigger
screens were invented. Until the banks called a halt. Now Hollywood is
more a city for television than for making films for the film theatres.
There is no time or money for the multimillion-dollar movie, or for a
lighthearted, unrealistic place like The Garden of Allah.

The serious young filmgoers of today, so many of them untidy
and long haired, demand a harsher reality in the films they line up to
see. For a new generation raised on McLuhanism, there is no place for
the manufactured glamor that was Hollywood's raison d'être. There is
no place for a Garden of Allah that, for one brief moment, was
Camelot.

It was inevitable that Hollywood as we knew it, and its satellite,
Alla's garden, should disappear together.

Sheilah Graham

the garden of allah

HOW IT BEGAN

IN THE BEGINNING THERE WAS ALLA. Then came Rudy and Pola. Gloria and Bart. Pavlova. W. C. Fields. The Barrymores. Dempsey and Dietrich. The Marx Brothers. Maugham. Wilder and Bromfield. Scott Fitzgerald. Donald Ogden Stewart. John O'Hara. Dashiell and Lillian. Marc Connelly. The Laughtons. Errol Flynn. Dorothy Gish and Louis Calhern. George Kaufman. Woollcott. John Carradine. S. J. Perelman. Bogie and Baby. A whole platoon of the British. The French. The Germans. The Musicians. The Pimps and the Prostitutes. And, finally, the big bulldozers that razed it into the ground. Now there is black hardtop and a savings-and-loan company where the playground and the prison known as The Garden of Allah housed the famous and infamous for thirty-two years.

It began as a home for Alla Nazimova, a Russian actress who had come to New York with the Orleneff Troupe in 1905. She arrived in Hollywood thirteen years later and paid fifty thousand dollars for a ninety-nine-year lease on a big Spanish house at 8150 Sunset Boulevard, with three and a half acres of tropical plants, ferns, fruit trees—orange, grapefruit, loquat, bamboo—and the banana trees that never bore fruit—bizarre birds, and two tall cedars guarding the entrance.

Nazimova was born on June 4, 1876, at Yalta in the Crimea. According to one report, she was discovered by one of the Shuberts, who caught her performance at a Jewish theatre on Fourteenth Street in New York City. Sometimes the credit is given to Charles Frohman,

13

the famed impresario of the early part of the century. Neither is true. Henry Miller (the producer, not the author) signed her in May 1906 to act in English although she understood only half a dozen words.

"Her appearance as Hedda"—as reported in the December 1906 issue of *Theatre Arts*—"under the management of Henry Miller, was a triumph." Her performance was described as "highly emotional." She was a "feline, pantherlike Hedda." As for her English, "Her enunciation is good, and her accent, though marked, does not detract from the favorable impression."

She had learned to speak English in three months. Her teacher was the mother of Richard Barthelmess, a small boy then, who hid under the table listening with great amusement to the lessons. Richard was to follow his mother's pupil to Hollywood, where he became famous as a silent-film star. I will always remember him as the quiet, kind Chinese who tried to save Lillian Gish from her cruel stepfather, Donald Crisp, in *Broken Blossoms*. Later he appeared with Alla and Valentino in *Camille*.

Nazimova was an admirer of Ibsen, whose name for a long time she pronounced Isben. But if her first producer was amused by her accent, he was amazed when he saw her for the first time offstage. The brunet actress had a clearly defined moustache. "You must do something about it," he told her. Alla stretched to the full height of her small slender frame and replied through an interpreter, "In Europe a moustache is considered very attractive." "Not in America," he said, and insisted she shave it off.

Most of the people who knew her in the early days are sure that she was married to Charles Bryant, a tall, good-looking English actor who had appeared with her in a play. Paul Ivano, a film cameraman who is still working at his craft in Hollywood, knew Nazimova when she first came to Hollywood early in 1918. "Everyone assumed they were married," he told me, "but with Alla preferring her women friends, of which she had a great many, and Bryant being a cold Englishman, I doubt whether they even had an affair, and I am convinced they were not married.

"It was rather awkward when Bryant married someone else in 1925," recollected Ivano. Hollywood already had a reputation as a godless, depraved city, and the press was hopefully believing the worst. "Aren't you committing bigamy?" the reporters asked Bryant. "They had to pretend they had been divorced."

Ivano designed the underwater lights of Alla's pool to enable him to take photographs under water. It has been written that the pool was shaped like the Black Sea to remind Nazimova of her faraway home. "It was more like an elongated figure 8," Ivano told me, although in the photographs it looks more like the Black Sea. There is another story that the pool was designed by Alla's astrologer to conform to her horoscope. When it was finished, and before the cement was dry, she carved her initials, A.N., on the right side, just below the watermark.

Nazimova was always ready to help the people she liked. She built the photographer a dark room at the far side of the pool. When she financed her film production of *Salome,* she gave Bryant credit as director, when in fact she directed the film herself. *Salome* failed, and Nazimova lost her entire investment.

Her first film, *War Brides,* was made in 1916 for MGM in New York. She was brought to Hollywood by the father of the late David Selznick. Nazimova was among the highest-paid actresses in the early twenties. The most highly paid of all was Mary Pickford, whose deal with Adolph Zukor gave her one million four hundred thousand dollars a year in salary, plus 50 percent of the profits from her films. The expensive fringe benefits included a ten-thousand-dollar weekly drawing account for her and her mother, who was vice-president of the company, and a three-hundred-thousand-dollar bonus on signing the contract.

When Nazimova worked, she was paid fourteen thousand dollars a week. But fearing that producers were exploiting her, she went into filmmaking on her own and lost most of what she had earned. Money was a cheap commodity in Hollywood in those rich early days. It was easy to earn, and Nazimova found it delightful to spend.

In 1918, Hollywood had not long been known by that name. Orange groves and vineyards were located on the hills opposite what was to become The Garden of Allah. The site had originally been the first post office in the area. By 1923 the population of Hollywood had increased from thirty thousand to one hundred fifty thousand. Today it is about two hundred fifty thousand. The streets were named earlier, between 1880 and 1900. In the latter year the new boulevards included Sunset, Hollywood, Santa Monica, and Melrose.

When Nazimova moved into her home, half of the property was considered to be in the city of Los Angeles, the other half in the county. Taxes were based in part on the value of the furnishings and

were cheaper in the county. When it came time to pay her taxes, Alla
moved her piano into the county and paid the lower tax, her only
economical gesture in the great years of her fame.

In 1936, a city ordinance put The Garden of Allah into the new
district of West Hollywood. West Hollywood extended from the west
side of Doheny Drive to Hyperion Avenue. The Culver City Chamber
of Commerce, where MGM is located, had wanted to use the profitable
name of Hollywood. But Hollywood proper protested, and each area
was now clearly defined.

But when Nazimova came to Hollywood in 1918, the home she

The front view of The Garden of Allah on Sunset Boulevard. *Wide World Photos*

bought was at the end of the line. The trolly cars from Los Angeles stopped where Schwab's Pharmacy was to be built in 1932. The Stage Coach for the tourists still continued up Laurel Canyon on the opposite side of the street.

It was a time of great activity, money, and overnight fame. The Mack Sennett Girls had been the pin-up beauties for the GIs of World War I. The most famous were Gloria Swanson, Marie Prevost, and Phillis Haver. There was also a pretty Sennett Girl, Madeleine Hurlock, who, according to the *Photoplay* issue of February 1927 was the first guest to register at The Garden of Allah. (Madeleine later married

Marc Connelly, then Robert Sherwood.) "Alla Nazimova's beautiful estate, the one far out on Sunset Boulevard, has been converted into a residential hotel of twenty-five separate villas, and Madeleine Hurlock is the first picture celebrity to occupy a unit. Rooms over the great garage of The Garden of Allah, as it is now called, have been transformed into a studio where Nazimova lives. At the moment, however, Madame is making vaudeville appearances."

When Nazimova arrived in Hollywood, Mary Pickford and Charles Chaplin were the top film stars. "Fatty" Arbuckle was riding the crest before the tragedy of Virginia Rappe ruined his career. Theda Bara was the Big Vamp, William S. Hart was the top Western star, and Norma Talmadge and Clara Kimball Young were becoming famous.

After World War I, propaganda pictures were very popular. Douglas Fairbanks and Mary Pickford starred in *War Relief,* with Julian Eltinge, the female impersonator, although what he was doing in a propaganda picture I cannot imagine. *Honorary Colonel,* another war picture, starred Mary Pickford. Other films made that year included *To Hell with the Kaiser, Fit to Fight, Lafayette We Come,* and Marie Dressler as a seaman in a wartime comedy.

The winsome sisters Lillian and Dorothy Gish starred in *Hearts of the World* with a very young Englishman, Noel Coward. Pearl White risked her life each week, tied to a railroad track or dangling over a cliff, to be continued next week. Tom Mix, earning ten thousand dollars a week, fifty-two weeks a year, starred in *Western Blood.* William Farnum appeared in *Les Misérables,* Will Rogers in *Laughing Bill Hyde.* Theda Bara was *Salome,* preceding Nazimova's version by seven years. Caruso, the great Italian singer, was at Famous Players Lasky that later became Paramount. Tallulah Bankhead, a pretty, shy, Southern belle, was the ingenue with Tom Mix in *Thirty a Week.* Constance Talmadge joined her sister Norma in the starring ranks. And Rudolph Valentino was a young leading man, appearing in a bit of froth titled *All Night.*

Hollywood in the early twenties, with Alla installed as a popular hostess in her mansion, was bursting with the excitement and vitality that made it a household word throughout the world. Nazimova starred in the film version of *A Doll's House,* silently mouthing the words of her favorite author. Mae Murray hurtled to fame in *Fascination.* Jackie Coogan starred in the first film of *Oliver Twist.*

Chaplin, cock of the walk, made *The Pilgrim* for First National.

The Garden of Allah Hotel in Hollywood 1928. The back view. *United Press International*

Douglas Fairbanks was Robin Hood. Mary Pickford swung her golden curls in *Tess of the Storm Country*. And Dorothy Gish, who was to live at The Garden of Allah in the forties with Louis Calhern, was again teamed with her sister Lillian in *Orphans of the Storm*. Can you hear the violins? In 1923, Pola Negri starred in her first American film, *Bella Donna*. Ronald Colman made his Hollywood debut in *The White Sister*. Nazimova made her first picture for Paramount, *Blood and Sand,* and met the late Joseph P. Kennedy, who was making films in the adjacent studio that later became RKO.

Kennedy was already a rich man in 1926 when he came to Hollywood to make cheap movies for his company, the Film Booking Office of America. The entrenched Hollywood moguls Marcus Loew and Adolph Zukor were suspicious of the cocky banker from Boston, and they had reason to be. During his two and a half years in Hollywood, Kennedy sold an interest in his company to RCA, acquired the Albee and Pathé interests, and almost swallowed up the First National Company, always enriching himself through shrewd stock manipulations.

Kennedy took over the career of Gloria Swanson, then the most glamorous star in Hollywood. Their film, *The Trespasser,* was enormously successful. He seemed to have come to grief earlier with *Queen Kelly,* which cost $800,000, a huge sum at that time. It was never released in this country. But the wily Bostonian had merely loaned the money for the film to Miss Swanson's "Gloria Productions." She was forced to repay him from the earnings of her subsequent films. "Friendship" was one thing, business another. When he left Hollywood, the father of the future President of the United States was richer by 5 million dollars.

The play *The Garden of Allah* had nothing to do with Alla's Garden but was based on the 1904 Robert Hichens novel. Starring the late Godfrey Tearle and the late Madge Titheridge, it played at the Drury Lane Theatre in London 1919–1920.

In the twenties, Rex Ingram directed *The Garden of Allah* (also based on the Hichens novel) in Africa, with Alice Terry and Ivan Petrovich. In 1936, Marlene Dietrich starred in David Selznick's remake of the film with Charles Boyer and Tilly Losch, the entrancing dancer from Vienna who had been a huge success for Max Reinhardt in *The Miracle*.

Nazimova's house was described in *Motion Picture Magazine* of March 1922 as "a square ocherous villa, which is discovered on the

Gloria Swanson was a frequent visitor to The Garden of Allah while making *The Trespasser* in 1929.
Springer/Bettmann Archive

road to Beverly Hills." In an earlier issue of the same magazine, the owner of the villa is sitting in an ornate garden chair in front of "the large house with exquisite gardens and sweeping lawns." Another paragraph refers to "Nazimova and Charles Bryant's beautiful home in the Hollywood Hills." Actually it was at the foot of the hills.

The starlets of the day were invited to swim in the pool, big even by Hollywood standards. Darryl Zanuck frequently appeared at the end of the afternoon to pick up Virginia Fox, who is still his wife although they have been separated for many years.

When Alla's garden and home were transformed into a bungalow hotel, the *h* was added to her name, to give an aura of the Arabian Nights. Nazimova protested the *h* to the day she died. She felt just as strongly against those who pronounced her name Nazeemova. Otherwise, in spite of her misfortunes, she was a happy person.

Frances Marion, the famed scenarist of the early and middle Hollywood days, remembers her last glimpse of Nazimova at the Garden in 1926. Frances lived at the Colonial House on the next street, with her husband, Fred Thompson, a famous film cowboy—she wrote his films.

"Nazimova was walking around her garden, pausing to look at her beloved cedars and vowing, 'Nobody, but nobody would ever dare cut down these lovely trees.'" They did, of course.

The house—dark and ornately Spanish, as they all were in those days—had a very large living room. Two huge antlers rose from the center of the floor in the hall and visitors had to be careful or they might be impaled on them.

A few years later, when Nazimova was in New York playing Olan in *The Good Earth,* after she had lost her house and garden, she told a magazine interviewer, "I had a beautiful home in Hollywood. For a long time I had dreamed of how happy I should be when I could have all the things that I wanted around me. One morning I was awakened by my maid saying the houses on the hill opposite were burning, and the fire would soon reach my house. I realized I must save whatever I wanted most. I went into my bedroom and looked around. I thought, there is nothing I want in this room. I went to the library. No, I said to myself, I cannot take all my books. I went from room to room and found nothing I could not do without, nothing I felt I had to save. I wandered back into my bedroom. There were some snapshots on the bed. I took them in my pocketbook and left. I had gone down the street only a block when the maid came running to me and said they had controlled the fire and it had not reached my house. I went back, but I did not like my house any more. I had discovered that when it came down to the last test, there was nothing there that really mattered to me today. Today I have not so many things and I am happier."

Rudolph Valentino was introduced to Nazimova by Paul Ivano, who told me, "We rode to her home on horseback on the dirt road from Paramount." Suspicious people at the time believed the dark-haired Russian and the great Latin lover were having an affair, but, according to Mr. Ivano, this was not true.

Valentino was made famous by Rex Ingram, the director, and June Mathis, the scenarist. A Mrs. Cudahy of the meat-packing family of Chicago had given him a Spanish edition of *The Four Horsemen of the Apocalypse* when he was an unsuccessful actor living in New York. Valentino learned that Metro was to make a film of the book. He hoped to get a dancing job in it and called at the MGM office in New York. He was greeted by an executive who demanded, "Where have you been? Rex and June want you to star in *The Four Horsemen* [made in 1921]." He recovered sufficiently from his surprise and excitement to sign a contract for $350 a week, the equivalent of $1500 today. Later, also in 1921, when he played Armand to Nazimova's Camille, she raised him to $450 a week.

Realizing he was to be successful, Valentino built his dream house, "Falcon's Lair," in the Hollywood Hills. All the walls were painted black, and the windows were draped in black.

Nazimova was distraught when Valentino fell in love with her set designer, whose real name was Winifred Shaughnessy. (Jean Acker, Valentino's first wife, was one of the first to live at The Garden of Allah.) Winifred had rechristened herself Natacha Rambova. She lived up to her new name, floating around in veils, satins, turbans, fancy earrings, and scarves.

Nazimova had introduced her to Valentino, never imagining that he would fall madly in love with her—the Sheik and the exotic Rambova. The impact was like a thunderbolt, and everyone could see that The Great Lover had fallen.

The difference in Hollywood coverage then and today is that Adela Rogers St. John, who had an exclusive on the story, broke the news of the engagement one month later in *Photoplay*. Today, with hundreds of reporters stationed in Hollywood, the story would be wired instantly all over the world.

Nazimova attempted to prevent the marriage, and invited Rudy to her home on Sunset Boulevard after work in the studio. They were both still in their *Camille* costumes. "She was older than he," Adela remembers, "but she spoke to him as a woman of the world, not as a mother. She warned him that Natacha would be fatal for him. 'She is eaten up by ambition,' Alla insisted. 'She will never really care about anything but herself and her own career. She will use you, your success, and your name. She will want to control you and direct everything you do. Oh, my dear Rudy, please, while there is still time, leave all this, go away. It simply will not work. No girl I know could be worse for you.' He was polite, courteous, but the impassioned words made no impression on him. Nazimova was right. Everything she had warned him against came true. Rudy and his career were destroyed, and his friends believed that the nervous reactions after the quarrels, the separations and, finally, the divorce from Natacha caused the agonizing stomach disorders that killed him."

But even in death he was to be disturbed. Natacha claimed she was in communication with his spirit.

Nazimova, a popular personality, drew the visiting celebrities to her home. Especially the Europeans. Chaliapin, the famed Russian singer, came to Los Angeles for three seasons, 1923, 1924, and 1925. After his performances, he invariably went to Alla's house to eat two big steaks, drink half a bottle of vodka, and tell dirty stories until morning. When Pavlova was dancing in Los Angeles with Fokine and Massine, they came to Alla's for supper after the show with Mary Pickford and Douglas Fairbanks, who made a screen test of Pavlova in 1924. Another guest in the same year was Madame Eleanora Duse.

Nazimova was accosted by Pola Negri at Marion Davies's lavish, fancy dress party in Beverly Hills in April 1926. Pola was dressed in the white-and-gold uniform of an officer of the Guards for Catherine the Great of Russia. Valentino was resplendent in his toreador costume from *Blood and Sand*. According to Paul Ivano, who was there, after some impatient polite conversation, Pola said to Nazimova, "I want to meet your friend Valentino."

Rudy knew the Garden when it was the home of his mentor,
Alla Nazimova. *Wide World Photos*

"They were introduced and left the party separately after midnight. Rudy went home, changed into ordinary clothes, drove his Isotta-Fraschini to Miss Negri's house, knocked on the door, entered without a word to the servant, and went upstairs." In Miss Negri's autobiography she states that the fiery mating did not take place until a few months later.

Valentino died on August 23, 1926, and Pola wept and wailed dramatically that they were to have been married, and we must take the lady's word for it. There was no autopsy in spite of the suddenness of his death. Valentino's family was in Italy, and apparently there was no one in the United States who cared enough to demand one.

Mary Pickford and Douglas Fairbanks invited Nazimova to join United Artists, the company they formed in 1921 with Chaplin and D. W. Griffith. It was the most powerful combine in the history of motion pictures. The original partners died or retired long ago, but the company still functions and is still very successful.

The partnership with Nazimova was brief. Alla believed that an executive of United Artists at that time wanted a cut of her *Salome* film. She refused his demands, and later accused him of underselling the picture. Charles Ray, the boyish silent-film star, also believed the same executive cheated him with two of his films, *The Courtship of Miles Standish* and *The Girl I Love*.

Because of these worries, Nazimova believed her manager, Mrs. Adams, was right when she advised her, "Turn your estate into a hotel and it will give you security for the rest of your life."

A company was formed and given a lease on the property. To build twenty-five villas around the pool would cost $1.5 million. A mortgage of $200,000 was arranged. Over what had been the handball court, an apartment was included for Nazimova's use in her lifetime. She left thankfully for New York to appear in a play with Eva Le Gallienne.

The Garden of Allah opened on January 9, 1927, with an eighteen-hour party, with troubadours playing madrigals from the middle of the pool, followed by a lush and stately dinner. Among the guests were Jack Dempsey, who had come to Hollywood in 1919 to make the *Fight and Win* series, his wife, Estelle Taylor, who was making a serial for Universal (they were divorced in 1931), Clara Bow, Gilbert Roland, Vilma Banky, Rod La Roque, Sam Goldwyn, John Barrymore, H. B. Warner,

Conrad Veidt, Edmund Lowe, Lillian Tashman, Marlene Dietrich, Marta Egert, Betty Blythe, and Frances X. Bushman. The latter pair attended the final party of The Garden of Allah before the demolition men moved in late in August 1959.

In the thirty-two-year span of its life, the Garden would witness robbery, murder, drunkenness, despair, divorce, marriage, orgies, pranks, fights, suicides, frustration, and hope. Yet intellectuals and celebrities from all over the world were to find it a convenient haven and a fascinating home.

the early settlers

AT THE END OF 1927, LESS THAN A year after its glamorous opening, The Garden of Allah faced bankruptcy. The mortgage payments had not been paid. The prices charged for a villa—two to four hundred dollars a month—were not enough to pay for the upkeep and make a profit. At first, celebrities preferred the older Beverly Hills Hotel, which had a dozen attractive bungalows. The midtown Ambassador Hotel on Wilshire Boulevard also had bungalows, and Scott Fitzgerald was there with his Zelda in 1927. The Alexandria was another famous hotel where the visiting greats stayed. There was a bar for men only, and on an average day it was patronized by Chaplin, D. W. Griffith, Louis B. Mayer, Douglas Fairbanks, and his brother-in-law, Jack Pickford. The ladies gathered in the lounge reserved for them—Mabel Normand, Mary Pickford, Gloria Swanson, Edna Purviance, and Adela Rogers, daughter of the famous criminal lawyer Earl Rogers.

But The Garden of Allah was the "in" place, Bessie Love told me in London, where she now lives: "With its beautiful pool, it was the place to go. I lived there in the early years." Her neighbors were Edmund Lowe, his wife, Lilyan Tashman, and Jean Acker Valentino. Miss Love had gone to Hollywood in 1915 and starred for Griffith in the twenties. "I began at the top," she assured me. Bessie left Hollywood in 1935 and could not remember much more about The Garden of Allah except "I don't remember going into the big house." Few of the guests did.

Unable to pay the enormous debts, the executives of the newly formed company wrote to Nazimova in New York and asked her to sell the place for the unpaid bills and taxes and she said, "Go ahead."

It was put on the block and bought by the same William H. Hay from whom Nazimova had bought the estate nine years earlier. Mr. Hay founded and owned most of Encino, in the valley, where he had a fabulous home, even by today's standards, with air-conditioning and solar heating.

Nazimova lost every dollar she had put into The Garden of Allah. The Wall Street Crash of 1929 took whatever she had left.

According to one report, Nazimova contracted cancer in 1936 and had one breast removed. In her last years she was ill and didn't do much acting. In 1941 she played Robert Taylor's mother in *Escape*. She was a lady riveter in *Since You Went Away* for David Selznick. But her role was minute, just three scenes, and she was virtually cut out of *Escape*.

Nazimova died in the summer of 1945, the same year that, in November, saw the passing of Robert Benchley, the genial but unhappy patron saint of the Garden.

Benchley had come to Hollywood for the first time in 1926 to be best man at the wedding of Donald Ogden Stewart and Beatrice Ames in Santa Barbara. Marc Connelly was an usher. At a prewedding party at a Santa Monica beach house, Benchley stepped out on the porch in the dark and fell off where a flight of stairs should have been but was not. He had to carry out his duties as best man on crutches. He was also singed when someone lit a fire under his chair at the bachelor's dinner. It was a foretaste of what his life would be in Hollywood. They were all to live at The Garden of Allah, but in 1926, it was still Nazimova's home, and they stayed at the Mark Twain, an inexpensive hotel in Hollywood.

Garbo lived at the Garden in the early days. Guests remember seeing her in the pool. She has always loved swimming, and the pool at the Garden was the biggest in Hollywood. In the early years, it was crowded with famous people from the film world.

Eddie Cantor, a hit in *Kid Boots* and *Whoopee,* stopped by to visit his eastern friends. Gary Cooper was often glimpsed striding through the side entrance from the old parking lot to visit his girl, the Countess Di Frasso, who taught him fancy manners and how to dress. Wally Beery who lived nearby was a frequent visitor. Harold Lloyd drove over from his million-dollar estate in Beverly Hills and Carl Laemmle was living on his sixty acres close by. Carl, Jr., often came to the pool to swim and to watch the starlets dipping and diving for attention. H. B. Warner, who was playing Christ for Cecil B. De Mille in *King of Kings,* was a resident. H. B. was ordered to lead a Christlike life. No smoking, no drinking, and no public appearances. He relaxed in the pool after the late working hours of those days.

Joan Crawford attended some of the parties, but she was usually at the Cocoanut Grove at the Ambassador Hotel. Joan was a star to be reckoned with after *Our Dancing Daughters* in 1928. In the same year, Walt Disney made a silent cartoon, *Plane Crazy,* that introduced a new character, Mickey Mouse, who would outlive all the stars except Miss Crawford.

In those early years, Claudette Colbert clattered carefully in high heels down the uneven, narrow, crazy-pavement paths. Ruth Chatterton, fresh from the New York theatre, frequently visited her New York friends who had preceded her to Hollywood.

William Powell and Carole Lombard lived across the way at the Colonial House and swam in the pool at The Garden of Allah. John Gilbert, at the height of his career following *Flesh and the Devil* with Garbo, cavorted with her at the Garden, where someone was always giving a party. Gilbert's romance with Garbo was fast and fairly short-lived, as Louella Parsons, the first of the Hollywood gossip columnists, chronicled in her column for the Hearst newspapers.

Janet Gaynor and Charlie Farrell, enormously popular since *Seventh Heaven* in 1927, enjoyed sitting under a bright umbrella near the pool, Janet sipping a soft drink. Charlie had something stronger.

Some of the dashing movie actors used to meet outside the Garden in their sports cars and big Dusenbergs, and then drive to what they called the Speedway. They raced at the unheard-of pace of eighty miles an hour on the narrow road by the sea, between Santa Monica and Venice.

Ronald Colman, who teamed with Vilma Banky for United Artists and later for Sam Goldwyn, rented one of the new villas, and his British neighbors—among them Clive Brook, Ernest Torrence, and Nigel Bruce —often stopped by for a game of poker. Ronnie's first marriage had been violently unhappy, and he was glad of the privacy afforded by the Garden. It was a good time.

"The atmosphere in Hollywood in the late twenties," Gloria Swanson reminded me, "was the same as it was in the Roaring Twenties of London, New York, and Paris, 1927, 1928, 1929, until the crash brought on the depression in Hollywood as everywhere else. I didn't live at the Garden, but I went there frequently to visit a man whose name I have since forgotten."

Gloria's marriage to the Marquis de la Falaise in the midtwenties, and the subsequent divorce, was more headlined than Elizabeth-Richard-Debbie-Eddie. "All the people—Chaplin, Garbo—who later shut themselves away from everyone," said Gloria, "were on the town. Joan Crawford sent me a fan letter. The Rhythm Boys [Bing Crosby's group] were singing at the Cocoanut Grove, where Paul Whiteman's band was playing. Men knew how to look after a girl. They sent you flowers, and sometimes there was a jewel concealed in a bud. Everyone was rich. Even the taxi drivers were millionaires, on paper. They were dancing the tango. Everything was gracious. We were flappers. We had bobbed hair and short skirts. Mine was the first movie-star home in Beverly Hills. It was on the corner, next to The Beverly Hills Hotel. I bought my house with three acres in 1922. In those days Beverly Hills was the country. I remember when Garbo came to Hollywood. I said, 'There goes a big star.' I was a star at Triangle in 1918 when Nazimova first came to Hollywood. She created a stir with the gatherings at her home on Sunset Boulevard. At this time I had a contract to make five films for C. B. De Mille. Only one of these films for C.B. featured me in a bathtub."

But it is the bathtub scenes by which Miss Swanson is most remembered.

When Ernst Lubitsch came to Hollywood from Germany, he lived at The Garden of Allah. Ramon Novarro, whom he directed in *Old Heidelberg,* was in a neighboring villa. Lubitsch was still at the Garden in 1929 when he was making Jeanette MacDonald and Maurice Chevalier international film stars.

Between marriages, John Barrymore lived at the Garden. Otherwise, until bankruptcy forced him to sell it, he owned a magnificent five-acre estate on Tower Road in Beverly Hills. He referred to the two houses, joined by a Turkish pergola, as "that Chinese tenement." The Barrymore retreat contained three swimming pools, a bowling green, a shooting range, an aviary, an English sundial for which he paid fifteen

Ramon Novarro lived at the Garden in the early days of his career. He is shown here as the star of the silent *Ben-Hur*. *Bettmann Archive*

Lionel, John, and Ethel Barrymore in *Rasputin*. John was forever falling into the pool at The Garden of Allah. *Springer/Bett-
mann Archive*

thousand dollars, and an English tavern room with a bar imported from Alaska.

There was no smog in those days. In fact, there was no smog when I first came to Hollywood to start my column in 1936. In the winter, however, the sun would sometimes be obscured by a gray haze from the smudge pots in the orange groves during the frosty nights.

Gilbert Roland, as trim today as when he courted Clara Bow at the Garden, had previously romanced Norma Talmadge, who chose him for her Armand in *Lady of the Camelias*. She was married to Joe Schenck, but it was obviously not a working marriage although she used Mr. Schenck's important position in Hollywood to impose silence on her lovers. When she spent a night with Edwin Justus Mayer, who lived at The Garden of Allah for most of his writing days in Hollywood, she threatened him in the morning, "If you tell anyone, I'll ruin you. My

Gilbert Roland when he courted Clara Bow at the Garden. *Bettmann Archive*

Clara Bow, an
early resident.
Bettmann Archive

husband is more important than you are." I can still hear Eddie's
amused laugh when he told me the story.

Some of the famed stars of the twenties deserted the pool at the
Garden when William Randolph Hearst built Marion Davies her
"shack" at the beach. Marion's pool was three times as big, with a small
pool for children. The Colonial-style house had forty-five rooms, twenty
baths, covered three lots, and cost Mr. Hearst seven hundred thousand
dollars. "If I tire of it," Marion giggled, "I can always turn it into a
bungalow hotel, as Alla has done." She never had to. Even without Mr.
Hearst's help, she would have been an important star.

When Alexander Korda came to Hollywood with his first wife,
Maria, they stayed at the Garden, which was becoming very popular
with film people from abroad. Elinor Glyn stayed there when she came
to Paramount to supervise the production of *It* with Clara Bow.

The young Cary Grant with the young Sylvia Sidney. Cary was too poor when he came to Hollywood to stay at the Garden, but this is where he courted and won Virginia Cherrill, who became his first wife, and later the Countess of Jersey. *Bettmann Archive*

Cary Grant, who arrived in Hollywood in the very early thirties, was enchanted by the Garden, with its marvelous pool, and he made inquiries about renting one of the villas, but during his early years the price was beyond his reach. When people like Cary couldn't afford the Garden, they usually stayed at the little Warner Pelton Hotel.

Jimmy Gleason, the sour-faced comedian, and his wife moved into the Garden when he expected to land in another film after starring in *Is Zat So*. Jimmy's villa was adjacent to Miss Bow's, a good vantage point to overhear some of the dialogue between Clara and Gilbert Roland. "We were a heavy thing for some time," Gilbert confessed to me recently, adding, "Everyone knew about it, so I am not telling tales."

When Clara left the Garden, she bought a house in Coldwater Canyon in Beverly Hills. Mostly those who had enjoyed life in the bungalows, when they moved, lived in a nearby street or in Beverly Hills, which was still sparsely settled in the late twenties.

Other early residents at the Garden included Buster Keaton and Buster Collier. Where the two Busters were, you would see Constance Talmadge. Connie, the blond new saucy type of film star, had known the Garden when it belonged to Nazimova. Her sister, Norma, took to drugs near the end of her life. She had been desolate over the end of her affair with Gilbert Roland, but being an honest lady, admitted to a friend, "Gilbert was too young for me." She was rather like Paulette Goddard, hiding her jewels for safekeeping. Norma kept her gems in her shoes. Her memory was bad, so the diamonds were secreted in white shoes, the sapphires in blue shoes, the emeralds in green shoes, the rubies in red shoes. Paulette kept hers in a cigar box on the theory that no gentleman would take a cigar without asking her permission first.

Louis Bromfield, the author, always stayed at the Garden when he came to Hollywood. He was one of the early guests in the late twenties, catty-corner from Nita Naldi. She had been a famous vamp, but with the advent of the talkies (and even before), vamps of the exaggerated style of Nita and Theda Bara had gone out of style. Nita had the young feminine lead in Valentino's *Blood and Sand*.

Jon Hall, whose real name was Charles Locher, was also an early resident. He was a fine swimmer, and the pool was the attraction. In the late thirties, he was to star with Dorothy Lamour in *Hurricane* for Sam Goldwyn. In this film, Dorothy wore a sarong for the first time. It became her trademark.

Francis Marion and her husband, Fred Thompson, were at the Garden frequently after it became a hotel. Gilbert Roland remembers that when Fred died, he and Norma Talmadge called on Frances. They expected to find her distraught, but she was consoling herself playing Brahms "Cradle Song" on her organ.

Jed Harris, the most prolific producer on Broadway in the twenties, usually stayed at the Garden when he visited Hollywood. "We had a stud poker game there," he recalled. "Irving Berlin, Joe Schenck, who had rented the Garden from Nazimova in 1926, Darryl Zanuck, and Sid Grauman" of Grauman's Chinese Theatre, which was famous for the big premieres of the top films, then as now.

"Sid had two jacks. Irving showed a queen. Irving raised Sid twenty-five thousand dollars. Sid was horrified. He was overextended. He looked at Irving, stricken. 'How can you do this to me,' he demanded. 'We're playing,' said Berlin stonily. Sid turned to Schenck who said severely, 'I can't interfere.' Sid walked around, muttering strong language. He looked out the window and contemplated the ground below. He turned back into the room and said, 'If I jumped out I'd only break an ankle—okay, I call, show me.' Irving burst out laughing and showed his cards. He had nothing."

Marlene Dietrich, fat and fresh from Germany and *The Blue Angel,* landed in The Garden of Allah. It was recommended to her by her monocle-wearing friend and director, Joseph Von Sternberg. Marlene did not stay long. As soon as she finished *Morocco,* with Gary Cooper, she moved to the more regal atmosphere of Beverly Hills, as Garbo had done.

Garbo had the perspicacity to buy up large tracts of land in Beverly Hills. When the crash came, she sent one million dollars in gold coins to her native Sweden for safekeeping. "Buy land," Mr. Hearst had advised Adela St. John when they drove the two hundred fifty miles to his "three cottages" at San Simeon in Northern California. If only we had all bought land!

Adela knew the Garden very well in Nazimova's day. "I remember going there soon after it became a hotel. A blond movie actress was sitting by the edge of the pool. I stopped to speak to her because she seemed sort of wild. I said, 'You look half awake,' and she replied, 'I haven't got this worked out yet. I'm taking sleeping pills at night to get some rest, and benzedrine in the morning to pep me up, and half the time they work backwards.' "

As I came to know the writers who stayed at the Garden, I realized that many of them took sleeping pills at night and benzedrine in the morning. It worked for some, but not for Robert Benchley, who had the same experience with the pills as the blond leading lady.

Marion Spitzer, the magazine writer, was sent to Hollywood in the early days of the Garden by George Lorimer, editor of the *Saturday Evening Post.* After reading some of Miss St. John's articles, he realized that Hollywood was a gold mine for stories. Marion was impressed by the first purple toilet she had ever seen, when she attended a party at The Garden of Allah. She returned to the Garden again in 1932. I met her there in the late thirties with Eddie Mayer.

The black marble bathtub used originally by Nazimova fascinated eastern visitors. Actress Natalie Schafer always tried to rent the villa in which it was installed. Unless you stayed at the Garden regularly, you were not likely to get the same villa when you came back, although regulars like Benchley and Marc Connelly usually asked and if it was available were given the same one.

Until the war years of the forties, the Garden was never completely full, and how it lasted as long as it did is one of its mysteries.

[III]

the british are coming

THE GARDEN OF ALLAH SYMBOLIZED an era of opulence and waste. The tiled Spanish kitchens were a delight, especially to the British who came in ever-increasing numbers. They loved the sun, the pool, the privacy, the kitchens, and the maid service, even though it was awful, the maids coming in late and whisking around. The colored tiles on the bathroom walls with bright blue painted peacocks were fascinating to the British, who had nothing like it in England or the Commonwealth.

Beatrice Lillie, Lady Peel, went to Hollywood late in 1926 to appear in *Charlot's Revue*. She was a great favorite in the show with Gertrude Lawrence in New York. Gertie became ill in Toronto and could not appear on the road. She was well enough to join her costar in Los Angeles.

"After the revue, Gertie returned to London," Bea reminisced to me, "but I stayed over and rented a bungalow at the Garden. It was a lovely place. Everything was new and shiny and very glamorous. The last time I saw it, in the late forties, it was pretty run-down."

MGM signed Miss Lillie in 1927 to star in *Exit Smiling*. The captions were by Marc Connelly. The film was directed by the late Sam Wood. It was one of the last and one of the best of the silent films. Jack Pickford, the handsome brother of Mary Pickford, costarred with Miss Lillie. It marked the debut for Franklin Pangborn, the comedy actor who always looked so bewildered and outraged. Harry Myers, the large

40

Beatrice Lillie and Doris Lloyd. *Exit Smiling*, 1927. Bea with the moustache. *Springer/Bettmann Archive*

man with the fierce moustache of the early Chaplin pictures, was also in the film.

Buster Keaton, Bea's neighbor at the Garden, had seen the English-Canadian comedienne in *Charlot's Revue,* and had fallen in love with her. He sat outside her door at the Garden all night, night after night. Bea was worried lest he catch cold in the chilly California air and tried to get him to leave and go to bed in his bungalow, but Buster shook his head mournfully and maintained his vigil. She was never quite sure whether he was protecting her from other admirers, or whether he merely found comfort in being so close, although so far from his idol.

Buster Keaton, shown here in a scene from *The General,* was in love with his Garden of Allah neighbor, Beatrice Lillie. *Bettmann Archive*

Chaplin had come to the Los Angeles opening of *Charlot's Revue,* and he and Bea became friends. "In Charlie's autobiography," she told me, "he quoted me saying that when we were in the hills looking at Los Angeles, I couldn't wait until all the light got together to spell Marion Davies." With Mr. Hearst's power, anything was possible. "I met Leslie Howard at the Garden," Bea remembered, "and Roland Young and Ronnie Colman. Even after they had their own homes they came to the Garden. I remember Clive Brook and C. Aubrey Smith, who started the first British cricket team in Hollywood."

Miss Lillie met Garbo at the Garden and was as thrilled as anyone else would have been. "I knew her when she was full of fun and loved to go to parties. Garbo was nothing when she first came to Hollywood. [She only came because Mauritz Stiller, the Swedish director, refused to come without her.] But her first film, *The Torrent,* made her an instant star. She was the first woman I ever saw who wore slacks."

Herbert Wilcox, one of the founders of the British film industry, stayed at the Garden in the late twenties and met Garbo there. "I had heard she was shy, but I found her very outgoing."

During his stay, Herbert made a deal with Howard Hughes to borrow Louis Wolheim who was under contract to Hughes. "I only needed him in my film for two days. I agreed to pay fifteen thousand dollars. But Mickey Neilan, who was directing the film, wouldn't have him. Hughes was adamant. 'You've got him and must pay me fifteen thousand dollars.' That is why," Herbert said wryly, "Howard is a millionaire and I am not."

Mr. Wilcox returned to produce *Black Water.* "It was the fifth talking picture and cost me forty-two thousand pounds. John Loder and Mary Bryant were the stars. When I arrived in England I was met by a bevy of reporters who asked me, 'Do you think talkies are here to stay?' 'They'd better be,' I replied, patting the can I was carrying, 'or I'm broke.' " He had made the film in five days.

Herbert remembers a party in Ramon Novarro's bungalow. Novarro was to die tragically forty years later, beaten to death in his North Hollywood home. During Novarro's days at the Garden, he starred in *One Heavenly Night* with the British musical-comedy star Evelyn Laye, who came to Hollywood in 1929, a year before Frank Lawton (of *Young Woodley* fame), who was also living at the Garden.

Frank played the older Copperfield in David Selznick's production for MGM, with Freddie Bartholomew as the young David and W. C.

Fields as an unforgettable Mr. Micawber. For six years Lawton had been asking Miss Laye, a beautiful blonde with a gorgeous voice, to marry him. When they spent the weekend at the La Quinta home of Herbert Marshall, Frank popped the question again, and perhaps because of the seductiveness of the desert, or whatever, Evelyn said yes.

"Frankie almost fainted," she told me during her run in London last year in *Phil the Fluter.* "When he recovered he said, 'How about tomorrow?' We eloped to Yuma, in Arizona, with Herbert Marshall as best man and Gloria Swanson matron of honor, then we all came back to La Quinta and had a brief honeymoon because I was still in the picture with Ramon. It was so sad about him. He was a gentle person. We were friends right up to his terrible death." Mr. Lawton died last year after a long siege of cancer.

Laurence Olivier came to Hollywood in the early thirties and rented a bungalow at the Garden for what he hoped would be a three-month stay. MGM had brought him from London to star with Greta Garbo in *Queen Christina.* He made the test, but Garbo refused to see it. After the first rehearsal, she insisted on having John Gilbert. She was no longer in love with him, but she wanted to help the man ruined by talkies because his voice was too high. As her lover in the film she expected the role to bring him back to public favor. It did not.

Olivier and his wife, Jill Esmond, returned to England completely discouraged. He would soon meet Vivien Leigh when they made *Fire over England.* It started the fire that led to their respective divorces and their subsequent marriage at the height of the publicity for *Gone With the Wind.* Tallulah Bankhead claimed I lost her the role of Scarlett O'Hara because I stated in my column that she was too old for Scarlett, which she was. She was younger when she first stayed at The Garden of Allah.

Bill O'Bryan, a top agent and manager, was living at the Garden with his wife, a green-eyed English actress, Elizabeth Allen. One morning at about five, Bill was awakened by an unearthly din. He got out of bed and hastened to the window. The scene was straight from a Hollywood movie. A group of people in full evening dress had obviously had one hell of a party, and two of them, Tallulah and Johnny Weissmuller, proceeded to dive off the top board, fully clad, into the pool. Tallulah was weighted down with a heavily beaded dress and diamonds, and she dropped to the bottom like a stone. Having an instinct for survival, she shed her clothes and jewels while weaving at the bot-

Queen Christina, with Garbo and John Gilbert. Garbo refused Laurence Olivier to give Gilbert a chance for a comeback.

Springer/Bettmann Archive

Tallulah preferred to run naked around the pool at The Garden of Allah. *Springer/Bettmann Archive*

tom of the Black Sea, emerging completely naked. "Everyone's been dying to see my body," she croaked. "Now they can see it." Johnny, an Olympic swimmer, took to the hills after dragging his intoxicated companion—who could not swim—out of the pool, where she lay panting. A Filipino gardener, coming on early duty, tried to snatch a hose from her neck—she was wearing it like a snake—whereupon she chased him around the garden, intending, no doubt, to murder him if she caught him. Dredging operations to recover Miss Bankhead's jewelry took some time, while Tallulah removed the Gar from the big sign on the outside wall, leaving it The   den of Allah.

Prohibition had yet to be repealed, and wild private drinking parties were the order of the day. In the 1928 issue of *Photoplay,* a picture of Dick Barthelmess with a decanter of wine in the background was considered pretty racy. John Barrymore usually had his valet following him with a portable bar that looked like a big hatbox.

Margaret Sullavan, fresh from a finishing school in Virginia and summer theatres on the Cape, came to Hollywood in the early thirties. Before her marriage to Willie Wyler and after their divorce, she lived at The Garden of Allah. It was here that she was courted by Leland Hayward. During their marriage she lived in a lovely house high up in Beverly Hills.

Marriage, divorce. Lillian Hellman and Arthur Kober stayed at the Garden in 1931 and decided to terminate their marriage. Lillian was a sexy dish in those days. Ginger Rogers, who lived there with her mother, remembers Lillian lounging around the pool in what was then considered a skimpy swim suit, ready and eager for conversation. "Anything," Lillian confessed, "to delay the work."

Robert Hichens, who had written *The Garden of Allah,* came to Hollywood during the war. His agent told the management, "We must have the biggest and the best bungalow for Mr. Hichens." "Who is Mr. Hichens?" he was asked. "He wrote *The Garden of Allah,"* was the reply. "I don't care if he wrote the Bible, we don't have a villa. Only a room in the main house." The manager shuddered, and took his client elsewhere.

No one who was anyone ever stayed in the main house that had been Nazimova's original home. You rarely saw people in the small bar to the left as you entered. Only the O'Bryans and Frances and Albert Hackett seem to have enjoyed eating in the gloomy dining room. The food was pretty bad, but Frances has assured me that the steaks were good. I ate there once with Scott Fitzgerald, and we had a watery soup. He had been drinking and was not up to chewing meat.

Heather Thatcher, a well-known English actress, came to Hollywood in 1932 to spend a holiday with the P. G. Wodehouses and their daughter. Ivor Novello, then working in Hollywood, suggested her to Metro to costar with their promising new actor, Robert Montgomery. The suggestive title of the film, *But the Flesh Is Weak,* embarrassed the English star, who received more publicity than she might have if she had not worn a monocle. English male toffs were supposed to wear them, but not a blond Englishwoman.

"They kept postponing the film," Miss Thatcher recollected. "I had a good career in England, and I hadn't really come to work. I decided to spend a week in New York with friends, then return to London."

Heather booked her passage and gave a cocktail party in New York the night before she was due to sail. The telephone rang. "It was a charming man from Metro's New York office who told me they were now ready to start the film, and would I go back immediately. When I told my guests that I was returning to Hollywood they were astounded. The Wodehouses had left Hollywood, and this was when I stayed at The Garden of Allah. Edmund Goulding, who was directing the picture, had recommended it to me."

Heather had her English maid with her, ". . . so we never had to eat in the restaurant. I liked the place very much and told my friends about it when I returned home. Sir Phillip Sassoon went there when I described the bungalows and the swimming pool. I went back and stayed there again in 1938 when I made some films. But when I returned there in the forties it wasn't the same, rather too noisy, and I stayed with friends at the beach."

During one of her visits, Heather rented a two-bedroom bungalow at the Garden, on a corner, near Benchley. She went to visit Ronald Colman at his ranch near Santa Barbara. "Miriam Hopkins," she told me, "was using my other bedroom the night she had to get up at six in the morning to attend the Rose Parade. She had a bath and went to bed. At about one o'clock in the morning she heard someone flicking the heating buttons on and off. Miriam opened the door and was confronted by a naked man. She screamed, 'What are you doing here, get out!' He ran out holding on to his penis." A minute later he rushed into Heather's bedroom, flopped into her bed, and went to sleep. Miriam called the management who, as usual, took a long time coming. Miriam was shouting, "You disgusting man, I want an apology! Arrest him someone!" Heather told me he was the son of a banker in Chicago. He telephoned Miriam the next day and apologized. He had urinated in Heather's bed, and she was outraged when the maid put a sheet over the wet.

While Herbert Wilcox was at the Garden, he discussed the filming of *Madame Pompadour* with Dorothy Gish, who was living there. He gave a party for Dorothy, with whom he was in love, as so many men were, and among the Garden inhabitants he invited were Dame May Whitty, D. W. Griffith, Ernst Lubitsch, and the New York stage actress, Hope Williams. Also invited were Frances Marion and Lillian Gish, who did not live there. Herbert remembers Frances asking Dorothy, "What do you think of The Garden of Allah?" and her reply, "It's a lie!"

Mr. Griffith liked the Garden "because the beds are soft." Sometimes they were too soft—as I found them when I stayed there with my infant daughter in 1942. Everyone agrees that the furniture and the service at the Garden were always atrocious. Most of the parties were prepared by the guests themselves.

"When Mickey Neilan gave a party there," Herbert recalls, "he didn't have caviar in a pot, he had great big basins—five hundred pounds, it seemed to me." Small wonder that Neilan, the most famous of the silent-film directors before Griffith, ended up playing an extra in the talkies. A man with a sharp eye visiting a set asked, "Isn't that Mickey in the crowd scene?" "We have a dozen former directors in the crowd," he was told.

These were the days before the business manager. They spent what they earned, believing it would go on forever. Some were smart and managed their money well, like Mary Pickford, Garbo, and Corinne Griffith. Corinne shrewdly bought up several of the business corners in Beverly Hills. She now has a beautiful home around the corner from one of her investments.

With the advent of sound, Hollywood—and the Garden—was flooded with writers for the actors and actresses who could talk. Except for a few people like Frances Marion, Donald Ogden Stewart, and Marc Connelly, most of the dialogue for the silent stars was written by the secretaries or the assistants to the directors. The actors had to be careful not to swear, although sometimes they did, and the audience could lip-read, but chiefly it didn't matter what they said as long as they seemed to be speaking what the story called for. But now the words could be heard, and New York and London were combed for established authors who came to Hollywood because of the high prices paid.

There was talk that George Bernard Shaw was prepared to sign on the dotted line, but this proved false. However, in England he worked on scenarios of his plays.

David Selznick brought Thomas Wolfe to Hollywood in 1935 to write a screen version of *Look Homeward, Angel*. During the first story conference, Selznick suggested some changes from the book. The big lumbering author regarded the producer coldly. "Mr. Selznick," he said, "you are offering me more money than I have ever received in my life. But this book is my baby, and I'm damned if I'll change a single word." He left the room, returned home, and never came back to Hollywood.

H. G. Wells was reported to be coming to write a picture for Paramount. If he did, there is no record of his work. He was in Hollywood in 1936 staying with Chaplin when I arrived. I had read some of his books and knew of his reputation, and I thought I should interview him. "Don't bother," a well-meaning friend told me. "Writers in Hollywood don't count." This was the attitude writers had to overcome during the next two decades.

Somerset Maugham came, saw, and was not conquered. Soon after his arrival, he was interviewed by our intrepid reporter Adela. (I'm glad I was never in competition with Mrs. St. John except during the Hauptman kidnapping of the Lindbergh baby in Flemington, New Jersey, in 1934. It was my first reporting assignment, and it was frightening enough to be competing with Dorothy Kilgallen.)

Mr. Maugham was interviewed by Adela at The Garden of Allah where he was staying for the duration of his assignment at Paramount. She knew about Mr. Maugham and was terrified of meeting him. She felt easier when, stuttering, he complained, "It's all very well. They send for me in order to get something new into films, to get them out of a rut. But every time I get my foot out of the rut, they shoot it off."

When Ronald Colman made *Raffles* for Sam Goldwyn in 1930, he had already left the Garden for a home in Beverly Hills. I was present at the 1935–1936 New Year's Eve party at the Sam Goldwyn house where Ronnie met Benita Hume. Jock Whitney was a guest and he wanted to take Benita home, but she left with Ronnie. It was a wise choice because she became Mrs. Colman, whereas Jock would never have married an actress.

Nineteen thirty was a good year for the actors. John Barrymore had not yet become the sodden drunk of his later years, although he was still falling into the Garden pool. He starred that year in *Moby Dick* and gave a fine performance chasing the big white whale. Gregory Peck did the remake many years later with less success.

Gable, who could not afford the Garden when he first came to Hollywood, was on his way up in 1931, with second billing to Garbo in *Susan Lennox*. Garbo, who had spoken for the first time on the screen in *Anna Christie,* burst into tears at the sound of her own voice.

Clark met Florence Desmond, an English actress, at a party at Joan Crawford's house. Florence was in Hollywood to appear in *Mr. Skitch* with Will Rogers and Zasu Pitts. Florence enthused, "Oh, Mr. Gable, you are so popular in England. The British are mad about you."

Clark Gable, here with Greta Garbo in *Susan Lennox,* was
snubbed by an English actress at the Garden. *Bettmann Archive*

He was modestly surprised, but pleased when she begged for his photograph. The next day, Miss Desmond had a call from the front desk at The Garden of Allah, where she was living. "Mr. Gable is here," she was told. Whatever for, she wondered. "Put him on," she said. "I've brought the photograph," he told her. She was not dressed or made up as she had been the night before. "Don't bother to come to my villa," she said. "Leave it at the desk." She met him again in England during the war when he was a captain in the United States Air Force. She was now Mrs. Charles Hughesdon. "Do you remember me?" she asked the famous actor. "Do I?" he replied. "You're the first gal who ever asked me to leave my photograph at the desk." It was the first and last time he had ever delivered a photograph in person.

Virginia Cherrill, whom I met in England during the war, was also at the Garden in the early thirties. Cary Grant was a constant visitor. He swam while waiting for Virginia to get ready. An angry divorce terminated their marriage. When I met her in England in the summer of 1941, she was the wife of the Earl of Jersey, and was living at Hampton Court.

Blond, girlish Ginger Rogers was always in tennis dress at the Garden. There was a court at the Ronda Apartments on the side street where Johnny Farrow lived when Maureen O'Sullivan was at the Garden. She was brought to Hollywood by MGM in 1931 to play Jane to Johnny Weissmuller's Tarzan. Mr. Farrow had a snake tattooed on the upper part of the inside of his left thigh. He posed for long periods at the end of the Garden's diving board wearing short swimming trunks, and the snake appeared to be emerging from his reproductive organs. Later he married Maureen. I attended the reception at the home of Loretta Young's mother in Brentwood, which was then becoming a fashionable area as Hollywood burst its seams in the direction of the Pacific Ocean.

Before the marriage, and while the mother of Mia Farrow was still living at The Garden of Allah, an actress who had made a name for herself on the British stage came to stay at the Garden. She called Maureen late one afternoon and said, "I'm sorry to ask you so late. But I'm giving a big party tonight. Joan Crawford and Clark Gable are coming, and I wasn't sure there would be room for you and Johnny. But you're my neighbor, and I suddenly felt awful that I had not invited you." Maureen said she understood and accepted the belated invitation.

Ginger Rogers. Take away the feathers and you would find her *Sitting Pretty* at The Garden of Allah. *Bettmann Archive*

"I arrived early with Johnny. There were thousands of hors d'oeuvres and dozens of bottles of liquor with hundreds of glasses. And nobody came, except Eddie Goulding and us, and all the press and all the photographers. We stayed for hours because we were sorry for her. It was so ghastly and embarrassing. The press had a marvelous time, eating and drinking and not having to work."

Maureen was still at the Garden when the Charles Laughtons arrived. Charles and Elsa lived there so long that when they finally decided to have a home of their own, they bought a house a few blocks away.

Johnny Farrow, writer and director, and the snake tattooed on his leg were star attractions on the diving board at the Garden, where his fiancée Maureen O'Sullivan lived. *Associated Press*

Charles came to Hollywood with his heralded reputation as Henry VIII in the Korda production. In 1933 he starred in *If I Had a Million*, and in 1934, *The Barretts of Wimpole Street*. The latter was written for Charles by Donald Ogden Stewart. Donald became the most highly paid screenwriter, with the exception of Ben Hecht, who received a thousand dollars a day in cash.

The Laughtons lived at the Garden when he was playing Captain Bligh in *Mutiny on the Bounty*. Miss O'Sullivan walked into their living room one afternoon to find Charles and Elsa trying all kinds of makeup on a plaster bust of him in the center of the room. They worked with tremendous concentration, and Maureen left without their being aware that she had been there.

The Laughtons came and went back to England, but until they bought their own house, they always returned to the Garden when they

Hunchback of Notre Dame with Charles Laughton and Maureen O'Hara. It was a hot summer and Charles swam in the Garden Pool wearing his hump. *Springer/ Bettmann Archive*

were in Hollywood. There was a prolonged heat wave in September of 1939 when Charles was making *The Hunchback of Notre Dame*—136 degrees on the set, ". . . and 110 degrees at home," Elsa remembers. "Charles came back to the Garden for his midday meal. We cooked all the English dishes that Charles loved—steak-and-kidney pudding, and Yorkshire pudding. He'd come in with this great hunchback on and he was hot enough to explode. He was forbidden to go into the pool as it would spoil the hunch, and his makeup took hours to apply." To get cool, Charles rolled over into the water and hung on to Elsa's ankles, floating in a half sleep with his putty nose up to the sky. It was a long hot summer. "At night the mattresses were burning hot." The scorching heat lasted for two weeks, and all night long the pool was full of residents, among them Tyrone Power, Forrest Tucker, and John Loder, and even Benchley and Butterworth, trying to cool off.

"Once," said Elsa, "we had the bungalow with the black tiles and the black bathtub, the original Nazimova tub. We thought it was hideous then, but today it would be interesting."

I told Elsa I had heard that her cat had drowned in the pool, causing a swimmers' boycott. She denied this with vehemence. "I had a cat who liked to swim in the pool. He would jump in after flies. The cat died, but on land."

Some of Elsa's clothes were designed for her by Madame Edward Mensior, who had a home adjacent to the Garden, at 1428 Havenhurst Drive. Her sons had a punching bag in her garage, and Charles often lumbered over to punch it. He enjoyed the exercise and hoped it would reduce his weight.

Franchot Tone was a constant visitor at the Garden to see the Laughtons. "When he was leaving Joan Crawford, Franchot came for dinner. He said he would call us the next day to play golf. He never called, and we didn't see him again until they both made *Advise and Consent* in Washington many years later. Franchot had cancer and knew he was dying." Charles also had cancer and knew he was dying.

Hugh Williams, the British actor and playwright who died suddenly last year, lived at the Garden from November 1933 until early 1935. Twentieth Century-Fox had signed him to a contract. He made five fi'ms in one year. "Three of them were listed among the worst ten films of 1934," he told me when I had cocktails with him last year at The Bath Club in London. He was still very handsome and distinguished, tall and straight and graying. He looked like a military man. He had five children and seven grandchildren, he told me with pride. He collaborated with his wife Margaret on the plays in which they usually acted. They had a home on the coast of Portugal. He was the picture of a happy, healthy man.

One of his Hollywood films was *All Men Are Enemies,* he recalled. Another was with Lillian Harvey, an English girl who had become well known as an actress in Germany in the early thirties. He played Steerforth in the early MGM production of *David Copperfield.* And in *The Life of Eleanor Merton* with Claire Trevor and Gilbert Roland in 1933 at Fox, Hugh was the villain.

"In my time at the Garden," said Hugh, "I saw a great deal of Charles and Elsa. And Robert Donat, who was fighting the studio tooth and nail about the picture he was making, *The Count of Monte Cristo.* Pat Patterson [later Mrs. Charles Boyer] was there, and I remember playing Ping-Pong with Ginger Rogers. Oh, yes," he laughed, "and Johnny Farrow's snake."

Frank Lawton and Hugh gave a stag poker party one night. "Bart Marshall, Bill Powell, and Ronnie Colman came. We had a weekly Saturday-night game at one of our homes and this was my turn. Gloria Swanson was Bart's girl and heard of it, and she and Liz Allen dressed up as men and came. We let them stay."

When Hugh came to Hollywood, the publicity people at Fox had arranged for Miss Allen, Florence Desmond, and Heather Angel to meet Hugh at the station. Heather did not live at the Garden but the other two girls did. "Liz had a party for me at the Garden," Hugh told me, "and it went on and on. It got very late and she rang up the manager and asked if they could give me a bungalow for the night. I stayed fifteen months." He remembers his villa, Number 10. "I never ate in the dining room, and no one ever had a drink in the bar. I had considerable difficulty giving my breakfast orders over the phone because they loved my accent and wouldn't listen to what I said."

Later Hugh shared a bungalow with another English actor, George Barraud. It was next door to Margaret Sullavan. George was a good actor and a brilliant pastel artist—he did a lovely poster of Fay Compton as Barrie's Mary Rose, which has been frequently reproduced.

Robert Benchley and the Bill O'Bryans were guests at a noisy party one night. Hugh believed that Miss Sullavan did not like him, and with reason. A few nights before, he had set himself on fire by attempting to sleep with a lit cigarette in his mouth. The fire had singed Margaret's walls and she had been terrified. He was worried what she would think of the din, and he sent her a note asking if she would care to join them. Her reply was shouted through the thin walls, and it is not printable here.

When Fox "flung me out," as Hugh put it, someone from the studio called him and said, "We have two thousand six hundred photographs of you in our 'still' department. Would you like to buy them?" Hugh's reply is almost as unprintable as Miss Sullavan's. He returned in 1938 for Sam Goldwyn's *Wuthering Heights,* with Laurence Olivier and Merle Oberon. He was the drunken brother, Hindley.

"I didn't stay at the Garden this time, but with the Ian Hunters at the beach. Do you remember the big flood in '38?" I remember it well. I was with the Ogden Nashes in Benchley's bungalow when Scott Fitzgerald came in very excited and told us, "There are bodies floating down the river under the Warner Brothers bridge and Jack Warner's body is leading them." Then he exploded into laughter.

When the late playwright, critic, and columnist Ward Morehouse married the play producer Jean Dalrymple in New York in 1932, he was in the midst of an assignment to script a film in Hollywood. They decided to go there for their honeymoon. He had been renting a villa at the Garden, and they arrived to find the pool full of mounds of rice and flowers.

"I love to cook," said Jean, who is famous for her culinary feats and her cookbooks, "and was delighted with the gorgeous kitchen in our bungalow. 'Let's not go out,' I begged Ward, who loved the bright places of Hollywood and the invitations we received from John Gilbert and other stars. 'Let me cook for you in this lovely kitchen in this darling bungalow.' " He grudgingly assented. Jean disappeared into the kitchen and soon a beautiful meal was ready for her husband. When she brought it to him in the little alcove that served as a dining area, he was weeping. She thought he was ill and asked solicitously, "What is the matter?"

"Here we are in the most glamorous place in the world," he sobbed, "and you're in the kitchen and we're eating at home. We might as well be any suburban couple in the Bronx!"

Within a month they moved to a two bedroom bungalow, and Natalie Schafer, who was at the Garden, thought it was the shortest honeymoon on record. Jean explained, "He liked to work at six or seven in the morning. I preferred a little more sleep and then to play golf with John Gilbert. Two bedrooms solved our problems."

The Morehouses found a friend at the Garden in Roland Petit, the French choreographer husband of Jeanmaire. He stayed there, he told them, because his idol, Rudolph Valentino, had stayed there. But he was mistaken. Rudy died five months before The Garden of Allah opened. Perhaps he meant that Valentino visited there frequently in the days of Nazimova.

When I telephoned Arthur Kober at Easthampton, Long Island, where he was staying last summer, he could not remember staying at the Garden, although he lived there in 1931 with Lillian Hellman while she was still Mrs. Kober. He had also lived there earlier when he was writing for Fox and Paramount, and later in 1937 during Scott Fitzgerald's time.

"Don't bother to come out and see me," he said when I called. "It was a long time ago. And in any case, so many people who stayed there are dead, including The Garden of Allah." To Kober in 1969, the whole experience was obviously very remote.

But I will not forget him at the Garden. It was soon after I had met Fitzgerald and I was still going out occasionally with other men. I had a dinner date with Arthur, and Scott was jealous. To reassure him, I asked him to call me at home at 11:00 promising, "This is going to be an early evening." Arthur, who can be interminably long in saying good-bye, continued talking to me after I got out of the car at my home. It was after eleven and I could hear the phone ringing. I called Scott at the Garden as soon as I was inside. But there was no answer. He was drinking, I learned later. It was his first drink in the three months I had known him. Yes, I remember Mr. Kober at the Garden very well.

I asked Miss Hellman, who always seems worried, what had she written in the few months she was living with Arthur at the Garden before they decided on the divorce. "I was just a wife," she replied. Then recollecting, "I used to swim a lot."

While Lillian and Kober were at the Garden, the Harpo Marxes lived there. Also Lila Lee, the first Mrs. Charles Chaplin. "I left Hollywood at the end of 1931," Lillian told me, "and I never lived there again, although I went back from time to time to work on the scripts of my plays"—*These Three, The Children's Hour, The Little Foxes, Watch on the Rhine,* etc. Her last Hollywood assignment was *The Chase,* which starred, disastrously, Marlon Brando. "I never liked Hollywood, and I don't like the look of Los Angeles."

Alexander Woollcott, who lived at the Garden in the winter, delighted in word games that were so intricate and intellectual that no one except Harpo could understand them. Perhaps this was when Robert Benchley acquired his hatred of all the games that were played at the Garden. George Kaufman—who came to Hollywood to write *Coco-anuts* and *Animal Crackers* for the Marx Brothers—and Marc Connelly were avid players. Woollcott refused to write for films. He had better things to do, such as visiting Laura Hope Crews when she worked with Garbo in *Camille.* He had come to Hollywood in the winter of 1936 especially to see Miss Crews because he was told they looked alike. He wanted to see for himself. Oscar Levant, who lived nearby,

was Harpo's closest friend. One evening they sent what Oscar describes as "a covey of prostitutes" to Alec Woollcott's villa. The eminent neuter failed to see the joke. He told Oscar wearily, "I had every form of sex by the time I was seven."

Zeppo Marx and his wife Marian lived at the Garden for a while. Later they bought a big house close by. Groucho was also a resident, but when I called him to chat about the place, he was watching Dick Cavett on television and was rather short. "In any case," he told me, "I didn't mix with that lot. I didn't fraternize. I was a family man."

Poor Groucho. His last "family man" marriage cost him one million dollars in the settlement.

From *Monkey Business*. All
the Marx Brothers lived at the
Garden in the early 1930s.
Springer/Bettmann Archive

In the early thirties, Sam, the father of the Marx Brothers, lived at
the Garden with Harpo and his wife Susan. Later he died there.

S. J. Perelman was at the Garden at the time of the Marxes. He had
come from New York to write *Monkey Business* for them. In a recent
piece in the *New Yorker* he mentioned that he was writing a vehicle at
Paramount for a quartet of buffoons. Their identity was not important,
but for those who insisted on a clue, "the ringleader wore a large
painted moustache and affected a cigar, and his three henchmen im-
personated respectively a mute harpist afflicted with satyriasis, a lar-
cenous Italian, and a jaunty young coxcomb who carried the love interest." He had often been their guest, and he and his wife invited them

to dinner at their Garden bungalow. Only a Perelman can describe the occasion, which was a disaster, ending with the Perelman schnauzer chewing up Mrs. Groucho's hat to the last feather and falling asleep on her mink coat.

A wife of one of the Marx Brothers was called from the Garden at four in the morning by an actress who had been a statuesque silent-film star and was then working infrequently in the talkies. "I'm dying," she moaned. "You've got to come over, I'm dying."

Mrs. Marx hastened over. She was far from dead, but her bed, her gown, and her body were covered with blood. The sadist, who is now dead—the father of a famous current young film actress—had made little cuts all over her with razor blades. Cutting soft flesh was his particular hang-up. There was lechery at the Garden, but nothing as cruel as this. The same man was always pretending to commit suicide. They would take bets at the Garden on whether he would surprise himself one day and succeed. He died of natural causes two decades later.

They were still talking of the big earthquake of March 10, 1933, when I arrived in Hollywood almost three years later. The damage had been enormous, and the terror was real.

Ward Morehouse was in his cottage at the Garden sleeping off the night before when the earthquake struck. Liz Allen was making a picture at MGM. Her husband, Bill O'Bryan, was strolling on a street in Hollywood. Ward was knocked clear out of bed. He telephoned his wife, Jean, in New York and told her, "Everything was shaking and I was knocked all over the place. I thought the roof was going to fall any minute. All the pots of geraniums on the top floor smashed to the ground." Ward was an extremely neat man, and he told his wife, "I'm getting out of here. The place is a shambles." "Don't," she replied, "you're getting one thousand dollars a week and we need it." He was working on *It Happened in Manhattan,* but he took off for that then safe city.

Willard Keefe, a young actor, was having a drink with Charlie Butterworth. "There was a sort of rippling movement of the floor, and a dousing of lights. Presently there were cries of panic outside, and guests charged out of their homes and made quite a crowd. When the danger had passed, all the guests joined in one big party. It was not a relaxed party. It was an excuse to find comfort in a crowd." Those present included Louis Calhern, Benchley, Eddie Mayer, and Ginger Rogers' mother. Ginger was at a studio working.

The way Liz Allen remembers the earthquake. "The scenery on the set fell all over us, and I was shoved under a table. The lights went out and the big doors wouldn't open. You can imagine how panicky everyone was. They finally got the doors open and told us to go home. I found Bill placidly reading a book. 'Didn't you feel the earthquake?' I shouted at him. 'Oh, it was an earthquake?' he said, maddeningly calm."

Bill had been walking back to the Garden. "I thought it was a little strange that so many people seemed to be running out of their houses. I climbed up to our first-story apartment and opened the window and noticed that the pool was lapping backwards and forwards and overlapping." "It was like the Atlantic in midstorm," Liz interrupted. There were small tremors for the next two months. "It was rather uncanny," said Bill, "to be lying in bed and awakened by a rolling motion, and turning on the lights to notice those lovely [sic] framed Garden of Allah treasures moving from one side of the wall to the other."

Frances Marion in her home across the street thought it was King Kong on the roof. Mrs. Basil Rathbone fell out of bed and accused her husband of pushing her. Everyone had a story about the earthquake when I first went to Hollywood.

There was only one earthquake while I was there—the big one at Tehachapi in the fifties. It was evening and I was writing in my office when I felt the floor swaying. The ceiling candelabra was swinging crazily. I called the operator and asked, "Is there an earthquake?" "I'm sorry," she said crisply, "I cannot give any information." The plaster of my home in Beverly Hills was cracked in many places, although the earthquake was eighty miles away. It was an awful feeling to have the earth move under your feet. You felt helpless and frightened.

In the early thirties, Anita Louise, blond and beautiful, was a conversation piece at the Garden. She used to swim in full makeup, with every hair on her head in place. She swam sideways so as not to ruin her makeup or hair. The residents watched to see if she would or would not wet her face or hair. No one saw Anita except when she emerged for her dip. But they could hear her in her villa, twanging away on her harp.

Maureen O'Hara stayed at the Garden with her mother when Charles Laughton brought them from Ireland, Maureen to be his leading lady in *The Hunchback of Notre Dame*. When the reporters met the boat in New York, Charles was asked, "What are you doing with a beautiful girl like that?" His answer was rather sheepish, but he was worried and called Elsa at their hotel to say everything was all right, no matter what she might read.

It was thought at the Garden that Miss O'Hara's mother was looking for a rich husband for her daughter. Maureen has had three, and not one was rich, although for many years she had a Mexican friend who draped her in jewels and houses that, according to Maureen, he wanted back when the affair had run its course. Mrs. Laughton describes Maureen at the Garden "sewing tiny stitches. She looked as though butter wouldn't melt in her mouth—or anywhere else."

Ruth Gordon was an early resident. Her husband, Garson Kanin, stayed there in the mid- and late fifties. Mrs. Patrick Campbell, with long black hair, could be heard reciting loudly, "The birch trees are moving in the wind."

"Pat Campbell," Elsa remembers, "was a trio at the Garden with Zoë Akins and Charlotte Greenwood."

Flora Robson, the fine English actress, also stayed there, and she and Elsa took a trip together to Mexico when Charles was involved in a film. It was dull for the woman when her husband was working, although Elsa had a good career of her own, mostly in revues at the little theatres around town.

The pool and the sun of the Garden were a godsend for the wives, and when Albert Basserman came to Hollywood in the midthirties to escape the anti-Semitism of Hitler's Germany, he stayed there with his wife. It seemed like the Garden of Eden to them. While Albert worked in the film studios, Mrs. Basserman and her sister wandered around the pool with vine leaves in their hair, reciting.

The women, who were along in years, were modest swimmers. They were covered in voluminous robes until reaching the edge of the pool. Dropping the robes they revealed skin-tight flesh-colored swim suits. Mrs. Basserman mounted the diving board and always fell off with a resounding belly flop. After each flop, she bravely got up on the diving board again and repeated the performance.

ben the bellboy—and other residents

UNTIL THE VERY LAST YEAR OF ITS existence, The Garden of Allah was a losing proposition. The ownership —from Williams Hays to Cornelius "Sonny" Whitney to Bart Lytton— was always changing hands, especially after the midthirties, the beginning of the golden age at the Garden. But even then it was beginning to lose its pristine freshness. Until the midfifties I doubt whether it had ever been repainted, inside or out. Or the heavy Spanish furniture replaced. There was not enough money in the till. The bar might have been lucrative, but the inmates of the villas preferred to drink privately at home. They sometimes needed more ice to replenish the heavy iceboxes. But usually they bought their own liquor and entertained in their own ugly pseudo-Spanish-style villas.

The main building, with its eight guest rooms that no one rented if he could help it, was very dark. The carpets at the Garden when I first knew it in 1936 had once been ashes of roses color, but were now gray, dark drab rose, soiled green, or worn-out burgundy. The kitchen walls were stained and ranged from a pale apple-green to beige. The double beds sagged in the middle under the heavy mahogany headboards. There were maple-framed mirrors with shoe boxes at the bottom of them. The tables were dark oak with thick spool legs. It was the worst kind of Spanish, with grillwork everywhere.

It was less desirable to live on the parking-lot side of the Garden, which was unpaved, dusty and impossible to use during the heavy rains. The regulars asked for the villas at the back of the pool or on the far side, away from the parking lot. The main house fronting Sunset Boulevard was always deserted and increasingly dusty and raggle taggle. The drab restaurant was the most deserted place in Hollywood. "It was like an old ladies' home," said Elsa Lanchester, recollecting the dark, dreary eating room and the indefinite quality of the food.

But the pool and the sun and the privacy recompensed for the ugliness of the buildings. The narrow uneven paths over which the women were always stumbling had charm. There were the flowers and the exotic trees. And the Ping-Pong table, and by the pool the telephone with what was claimed to be the longest extension cord in the world.

Mrs. Vaughan Thompson—who was eight, nine, and ten when she lived at the Garden with her parents, Arthur Sheekman and Gloria Stuart (he wrote mostly for the Marx Brothers in his early years in Hollywood)—remembers the Garden with affection.

"As you came down the long walk, Louis Calhern's villa was on the right-hand side beyond the pool. The Ping-Pong table was on that side and someone was always playing. You could always hear the sharp click of the balls. The telephone was on the wall near the pool, also the banana trees where I used to play. There were two loquat trees. The shrubbery was wild to the waist. The stucco was also up to your waist. Schwab's, the drug store, was like an extension of the pool. You'd walk across the parking lot to Schwab's. My memories of The Garden of Allah are the only things I have from those lonely years, the smell of a room, of a flower."

Children were not encouraged at the Garden. It was for sophisticated adults. When Walter O'Keefe's two sons stayed with him and raced around the place and played tricks, they were nicknamed Leopold and Loeb. They were ten and twelve respectively. Jackie Gleason was downing bloody marys in a villa when he remarked that he had seen a couple of boys throwing furniture into the pool. "Oh," said Jay C. Flippen, "you mean Leopold and Loeb." The nicknames stuck, much to the annoyance of Mr. O'Keefe.

At this time Perry Como was new on the Hollywood scene and CBS gave a party for him at the studio. As Mrs. Como walked past the Garden pool to the parking lot, the two boys, who were swimming in the pool, drenched her with a hose. It was Leopold and Loeb in action.

Mrs. Marie Weatherwax, wife of the film editor, was a frequent user of the pool. One afternoon she was introduced to Jack Doyle, whom sportswriters referred to as the Irish Thrush and music critics called the Pugilist. Doyle was having a romance at the Garden with a wealthy heiress. He was bragging about his accomplishments and Mrs. Weatherwax said, "You are the most conceited Irishman I have ever met." He laughed and moved towards her with outstretched arms. She ran clear out of the Garden.

The walls at the Garden were extremely thin, and Marc Connelly remembers that very frequently you heard intimate conversations in the next bungalow. "Sometimes they kept you from going to sleep and sometimes they compensated you for not sleeping."

There is the famous story that Robert Benchley was sleeping soundly when a feminine voice said, "Darling, please get me a glass of water." He stumbled into the kitchen, came back with it only to find he was alone. The lady who asked for the water was in the next bungalow. Sometimes the story is attributed to Arthur Kober. But this sort of thing could have happened only to Benchley.

In spite of the lack of beauty indoors and the various outdoor hazards of life at the Garden, the celebrities of literature and the acting world loved the place and would not live anywhere else, if they could help it. They were proud of their address. When Benchley wrote to his family in the East he informed them, "I am, if you can believe it, in a place called The Garden of Allah on Sunset Boulevard."

Thomas Wolfe refused to believe it existed. "I'll be damned," he wrote to Scott Fitzgerald on July 26, 1937, "if I'll believe anyone lives in a place called The Garden of Allah . . ."

The Garden reflected the times. When conditions in Hollywood and the United States were good, things would simmer down at the Garden. When conditions were bad, more inmates would be drunk, more people fell in the pool, more shrill laughter. From 1927 to the Wall Street Crash in 1929, the place was gay, the scene of elegant parties. The high life started up again after the depression. In 1934, things started to zoom.

The golden age of the Garden was between 1935 and 1945. When the war was over, there was an exodus of the illustrious writers, musicians, and stars, accelerated in the late forties by Joe McCarthy and the House Un-American Activities Committee. By the early fifties The Garden of Allah was going downhill. This was also true of the motion picture industry. But it was not apparent in the decade between the midthirties and midforties.

"Nothing—," wrote the elegant food-and-wine connoisseur Lucius Beebe, who was a steady visitor at the Garden during its best years, "nothing interrupted the continual tumult that was life at The Garden of Allah. Now and then the men in white came with a van and took someone away, or bankruptcy or divorce or even a jail claimed a participant in its strictly unstately sarabands. But no one paid any mind."

Beebe's last sentence is the clue to the popularity of The Garden of Allah. No one paid any mind. Your neighbor could be Hemingway making impassioned speeches for the Spanish Loyalists or Scott Fitzgerald on a tear, but no one paid any mind.

Bachelors, or men separated from their wives, could have a girl there, and no one would know or care. They did not have to go through the main house, or even to register until they felt like it. There were many entrances into the Garden—from the parking lot, or from the side paths that paralleled Havenhurst Drive on the right, or from North Crescent Heights on the left from Sunset Boulevard. If you were athletic, you could scramble through the jungle of bushes at the back. You could be as private as you liked by locking your front door; or keep it open and the inmates would drop in. It was a glorified house party if you belonged.

"The Garden of Allah," said Arthur Sheekman, "was one of those places where people were always in transit—even if they lived there for five years."

"There were no house detectives," said Walter O'Keefe. "There was great freedom to come and go without being noticed."

"The place was full of producers, writers, actors," said Bill Spier, who had gone to live there when he went to Hollywood to write and direct the *Suspense* series for radio. "People often sat outside their bungalows, writers on wooden slat chairs, typing. People wouldn't bother them during working hours. It was like an artists' colony."

S. J. Perelman remembers Ward Morehouse diving into the pool in his dress suit—people dressed more often in those days than they do now.

In the daytime, some of the residents sat around the pool and read their papers and chatted. But usually the Garden was quiet during the day. The occupants of the villas were either sleeping off the night before or working in the studios.

When Nat Benchley went to Hollywood to visit his father in 1939, he remarked that there were not many people around the pool. "The first person I ever saw in it was Joe E. Lewis," Nat recalls. "It was the afternoon following his opening at one of the Hollywood nightclubs. He hopped into the water, did an ungainly breast stroke, then announced, 'You see twelve scotch and sodas in the wake behind me.' " Nat probably remembers this because he was an easterner and this sort of exhibitionism had not come into his life before.

The first Mrs. Donald Ogden Stewart remembers the pool vividly— but with dislike. "In the later afternoon every day, it got damp around the pool." [The Hollywood sun is the fastest going down—literally one minute up, the next completely gone.] "It was lonely there during the day. The place only came to life in the late afternoons. As soon as the chill settled in, you would see people. The doors opened, you heard the chink of ice in the glasses and people laughing uproariously."

Benchley, especially, always laughed at what I or anyone said and made us feel very witty, although Bob did not consider himself a wit. "I'm considered funny," he told me once, "because I laugh so heartily at the witticisms of others, including mine, and they are sometimes pretty tired."

The screenwriters staying at the Garden did not swim much, although these paunchy, pale men occasionally strolled to the pool in their swimming trunks to watch the little starlets giggling in and out of the pool. They made audible remarks about the girls, how beautiful and glorious they were. Benchley usually appeared to say something affectionately funny and they would all laugh.

When George Kaufman lived at the Garden he was asked, "Why do you stay here?" It didn't seem the right place for a writer requiring the quiet and tranquillity necessary for his trade. He replied enigmatically, "It reminds me of Hollywood." Not really. It was more a refuge from what was going on outside and in the studios—an escape.

It was the first real communal living in Hollywood—a longing to be a part of a congenial group, which is what the young people of today seem to be seeking and finding.

Artie Shaw lived there at the height of his popularity as a band leader, and during part of his brief marriage to Ava Gardner. "I really miss that place. Now, I have to stay at the Beverly Hills Hotel," he reflected recently. "It was very relaxed there. Not like the formality of the Beverly Hills Hotel or the Beverly Wilshire Hotel. At the Garden it was like having your own home. The bungalows were all around the pool, so there wasn't that mile-long walk down a hotel corridor to

get to it. It was always a little shabby and run-down. You'd expect
the rats to come. No one was polishing the tops of the palm trees. The
Garden was one of the few places that was so absurd that people could
be themselves. Also no producers—the common enemy—hung around
there, just hip actors and good writers. It was a colony of expatriates
in the middle of Hollywood."

Jed Harris thought of the Garden as a place for a man to go to
when he was breaking up with his wife. Charlie Butterworth hastened
there when his marriage with Ethel was over. Errol Flynn was always
there between marriages. Humphrey Bogart first stayed at the Garden
with his second wife, Mary Phillips, then with Mayo before he married
her, and afterwards with Lauren Bacall.

"People went to the Garden," said Jed, "because it was a deluxe
hotel without the inconveniences. It was like having your own home,
your own privacy. But it was always a place for transients. It was a
short distance, a short drive, from anywhere you wanted to go, the
studios, and the restaurants. You were anonymous. It was made for
people like Benchley. The anonymity of the place was its chief virtue.
It was a compound of peace. You didn't have to dress, you didn't have
to leave your bungalow to eat if you didn't feel inclined. It was an in-
formal place where you could always arrive and be accommodated. It
was always on the verge of being a glorified whorehouse, a place where
a man could have a girl."

Also, when the war was on and you could not get a maid no matter how rich or successful you were, the Garden provided room service
and a home when you could not rent or buy a home. It was less expensive than the luxury hotels, and ideal for couples or bachelors who
were not too rich. People stayed there who didn't want the bother of
running a home.

"It was," said George Oppenheimer, the writer and critic, who
lived there until he moved into his own home, "just a liquor closet. It
was a night hotel." It was more of a cocktail hotel. At cocktail time the
place was at its liveliest, except for the nocturnal revelers who came in
late, yelling and laughing and falling into the pool.

Muriel King disliked Hollywood, except for her life at the Garden.
She hated the climate, the fog, the heat. "I never really fitted in," she
remembers. At a party, Muriel was asked why she wanted to return to
New York. Before she could reply, the wife of a well-known producer,
a lady who had started life as a poor actress and was now proud of her

Jed Harris, famed play producer of the thirties and forties. "The Garden was a place for transients—a glorified whorehouse." *Springer/Bettmann Archive*

butler and of living rich, said, "I can understand why you want to get back to New York. In New York what you do is considered distinguished. Out here you are on a level with the props."

I wondered why the expatriates in the Garden always spoke so nostalgically of New York, why they contrasted it so much, and so often, with life in Hollywood.

"New York," explained Muriel, who now lives in Connecticut, "used to be full of simple gaiety. In Hollywood, people only cared about how much money they were making. But New York had an almost innocent gaiety." This will be a surprise for those who know the dangerous, dirty, noisy city of today.

I never thought it had an innocent gaiety, not even when I first went there in the summer of 1933. It was a safer place. A woman could walk alone at night without the danger of being mugged and robbed or murdered.

Miss King mentioned the Hollywood dress designers who had committed suicide—Irene and Vera West. "It was difficult for us when I was working in Hollywood. There was always trouble with someone. It might be the producer, or the producer's wife. But I liked working and I managed to have a good time, especially at cocktail time at the Garden and the parties afterward at the exquisite homes."

She was taken by Tony Duquette—the designer of beautiful theatre sets and interiors for the rich people of Hollywood and elsewhere—to dine with Dugie Bucocks, a very rich lady. When they brought Muriel back to the Garden, they serenaded her in front of her window, causing some howls from awakened neighbors. "They leaped away down the steps into the patio. It was like an Italian opera."

Muriel had come to Hollywood in 1935 to design the clothes for Katharine Hepburn in *Sylvia Scarlet*. Previously Kate had visited Muriel's shop at 49 East Fifty-first Street in New York and asked her to go west for her picture, urging, "It's a marvelous clothes story." Muriel went to Hollywood and stayed at the Chateau Marmont, a turreted imitation castle that is still in existence and still patronized by actors and writers.

Later Muriel stayed at the Garden until she found a house, but even when she had her own home she was always there visiting her friends Benchley, Roland Young, and Eddie Mayer, with whom I first met her.

"The clothes I made for Kate in *Sylvia Scarlet* were gradually cut out of the film," she told me wryly, "until all that was left were two cotton dresses, a raincoat, and some clown suits."

Muriel, like Benchley while he still held his job as play critic for the *New Yorker,* usually went to Hollywood to escape the hot New York summers. Woollcott didn't mind the summers, he hated the winters, and he preferred Hollywood in the winter. There was no business for Muriel and Bob in the summer in New York. There were no plays to criticize, and the rich women who patronized Muriel's shop were all away at the beach or, before the war, in Europe. Among the films "dressed" by Miss King were *Back Street* with Irene Dunne and *Appointment for Love* with Margaret Sullavan, *Casanova Brown* starring Teresa Wright with Gary Cooper, and *Woman in the Window* with Joan Bennett.

Managers came and went in rapid succession as new owners appeared and took over the Garden. The servants did not stay long either. There was always a new girl making your bed. But one employee outstayed most of the owners and most of the guests: Ben the Bellboy, a short man in his early thirties, with sandy receding hair and the freckles that go with it. He was the servant, but the residents were in bondage to him.

Kyle Crichton mentions Ben in his book *Total Recoil* (1960). "The great character at the Garden of Allah was Ben the Bellboy. He was a bulky rather pudgy man of about thirty-five, and not only was he the bellboy, but he was the only bellboy. He was also the man who knew where everybody was, what everybody was doing and where everything could be had. He represented a laundry and a car-renting agency. When liquor was scarce during the war, Ben could always get it."

Part of Ben's duties was to deliver the mail in the morning, and he must have been able to read through the envelope because after dropping the letter nonchalantly on a table he would observe, "You don't want this one," or that one. "So," as Kyle wrote, "Ben must have had second sight or have steamed the letters open because he was always right."

If there was a party in any bungalow, Ben would appear as though on cue and offer to help out. During the war this was something of a handicap for the host because invariably part of a bottle of scotch would disappear with Ben. He knew where everyone kept their precious supplies of liquor. He had come to the back door late at night when Kay Thompson was married to Bill Spier, rapped loudly, demanded, "Give me a bottle of gin and a bottle of whiskey." He had a rush call for a party. "But," said Kay, "I don't have any." "Oh, yes you do," said Ben, and led her to the place where it was hidden.

When Dorothy Parker asked him to go to Schwab's and bring back some scotch he replied, "But you have some. There's scotch in your underwear drawer."

Ben carried his liquor no better than the people on whom he waited, and this was not surprising because he was credited with taking one drink from every bungalow where he had business, and he had business in them all. It was his recognized tip. When he borrowed a bottle from one bungalow to sell to the next, he replaced the bottle without the owners being aware of it.

"One time when Ben returned a bottle, he told me he had taken it the week before, and we hadn't missed it," said Miss Thompson, who loved her life at the Garden in spite of some horrendous experiences. "Ben was the most amazing man. He supplied everything, for the men and for the women. He had four or five girls that he could bring to the parties for the men—married men, some of them—who would get in a fast frolic when the wife was out shopping. Some men enjoy a life like Ben's." Her slim frame shuddered.

Ben started at the Garden in the very early thirties. He was there when Tallulah Bankhead was rampaging naked around the pool, and for once he was nonplussed and had run across the street to the drugstore, yelling to Leon Schwab, "Come, you gotta help me. Tallulah's running around the pool naked and I can't catch her." He carried the bath towel in which he hoped to wrap her up and carry her to her bungalow.

Jed Harris remembers Ben possessing "a built-in sense of accommodation. You could get things from Ben that you could not get at a hotel." There was talk that he was involved with the robberies at the Garden. But this was never proved and I think he was too shrewd to steal. Most of the residents liked him for the favors rendered. He sneaked liquor to Louis Calhern when Natalie Schafer was trying to keep him on the wagon, an impossible feat as it turned out.

When it came to helping a client, Ben was strictly business. He received a cut from everything he brought his customers. He went to Schwab's when he had a big order and announced grandly, "I want to make a profit on this." He paid for the order, then charged the guests what he thought they should pay. He never used a car on his errands. He always walked to Schwab's, no matter what he had to carry back, whether it was a band-aid or a case of whiskey.

At the Garden when he made his deliveries, he rode a bicycle with a tray aloft in one hand, singing to himself. He had good reason to sing. He was richer than many of the people he waited on. Muriel King remembers Ben's blond hair. "You know, the wet kind of blond hair and square shaped. He was often bawled out by the people whose liquor he helped himself to."

He was at Benchley's bungalow day and night. Bob was so un-mechanical that he was incapable of taking ice out of an ice tray, and Ben was always there shagging ice for him.

Bill Spier describes Ben as a young Stuart Irwin. "He had a whimsical grin. If he liked you he would do anything for you. If not, he wouldn't lift a finger. If he liked you and you wanted a bottle of whiskey at 4:00 A.M., he'd get it. I used to see him at nine in the morning wearing a green baize apron with a pocket in it for a cork-screw, delivering a bottle of gin to Benchley," who had probably been up all night unable to cope with his frustrations.

One time Eddie Mayer had returned from New York where he had gone to see about his play *Sunrise in My Pocket*. Oh, the frustra-tions of Eddie trying to put the play on. He had Tallulah Bankhead set. After a year of preparation she was no longer available. Eddie returned rather bitter, but never too much so because he accepted this as part of his life. He had been gone three or four weeks, and when he arrived at his villa in the Garden, he looked in his closet and all his clothes had disappeared. He called Ben to discuss the unexpected de-velopment. "Oh," said Ben, "I thought they looked dirty and creased. I sent them all out to be pressed and cleaned." To his own cleaning com-pany of course.

"Ben was one of the most kindhearted people," Hugh Williams was sure. "He was on night and day. He did all our shopping for us. Yes, it is true that he would take a drink from every bungalow, gin from one, scotch from another, bourbon from the next, but only one. If he borrowed a whole bottle of whiskey, he always replaced it."

The young Sylvia Sheekman liked Ben very much. "He was the confidant of everyone. He bought bubble gum for the few kids around. Once I gave him a check, 'Pay to the order of Sylvia Sheekman, One

Dollar.' He took the check to Schwab's to cash it. He came back and said sadly, 'Sylvia, it won't work. You don't have any money in the bank.' "

According to Sylvia, who is now an authoress of distinction, Ben could never walk straight. He was always drunk. "There were a lot of fish ponds at the Garden, so it was rather hazardous." Walter O'Keefe agreed. "Ben was always reeling."

One day John McClain, for fun, not rancor, decided to teach Ben a lesson. He filled a dark whiskey bottle with soap bubbles, and when Ben came to John's bungalow he took his usual swig from the bottle which John had craftily hidden at the back of a cupboard knowing that Ben would search for it. The poor man was forever blowing bubbles, and muttering fiercely as he teetered around the pool, "Ivory soap! Ivory soap!"

Ben had a line of clichés that almost drove the nondrinking guests at the Garden to alcohol. When you asked him to do anything he always replied, "Why shore." If he had anything good for you he said, "Just like downtown." If it was bad, "Main Street all the time." To start a conversation, "What's the state of the constitution?" He meant *your* state of health, not the government's.

For nearly twenty years Ben was the go-between in most of the transactions of the guests at the Garden. There was nothing too unimportant or financially meager for him to attend to. For a small sum he walked the two scotties belonging to Jim Andrews, usually in the late afternoon after a generous day of tippling. The dogs abhorred the smell of alcohol, and when Ben came for them, they hid under the bed. You could hear him all over the Garden, pleading, "Come doggie, come." They were known as Ben's Seeing Eye Dogs.

Joe E. Lewis once quipped to Ben, "I act crazy for money. What's *your* excuse?" And, "I'd put you in your place if there was a zoo handy."

Finally a new manager came in after the more colorful celebrities had left the Garden. He was strict and would not stand for Ben's behavior, and in the late 1940s he gave Ben an indefinite leave of absence. He vanished and for years no one heard anything about him. Two years ago he was reported working as a bellhop in a Las Vegas hotel. He had been recognized by one of the habitués of the Garden. But I checked them all and no one knew anything about him. Perhaps he had changed his name. If he is still alive, he would be in his late sixties or early seventies.

Another character who did good business at the Garden was known as "Doc" by those who required her services. She was small and dark and carried a black leather bag like a doctor's. It contained her vibrator, ostensibly for massaging the entire bodies of her patients. She had an office near Paramount and was always being called by the producers. She did more to ruin Paramount than Paramount pictures. She came to their offices and masturbated them with her vibrator and then they were not so restless and could go back sleepily to work.

In addition to the little black bag she always carried, Doc is remembered for the black Salvation Army cloak and cap she wore when she came to the Garden. "I was always amazed at the speed of her massages," Natalie Schafer reminisced in her exquisite Park Avenue apartment in New York. Natalie was the most beautiful blond at the Garden. She has deep blue eyes, and the deep blue on the walls of her New York dining room matches her eyes. She is still a very elegant woman. "One day when I was tired," she recalled, "and not knowing the true nature of Doc's calls, I asked David Niven, 'Do you think she will give me a massage?' David choked a bit then said crisply, 'Darling, I don't think she's for you.' "

[V]

the hangouts

THE GARDEN OF ALLAH PEOPLE HAD their favorite hangouts. The Garden was within walking distance of several good restaurants and nightclubs. Nearby was the Trocadero, where the stars and Louis B. Mayer danced. It was thriving in 1936 and 1937, and I went there frequently with Scott Fitzgerald. He smiled wryly when the cameramen pushed him aside because Lupe Velez had just come in with Gary Cooper. You knew how important you were in Hollywood by the attitude of the photographers, who opened the cars as you arrived and, if your face was unknown to them said, "Nobody here!"

There was also the Little Troc, a bit further on Sunset Boulevard, where Mary Martin and Lena Horne appeared at the beginning of their careers. Lamaze was also very popular. One night every week—I believe it was Thursday, but it might have been Wednesday—a trio of actors dined together, Jimmy Cagney, Spencer Tracy, and Pat O'Brien. They had known each other on the stage in New York, and this was one way of keeping in touch in the spread-out city of Los Angeles.

Bob Benchley often took me to Lamaze for dinner. There were big bowls on each table, the cracked ice stabbed with celery and green-and-black olives and radishes. It was something to chew on while waiting for the food, chosen from a big slate board. Marcel Lamaze was a genial host. I don't know why he had to sell his restaurant. But later it became Dave's Blue Room. Florabel Muir was interviewing

Mickey Cohen there when a rival gang attacked. Mickey's henchmen ran out of the restaurant and were shot in the street. Florabel, a fine reporter, also ran out and was shot in the girdle.

For many years, Mocambo was *the* place to go at night. It was owned by white-haired Charlie Morrison, whom I socked one night when he bawled me out for what was meant to be a complimentary item in my column. He apologized the next day. "Besides, you hit too hard."

I said I was sorry and was glad to be persona grata again because it was a cozy haunt and a good place to pick up news from the celebrities. Later one of Charlie's partners bought The Garden of Allah. I'll always remember Johnny, one of the waiters at Mocambo. After the fight with Charlie, when I was in tears and looking blindly for the exit, he said, "Miss Graham, allow me to get your coat." With a less generous boss than Charlie, it would have meant instant dismissal. Mocambo is now the parking lot for the Playboy Club. Ah, progress.

Ciro's also was popular with the Gardenites. It was run by Herman Hover, a short, rotund, dark-haired man, and backed by several film magnates and Billy Wilkerson, who owned the *Hollywood Reporter*, and had owned the Trocadero. You could walk there in ten minutes. Hover brought in all the top attractions, including Jerry Lewis and Dean Martin, Sophie Tucker, and Josephine Baker, among so many.

La Rue's, nearby on the Strip, also owned by Wilkerson, served the finest French food in the area. Dave Chasen's, which opened in December 1936, had the best steaks and marvelous French bread toasted with garlic. Bill Grady, the casting director at MGM, had his special table, as did Ronald Colman, Leslie Howard, and Cary Grant. Scott and I went there very often. Bruno was among the top three headwaiters in Los Angeles.

When Benchley or Eddie Mayer was in the mood for something special, we drove to Perino's opposite the Ambassador Hotel. Oh that wonderful pale green creamy pea soup! I took Scott there and he had two big bowlfuls. The original Brown Derby was near Perino's, but none of the Garden crowd went there. They preferred the Derby in Beverly Hills or in Hollywood on Vine Street. I went there with Scott when we attended film previews on Hollywood Boulevard.

The Players Club, almost opposite The Garden of Allah, was very popular. It was owned by Preston Sturgis, a playwright who had come to Hollywood following his successful Broadway play *Strictly Dishonorable*. He built the Players with his first movie profits, and, like Nazimova's Garden, it was to consume most of his money. The original idea had been to make it resemble a Swiss chalet. It was always just on the verge of breaking even.

Preston, grizzled, short gray-brown hair, with small twinkling dark eyes, was so enthusiastic about his restaurant that he didn't really care if it made money. He was so happy with his toy. Whatever he earned from writing or directing a film went into the Players. He owned the whole building. The bar was on the ground floor and was well patronized by the residents of the Garden who disliked their own bar. Humphrey Bogart and Mayo Methot among others were often there, Bogey lingering over his drink.

I remember Preston's pride when he showed me the small theatre he had built at the very top of the Players. It was very elegant, with its French or Venetian decor—I have forgotten now, except that I thought it was too small to be practical. He was indulging his wish to own a theatre.

Donald Ogden Stewart once ate twelve dozen oysters at the Players on a dare. Before Preston built his theatre on the top floor, Howard Hughes dined there in solitary splendor or with his latest girl. He would write things on the table cloths. They might be valuable today if anyone had thought to keep them.

This eating alone on the top floor was the beginning of the hibernation of Hughes. He did not wish to mingle with the other guests, a fact I had not known. When I saw him slipping into the Players, I mentioned it in my column, and Preston lost a good customer. He told me without rancor that Howard never went there again. But it might not have been my item. They had a fight about something else, and Hughes, a bitter enemy, is reported to have said that Preston would never work for him or anyone else. When the Players closed down, Preston took his family to Paris, where he died.

The Ronda was a satellite of The Garden of Allah. In the war years, when you could not get into the Garden or the Chateau Marmont, you might get into the Ronda, where I often played tennis with Johnny Farrow when he lived there.

The most popular restaurant of all for the sophisticates at the Garden was Romanoff's, when it was located at North Rodeo Drive, on the north side of Wilshire Boulevard. Mike was always at the Garden, visiting his friends, who considered him a protégé, and when he decided to open a restaurant, they chipped in and became his partners—Benchley, Jock Whitney, Dorothy Parker, and, I believe, John O'Hara.

Mike was poor before he became rich with his restaurant. David Miller, the director, passed him once on his way to the slot machines at The Clover Club (where gambling took place on one of the floors). Mike was dressed exquisitely, David remembers, and he was surprised when he said, "Brother, can you spare a couple of bucks?" When I asked Muriel King, "What did Mike do before he had his restaurant?" she replied, "He sat at your table and told stories." About Old Russia, no doubt.

The opening night at Romanoff's, Mike was milling around tugging delicately on his shirt cuffs as he still does when he is nervous, and suddenly there was a crisis. There was no money in the till to pay the waiters. The investors passed the hat, and the waiters were paid.

For a party at Romanoff's, Irene—the dress designer who was to die tragically later—had taken over the place, and in the middle of all the drinking, the laughter, and the conversation, I saw Clark Gable, all alone. And alone at another table across the room, Gary Cooper. No one was talking to either of these film giants. Hollywood has always been this kind of lonely place. The great are so mighty that people are afraid to talk to them. As for the women stars, you could call almost any one of them late on a Saturday afternoon, and they would be doing nothing that night.

Later, Mike moved to the south side of Wilshire Boulevard in Beverly Hills to take care of his overflow, and, like most restaurants when they expand, it was not as good. Mike had often been angry in the old place—which is now the Daisy, a discotheque—because the customers always wanted the tables with banquette seats near the door. "Every table is a good table," he stormed to me when a disgruntled customer had finally settled for a table at the back. The new place was *all* banquettes and everyone could see everyone. When the regulars at the old place died or moved east, Mike was championed by Frank Sinatra and Humphrey Bogart.

Benchley's original piece of Romanoff's proved useless after his death. When gangsters tried to buy Mike out, he asked Bob for his stock for safekeeping. When Bob died, the original stock was still with

Romanoff's, but when lawyers for Bob's estate claimed it, Romanoff's lawyers countered, "Well, we have here a bill of Mr. Benchley's which is still owing. It is fifteen hundred dollars." Thus nothing was gained by either side. So much for lawyers. Mike had loved Bob, and Bob had loved Mike, who was often in Bob's bungalow at the Garden.

Schwab's Drugstore, on the Sunset Boulevard corner of North Crescent Heights, was a two-minute walk from the Garden. In the afternoon you saw Garden people browsing through the magazines, buying newspapers, giving in prescriptions, or having a soda or a sandwich at the counter.

It was a favorite place for Scott and me in the last year of his life when he was on the wagon. "Let's go to Schwab's," he often said after dinner, and we always laughed. It seemed incongruous that a drugstore would be the high point of the evening for the sophisticated man who had chronicled the Roaring Twenties. We looked through the magazines, and Scott had his chocolate malted milk and bought me the Bavarian chocolate mint bars they always had on the counter. They still do, in all three of their drugstores, one still on the original site.

Billy Phipps was the delivery boy for Schwab's. He was known at the Garden as "The Schwab's Boy." Unlike Ben the Bellboy, Billy came and went on his motorbike. "I'd take over mostly sandwiches and whiskey," he recalls. He is now an actor. "The service was great. Sometimes they'd call for a couple of aspirins only. Or a single Baby Ruth candy bar." The first merchandise delivered by Billy to Benchley was a urinal.

Doctor Frank Nolan had an office over Schwab's. He treated all the hangovers, and some were giant-sized. The Schwab's owners were rather perturbed at the magnitude of the sedatives ordered by the late Alexander King who, before he became famous, worked for *Life* and lived at the Garden.

"King was always sending over prescriptions," Jack Schwab told me while we had coffee in one of his Beverly Hills stores. He gave me some Bavarian mints for old times' sake. "After three really big ones, I was very worried and said to Sidney Skolsky [the columnist who did his share to make Schwab's famous all over the United States], do you know what they are for? They're for dope!"

Fade in. Fade out. Mr. King is on the Johnny Carson show to publicize his book *Mine Enemy Grows Older*. It dealt with his **drug** taking, among other bad habits. He tells the audience how he obtained such a quantity of drugs. "I brought all of my New York prescriptions to Hollywood and had them refilled, and brought my Hollywood pre-scriptions to New York."

In the late fifties Arthur Miller sometimes rapped on the door of Schwab's after midnight to collect the prescribed sleeping pills for his wife, Marilyn Monroe. Errol Flynn after a night out often walked over from the Garden and banged on the door until someone came to tell him they were closed. But if the request was legitimate—and I'm not talking about sex—they would give him the aspirins or the band-aid he wanted.

During her marriage to Artie Shaw, Ava Gardner came over late one night from the Garden and slapped hard on the door. All she wanted was to make herself an ice cream soda. Pretty soon the place was full of people who asked Ava to serve them sodas. They had a marvelous time.

But Mr. Benchley always relied on Ben to get him what he wanted from Schwab's because of the phobia that terrified him.

[VI]

mr. benchley

Every party needs a host. Robert Benchley was the host of hosts at The Garden of Allah. He would have resented the title, but if the leaf is a photograph of the tree, then Mr. Benchley was the reflection and the heart of the Garden. When he finally left in the late summer of 1945 to die before the year's end in New York, the Garden started the decline that would also end in death.

The Happy Walrus, I used to call Bob to myself. I wouldn't have dared say this to his face. Especially not in the last two years of his life when the frustrations sometimes made him difficult, but only when he was in his cups. Then it would all come out, the anger for what Hollywood had done to him, and the hatred of himself for having wasted his talent.

It wasn't all wasted. We still have the collections of his articles for the *New Yorker,* the columns preserved in books, the forty-eight marvelous film shorts including *The Treasurer's Report* in 1928 and the last, in 1945, *I'm a Civilian Myself,* for the United States Navy. And the great affection from everyone who is alive who knew him. They tell the stories of his kindness, his wit, his excruciatingly funny behavior. And his phobia.

He had a great fear of being killed while crossing Sunset Boulevard and North Crescent Heights. I was at Schwab's one evening having a prescription filled when Bob panted in, dressed as usual in a derby hat, pearl gray spats, silk shirt, dark suit, restrained tie, and announced

Robert Benchley, the patron saint of The Garden of Allah.
Wide World Photos

tremulously, "I just made it," repeating as his eyes rolled, "I just made it."

He had had a dinner date at the Players, he explained, after swallowing his breath. He had been too afraid to cross Sunset Boulevard from the Garden, and too ashamed to call a cab for such a short distance. Although sometimes when he felt that he could cope with the taxi driver's contempt, he would.

But now he said, "I just can't face the crossing. Will you call me a cab?" He fumbled clumsily in his pocket for the dime—his fingers were always all thumbs. The cab arrived and Bob was suddenly shy of asking the driver to take him across the road. Instead, he muttered, "Take me to the Little Troc," which was several hundred yards down the Strip. When they arrived Bob said casually, "Wait for me. I'm just going in to get a drink. I'll be right back."

He did not emerge until two in the morning, and he was very drunk. The cab was still waiting. This was Hollywood where, when a man went in for one drink, it might take hours.

The extremely intoxicated Benchley slurred, "Take me back to where you picked me up." The driver took him back to Schwab's. The very drunken Bob had to negotiate North Crescent Heights. God takes care of children and drunks, he once told me, and the good Lord saw to it that he arrived back safely at the Garden.

Bob had some reason to fear this particular part of Sunset Boulevard. The corner was a blind spot, the road veering sharply to the left. There were many auto accidents, and his greatest friend, Charlie Butterworth, was to wrap himself and his car around a billboard nearby on Sunset and be killed a few months after Bob's death. It was a dangerous crossing. Terry de Lapp, when he was head of Paramount publicity, was killed walking across to North Crescent Heights.

Kyle Crichton remembers, "The Players sat in a bend of Sunset Boulevard, with the most ferocious traffic in the Western Hemisphere roaring by. It was worth your life to go in against the traffic, and most people stopped trying." Kyle was staying at the Garden, and he said it sometimes took him fifteen minutes to negotiate the crossing.

Usually when Bob took me to dinner at the Players, I said, "Let's walk it." He'd look doubtful, then agree. Taking a fierce grip on my arm, we waited and waited for the rare moment when there was no traffic coming or going. When we reached the other side, Bob raised his head triumphantly as though he were Washington who had just crossed the Delaware.

Today there is an island in the middle of the crossing, and they have widened the corner. This would have pleased Bob.

Bob knew he had sold out to Hollywood, and he knew he should be doing something better than playing bit parts in films, although he rather enjoyed acting in his own shorts. But first he was a writer, and this is what he ought to have been doing—in New York, not in Hollywood where the writers were degraded by the producers who treated them like office boys.

Benchley's lifeline was his plan to write a book about Queen Anne. Eddie Mayer's escape hatch was the book he intended to write about Pitt the Elder and Pitt the Younger; Scott Fitzgerald was planning a book about Irving Thalberg and Hollywood. At least Scott wrote half of his book, *The Last Tycoon*. After Bob and Eddie died, the notes for Queen Anne and the Pitts were still in the research stage.

Benchley's opinion about Hollywood was revealed soon after he had come to stay at the Garden, when his wife Gertrude was visiting him from the East. She was lounging around the pool loving the sunshine, the flowers, and the prettiness of the hills opposite, and she said to Bob that it might be nice for her to move with the children to Hollywood, that it would be a fine warm place in which to bring them up. Bob became very angry, as he could when he thought something was wrong.

"Don't you ever let me hear you saying that again!" he shouted. "Ever. This is nothing for the children, and nothing for you. You keep away from it!" [Nat recalls in his biography of his father].

Nat remembers sitting with his father and St. Clair McKelway, the writer for the *New Yorker,* in the white slat chairs of the Garden, looking lazily at the nearby hills sharp against the blue sky. "It's just like a stage set," said his father. "And one day a monstrous giant will raise his head above that mountain and shout, 'Strike!' "

Bob always felt that Hollywood was an artificial, irresponsible place, a mere facade, no more real than a stage set.

In spite of all the years he spent in Hollywood, Bob considered himself a transient at the Garden. While he always kept the same rooms at The Royalton Hotel on West Forty-fourth Street in New York, when he left Hollywood he gave up his bungalow at the Garden and rented whichever one was available on his return. For several years he retained his job as drama critic on the *New Yorker,* but as he stayed more and more in Hollywood, the job was given to Woolcott Gibbs. When he wanted it back it was too late.

He was lunching at "21" in New York with Harold Ross, the acidulous editor of the *New Yorker,* James Roosevelt, Deems Taylor, and the first Mrs. Donald Ogden Stewart. Bob suddenly said to Ross, "I'm tired of being a mime, Harold. Can I have my old job back on the *New Yorker?"*

"Why, certainly not," rasped the editor. "You can't have your job back. Woolcott Gibbs is doing a better job than you ever did, or ever could." Bob said nothing, but as Bea Stewart said afterwards, "You could see him age visibly at the table." Deems Taylor was not as silent. "You know what, Harold?" he said indignantly. "You're a son of a bitch." James Roosevelt added, "I second the motion." Ross got up and left the restaurant.

Bob had once said to Harold Ross, "I'm not a writer and not an actor. I don't know what I am." In spite of his confusion, he had for a long time kept busy at both professions. At one point in the late thirties, he was writing three syndicated columns a week for the Hearst newspapers, doing his theatre review for the *New Yorker,* performing in a weekly radio show, making his shorts and playing parts in full length Hollywood films.

His unhappiness in Hollywood was furthered by his debts. The system to keep writers pinned down in Hollywood was to give them a fancy salary for six months. They were encouraged to spend extravagantly. Most of them, after staying at the Garden, bought lavish homes with expensive mortgages. When option time came around they were so in debt that they were glad to be picked up for another six months, and so on and on.

I was startled when Bob confided to me that he had borrowed five thousand dollars from his close friend, Jock Whitney, and that Jock was charging him 5 percent interest.

"How can he?" I demanded, "He's so rich."

"I insisted," Bob said. "It's a business transaction. And that's the way I want it."

Nat Benchley, when I talked with him recently, was sure that Jock had not charged the interest. He was shocked at the idea, as I was, but Robert told me this himself. He had borrowed the money from Whitney on his life insurance policy. They had met when Jock was at Yale and he at Harvard. When Bob died, Whitney, according to Nat, cancelled the debt. But Whitney's lawyers insisted that it be paid. I find this hard to believe. Surely they would have consulted Mr. Whitney on this matter.

I wondered whether the debt had been paid from Bob's estate. "What estate?" said Nat. "I inherited a gold watch and a bill from "21." The debt was paid out of the life insurance."

Jock was always a strict businessman. The millions he inherited he increased many times over. There was only one time that he was irritated with Bob. He had given him the manuscript of *Life with Father* to read, as he was interested in backing the play. Bob advised him, "Don't put a penny into it." As you know, the play ran for seven years on Broadway, is still revived on the road, and was made into a film.

Benchley's unconscious connection with the Garden began in 1917. He was pinch-hitting for P. G. Wodehouse as drama critic of *Vanity Fair*. He reviewed a raunchy play, *Ception Shoals,* starring Alla Nazimova. Bob, despite some aspects of his behavior, was a straightlaced New Englander, and the play offended him. He concluded his review with the complaint that it was too obstetric for his simple soul and too tragic for anyone. He referred to the leading lady—although not in the review—as the leading spermatozoa. His reviews were constructive and he usually found something to like. When he hated the play completely, he hated with humor, which perhaps is kinder to the actor and to the author.

Bob had worked in Hollywood before the talkies, writing subtitles for silent films. His friend Don Stewart was at MGM writing *Brown of Harvard*. As Don had gone to Yale they thought he would know all about Harvard—as Scott Fitzgerald, who went to Princeton, was put to work on *A Yank at Oxford* ten years later.

Late in 1926 Bob had accepted an offer from Jesse Lasky to write the dialogue and subtitles for a film at Paramount, *You'd Be Surprised,* starring Raymond Griffith. It would only be for two months, he thought, as so many other writers were to think later. He believed Hollywood was a frivolous place, but it might be amusing for a little while. There was no Garden of Allah then, and he stayed at the Mark Twain Hotel.

He returned to New York but came back in 1927. Fox had bought his *Treasurer's Report,* which he had written in 1922 for an amateur theatrical group. The sketch had appeared in the third Music Box Review and also in vaudeville. Fox didn't quite believe that talkies would ever be successful, but decided to experiment with the *Treasurer's Report*. It was successful, and the critic for the *World* wrote, "Mr. Benchley leads us to suspect that if he really cared to do it, he might go to Hollywood and be funny most conspicuously and successfully." It was the first motion picture in which, for one minute, you could hear the human voice.

In the next year Bob wrote and appeared in his short *The Sex Life of the Polyp,* also for Fox. He did three in 1929, *Lesson Number One,*

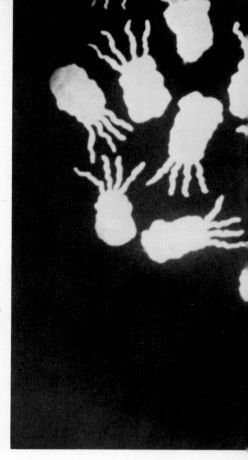

Robert Benchley making his short *The Sex Life of the Polyp.*   *Springer / Bettmann Archive*

Stewed, Fried, and Boiled (Bob was a culinary expert, although the title had nothing to do with food), and *Furnace Trouble.*

He returned to New York, permanently he thought. But the money offered was enticing, so he came back to Hollywood in the summer of 1932 to play a radio announcer in a full-length feature, *Sports Parade.* Bob wrote his dialogue, and his reviews were better than the films.

Bob enjoyed acting. He was remarkably at ease in front of the camera, and he was popular with the public, with his shy hesitation, his diffidence, as though apologizing for being there, which is how he sometimes was in real life.

He collaborated on forty-seven full-length pictures, in addition to the shorts, of which the most famous was *How to Sleep.* Pete Smith, who was then the best-known voice in the short films seen with major pictures in all the theatres, had signed to make a brief film for the

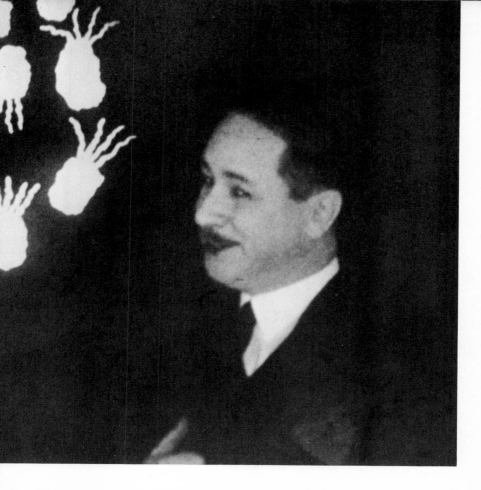

Simmons mattress people. They tried several comedians, then someone suggested Bob. *How to Sleep* won an Academy Award. Originally, Bob was asked to write the story only, then it was decided he should act as well. It was no strain because all the acting was based on material he had written. After this he did *How to Behave, How to Vote, How to Train a Dog, How to Raise a Baby,* etc., etc. In one short he shows the predicament of a man who is wedged into a corner seat at a table. A lady comes over, and he tries to get up but can rise only a few inches. I remember this short because it was exactly how Bob behaved when anyone came to our table.

The first time we conquered the hazard of the road and were dining on the middle floor of the Players, a reporter across the room waved to us and queried in a loud voice, "An interview?" "No, sex," snapped Bob, who was annoyed that the man assumed I was not interesting or attractive enough to be taken to dinner for the pleasure of my company. He always became very angry when anyone he liked was slighted, or if he imagined they were.

I met Bob in January of 1936, after he had been at the Garden for several years. I had no idea what I was getting into when I telephoned him at the Garden and said I had a letter of introduction from my North American Newspaper Alliance boss, John Wheeler. He asked me to come to his villa for a drink and he got me drunk. After a tall gin drink, he took me to dinner at the Hollywood Brown Derby, where he ordered a long, strong whiskey for me. I was somewhat dubious. I don't drink much, but I knew enough not to mix drinks. "It's all right," Bob assured me. "This can't do you any harm." He was my first important contact in Hollywood, and I didn't want to seem like a sissy. I was ill fairly soon, and Bob took me home, apologizing every few minutes but laughing secretly behind his eyes, which became thin slits when he laughed.

Bob called me the next day, and I became part of his group. They would always be there when I went over at cocktail time—Dorothy Parker, John O'Hara, John McClain, Eddie Mayer, Muriel King, Frances and Albert Hackett—when they lived at the Garden. And Charlie Butterworth.

The story that John McClain trundled Robert in a wheelbarrow from villa to villa is not true, according to his son Nat. He might have done it once during one of the games, he told me, and that is how the story grew. Any story that was wild was always pinned on Benchley. Anything you could imagine, he was capable of doing.

Later, when Bob could not hold his liquor very well, the evening was a complete blank for him. The next day, he called the people with whom he had started the evening and asked if he had done anything nasty. He must have had a deep-seated resentment against waiters. When he was drinking he was horrible to them. Snapped their heads off.

But he could also be unkind to his guests. I was dining with him one evening, in the very early days of Scott, when I was still seeing other men. We were at Lamaze. Once you were wedged into your seat, it wasn't easy to get out. Charlie Butterworth was with us. I made a harmless remark and Bob said suddenly and viciously, "If you don't like it here with us, why don't you leave?"

The unexpectedness of the attack made me choke with tears, and, not wishing them to see me crying, I pushed the table away with angry strength and walked out and had the man at the door get me a taxi.

The next day I received a hand-written letter by messenger, in which Bob apologized and begged me not to let a momentary rudeness spoil our friendship. Of course, I called him and we were friends again.

I was never quite sure whether he liked me as much as he did some of his other friends. I don't smoke, and drink very little, and I felt he regarded me with a sort of affectionate contempt. Especially when, instead of drinking, I preferred the German sausage on crackers prepared by his German houseboy, Albin. Albin also drove Bob—I never asked him but I am sure that the unmechanized Mr. Benchley was unable to drive a car. His servant never said, "Good morning," or "Good evening." It was, always, "Here is Albin." He was not a very good servant. And he never seemed to be around when Bob needed him. That is when Bob would get Ben to come over.

Bob, the kindhearted, kept Albin in his employ because once when the car had overturned in an accident he had had to step on Albin's neck to get out of the wreckage. Bob always felt guilty about this. Finally he set Albin up in business in a waxworks museum.

Albin was with Bob when he shared a bungalow with John McClain who, in his casual insouciant way, was more a part of the group than John O'Hara, who always seemed somewhat morose and uncomfortable. McClain also had a valet-driver and, as Benchley and McClain always ate out and usually took taxis, the two servants had a marvelous time cooking exotic meals for themselves in the kitchen. The food bill for the first month came to six hundred dollars—the equivalent of eighteen hundred dollars today. Bob and John had a meeting with the two servants to decide what to do about it. McClain's valet came up with what they all thought was a brilliant idea: have an adding machine installed in the kitchen. I don't quite know how this solved the problem, but they all loved the machine.

In some ways, Benchley—while being everyone's friend, if he liked you—was also everyone's sucker. No matter how rich his Santa Barbara and Pasadena friends were, it was always Bob who picked up the check. Bob took it upon himself to get his girls married off or to be the mistresses of richer men than he was. Louise Macy had been his girl before she married Harry Hopkins and was at the White House during the time of Hopkins and President Franklin D. Roosevelt.

But one could only go so far with Bob. He became annoyed when it was obvious that he was being taken advantage of. He had finished a job at RKO and was heading back to New York for relief. He departed from the Garden, leaving the usual gratuities for the staff. A man approached him with a subservient palm. Bob had never seen him before, and his Yankee blood revolted at the thought of being taken. He started to brush past, as Corey Ford relates in his book *The Time of Laughter,* but the other stood his ground and asked pointedly, "Aren't you going to remember me, sir?"

"Why, of course," Robert replied with a bright smile as he climbed into the taxi and, over his shoulder, "I'll write to you every day."

In the early thirties, when Bob was in New York at the Royalton and his wife was living with the children in Scarsdale, he took his two sons to lunch every Sunday at the Oak Room in the Plaza. After lunch he returned the boys to suburbia. This ritual, he told me, always shook him up, and upon depositing his offspring at home, he was so nervous that he had to stop at the nearest bar for a drink.

One Sunday after saying good-bye to the family in Scarsdale he was on the local train going back to the city, and he had to go to the men's room. The door was unlocked, and he surprised two homosexuals who sprang apart on his entry. They recovered and, smiling at Bob, said, "Watch the door. Look out for the cops." The always obliging Benchley obliged, until he suddenly thought, What am I doing? Two queers are performing indecencies and I'm the lookout man!

In the winter of 1940, when he was rooming with McClain, they ran into Jock Whitney at the track. Whitney raced his horses every season at Santa Anita. They always lost when I bet on them, and Jock said thank you very much but will you bet on someone else's horses. The millionaire had a horse, Sharpy, who showed so little promise that Jock told his trainer to get rid of him. Benchley felt sorry for Sharpy, and he and McClain decided to buy him. They got him cheap for one thousand dollars.

A problem arose instantly. They were owners of a racehorse and had nowhere to put him. Even Ben at The Garden of Allah was unhelpful. Sharpy had been entered in a fifteen-hundred-dollar claiming race in three days' time. They were unregistered without a jockey or colors. They stabled Sharpy at the track. Then they joined the California Racing Association, which wasn't cheap. They had fun deciding on their colors, which were a mixture of crimson for Bob's Harvard—*Havv*ard he used to pronounce it—blue for Whitney's Yale, and brown for McClain's Brown University. They called the tailor to work these colors together as best he could. The horse was listed on the program as belonging to The Garden of Allah Stud Farm—a rather appropriate name.

Benchley and McClain rented a limousine for the great day, with owner stickers on the windshield and paddock passes in their lapels. What a sight when Sharpy appeared for the race. Or rather, the jockey was a sight. His cap was an off-color brindle brown. His jacket a crazy jumble of crimson-and-blue stripes. "The overall effect," Nat Benchley writes, "was that of a stained window in a funeral parlor." The horse didn't look much better.

McClain got cold feet. "What if he doesn't win and no one claims him," he demanded of Bob. Bob's face creased in a huge grin. "So what," he said. "He can have my room at the Garden, and I'll sleep on the couch in the living room."

If this story were like the movies, Sharpy would have lost, and Bob and John would have been sleeping platonically on the floor with a girl. But Sharpy won, paying four to one and was claimed. The two new racehorse owners were almost sorry to see him go.

According to Nat Benchley, Roy Rowland, who directed some of his father's films, was able to pick nine out of ten winners. If he liked the name of the horse, he bet on him. One afternoon at the Garden, Roy picked eight winners out of seven races, calling his choice a second before the radio announced the name at the post. In one race he was undecided between two horses, and they finished in a dead heat. Benchley thought he could make a fortune with Roy, so he took him to the track to pick winners at close range. But Roy became nervous— he could win a five-dollar bet, but with five thousand dollars he questioned his hunches and lost.

Bob went to the track with Jock Whitney, who had a box in the owners' stand at Santa Anita. I sometimes went with them, and it was exciting being in the thick of the rich racing crowd—Louis B. Mayer was an owner; Alfred Vanderbilt always had a fascinating group in his box; and Hal Roach was the president of the track and had made millions from his *Our Gang* comedies. Gable was sometimes there, along with many of the horse-loving film celebrities and the well-dressed owners from the East. The air reeked of horses and money.

Whitney, the owner of Greentree Stables, was Benchley's junior by fifteen years, but he always called him Gramps. He named a horse Gramps in Bob's honor. But Gramps never won a race except one time when Bob was not betting on him.

At the presidential election of 1936 Bob was in New York and so was I. We were both Democrats and were dining at "21" when Jock Whitney came in. Jock has always been a staunch Republican, and you could see by his face that things were going badly for his man, Alf Landon. Bob and I were delighted under our seeming condolences. Jock could have all the money and power in the world that goes with it, but our man was winning.

Benchley's humor lay in the comedy of errors. He had a sharp eye for the ridiculous side of human behavior. It was the little-man-in-a-predicament humor. But surprisingly he did not care for Chaplin, who was another little-man-in-a-predicament comedian. He described Charlie's acting as "ass-kicking humor." I'm not sure what he meant by that. But it was chiefly directed against the slapstick type of humor. There was never anything remotely slapstick about Bob's sense of humor.

Among his dislikes were the blackface comedians Amos and Andy, who were very popular at this time—the thirties and forties. "Those guys never do anything but mispronounce words," he complained. He thought they were being condescending to black people, and he hated this.

The humorists he liked and respected were W. C. Fields—they drank at the Garden, at Chasen's, and anywhere there was a bar—Jimmy Durante, Fred Allen, and Stephen Leacock. He agreed with Leacock's definition of humor: The kindly contemplation of the incongruities of life and the artistic expression thereof. *Kindly* is the key word here. Bob was the kindest man I ever knew.

I remember his kindness to my friend Margaret Brainard when she came to Hollywood for the first time to open the beauty salon at Saks Fifth Avenue in Beverly Hills. He took her everywhere, introduced her to all his friends. He teased us both, especially me when I became pregnant with my second child. I had a craving for chocolates then, even more than now, and he usually had what he called a box of chocs for me when I called at the Garden. This was during the war, and my husband was in Canada for the British government, making planes. Bob saw to it that neither Margaret nor I was lonely.

In all the time I knew Bob, nearly ten years, he never made a pass at me, although he sometimes said suggestive things, and he always told me when Doc had been at his villa. Then he giggled like a schoolboy who has told a naughty joke.

He could be irritable even when he was not in his cups. Reginald Gardner was visiting his chums at the Garden. "There were three or four of us sitting on the patio outside Bob's window," he told me. "We didn't go in because we could hear his typewriter going. We had ordered drinks when Ben arrived with a formal note: 'Dear Mr. Reginald Gardner: I'm afraid you'll have to be a great deal more fucking quiet. Sincerely yours, Robert C. Benchley.' "

One night when he tried to telephone New York, he failed to arouse the switchboard operator. He went to the lobby, turned all the furniture upside down, and left a note: "Let this be a lesson to you," adding, "I might have been having a baby."

Once Robert complained to the management about the hideous violin practice that was going on in the villa next door. It started in the morning and Bob's head was sometimes splitting in the morning. He sent his neighbor a note demanding, "Why don't you practice in the afternoon?" The man making the "hideous noise" Bob learned later, to his chagrin, was the great violinist Mischa Elman.

Elman had a better reception from Philip Lees, a screenwriter living at the Garden. "I was at the pool one morning about ten," said Mr. Lees, who is now the manager of the Hollywood office of the California Motor Vehicle Department. "I heard someone playing Saint-Saëns's 'Rondo Capriccio' in a nearby villa. I walked towards the music, which suddenly stopped, and a man came out of the bungalow whom I recognized as Mischa Elman. I told him how much I had enjoyed the music. I told him I had once studied violin. 'Then you must play for me,' he said. Of course I didn't. The next morning, Sally at the desk handed me an envelope. It contained two tickets for the concert Mr. Elman was giving at The Hollywood Bowl."

In the early forties the Garden was jammed with musicians. In addition to Elman, Rachmaninov and Jascha Heifetz stayed there for brief periods. At the same time Artie Shaw and Woody Herman, the clarinetists, were there, and Al Jarvis and Frankie Laine, who was then Frankie Lo Vecchio, a young shipyard worker with a passion for singing. Jarvis rented him a cot in his living room for thirty-five dollars a month.

Benchley was working on a short in which he had to do a jitterbug.

Mischa Elman, violinist. Benchley complained about his practicing. *Springer/Bettmann Archive*

Woody Herman, the band leader. He played while Benchley jitterbugged. *Springer/Bettmann Archive*

To my knowledge, Bob had never danced, and he asked Woody Herman to help him out. "We practiced when the Garden was less crowded, after it was dark and before the cocktail hour," Woody told me. "I put on a record and showed Bob how to jitterbug. Bob clipped his peg trousers with bicycle clips and attempted to dance around the patio." It would have been worth the price of admission to see his determination mixed with his embarrassment.

There were four things Benchley detested above all others—phonies, cruel people, charades, and birds. Dorothy Parker and Marc Connelly loved to act things out. Connelly was a madly enthusiastic player of the Game. He was so serious about it that when his team was to play Dorothy Parker's or Ira Gershwin's, he rehearsed his group all afternoon. Fights sometimes broke out because Marc was such a perfectionist.

The Game always excited me. How proud I was after my scholastic briefing by F. Scott Fitzgerald, when I acted out Picasso's Blue Period, and Miss Parker came up with the answer.

But Bob hated the Game. He became volcanic one evening when he had to act out the Dow Jones Report. Everyone was running out of his sight and range, laughing because Bob looked so funny in his fury. Suddenly he exploded with a non sequitur, "I don't give a goddamn about Bush Fekete,"—the unusual name of a foreign writer in Hollywood. The next day the ladies who had been present received flowers and an apology from Bob.

The experts among the intelligentsia of Hollywood practiced their signals the way football teams do. Once Bob found himself crawling around the room on his hands and knees trying to impersonate the words *Of Mice and Men*. Suddenly he could stand it no longer and shouted, "To hell with you all!" and, still on his knees, crawled through the French doors and disappeared. No one could find him that evening. He probably went to his bungalow, turned out the lights, and locked the door.

Robert had his revenge on the game. He invented Subway, an antigame, during which Bob and Butterworth pushed each other around the pool in a wheelbarrow. This wheelbarrow, belonging to the Garden, apparently had a great deal of use.

The only time Bob defended a feathered friend was when someone gave him a myna bird. It had been trained to say, "Fuck you," and when some of the people at the Garden complained, Bob stated obstinately, "It's my bird and I won't hear a word against it."

David Niven, who stayed at the Garden briefly, asked Bob, "Why do you hate birds so much?"

"Because they look so awful," replied Robert. "In profile they're not so bad, but have you seen the sons of bitches head on?"

"I was in San Francisco courting a lady," Niven continued. "I hadn't told anyone where I was, for certain reasons. But Benchley tracked me down. In those days, making a call to San Francisco wasn't all that easy, and it took him some time to get me. After he did, he roared with laughter for twenty minutes' worth. I said, "What's so funny?' He laughed for another five minutes and, still choking from laughter said, 'An enormous black bird just landed on the pathway outside in the pissing rain and skidded on its ass. I just had to call someone.' "

Niven was a good friend of Bob's, and when Bob went to Venice for the first time, Niven gave him some addresses. From Venice, David received a cable addressed to Niven Travel Service: "Streets full of water. Please advise."

Nat Benchley believes the reason for his father's aversion to birds was that he felt they were a nuisance. (It's a good thing he didn't see Alfred Hitchcock's film *The Birds*.) "He also had a feeling that birds knew more than they were telling."

All his adult life, Bob and the birds were at war. He claimed one great victory. He was awakened by a great noise, something rustling and moving about in the mock orange trees outside his bungalow window. Finally, the loud thrashing caused him to look out to see what it was. There was a great bird flitting around in the tree. Bob, in telling the story, said it looked like a cross between a flamingo and a sea gull. With a warlike shout, he rushed outside and hit the bird, so he says—a solid right, on the side of its beak. "I was just about to give it a left hook when the bird scrambled into the air, leaving me with some feathers to remember my triumph." Exhausted but triumphant, Bob watched the bird flapping erratically over the bushes. Then he went back to bed to resume his interrupted sleep.

He didn't mind penguins, according to his author son. They seemed even more clumsy than humans, and of all humans, Bob was the clumsiest. He worked in a movie with a penguin called Eddie who could not walk ten feet without tripping over something, usually its own feet. A carpenter on the movie set watched Bob in amazement as he dropped things and fumbled around. With a kind of awe he said, "My God, he's a born one—he does it without thinking."

For a man who drank as much as Bob, he was surprisingly interested in the art of cooking. He wrote special recipes for his friends. He had two for Muriel King—Eggs à la King and string beans with chives.

For Gloria Sheekman, a fine cook who often invited him to her bungalow for dinner, he laboriously wrote in red:

Benchley's New England Boiled Dinner for Boiled
New Englanders

INGREDIENTS: A quarter tablespoon salt

Three tablespoons mustard (this is for jaded palates, the rule calls for one tablespoon)

One-and-a-half tablespoons sugar

A few grains cayenne pepper

Two tablespoons flour

One egg or yolk of two eggs

One and a half tablespoons melted butter

Three-quarters of a cup of milk

A quarter cup of vinegar

Add yoke of eggs, slightly beating in butter, milk, and vinegar *very slowly* till mixture thickens.

Strain.

Add pepper.

Add one-fourth tablespoon salt, few grains of pepper, and gradually two tablespoons vinegar.

Serve with cucumber sauce.

Beat half an egg and heavy cream (ha, ha) until stiff (ha, ha, ha).

Add one cucumber pared, chopped, and drained through cheesecloth.

Then take off your clothes and call villa 16.

more of benchley

NAT BENCHLEY SHARED HIS FATHER'S distaste for Hollywood. "Hollywood is basically a frightened society," Nat said when we were discussing the Hollywood of the thirties and forties. "People went there for a buck and were paid a great deal of money. They were afraid they were going to be found out. As a writer, it's humiliating working with a bunch of bums who have no artistic sense. The whole criterion out there for judging any picture was, and perhaps still is, 'What did it gross?' Hollywood has always been a lot of dull people doing dull things. But it's also vicious. If you got fired, you were so unimportant that you couldn't even get arrested."

Nat had first gone to the Garden in 1939, following his marriage. He was on vacation from the *New York Tribune,* and he went out to see his father. He returned there for his vacations in 1940 and 1941. For the next four years he was in the Atlantic serving in the navy. In the spring of 1945, Nat was transferred from the Atlantic to the Pacific, and he stopped at the Garden on his way out to visit his father. In November of 1945, Nat was again in Los Angeles on his way back from the Pacific, and he went to the Garden. His father was not there. By the time Nat reached New York, his father was dead.

"Acting was no strain for my father," Nat told me. "But the writing got harder and harder. When he gave up doing the *New Yorker* pieces in 1942 or 1943, he said it was because no humorist was funny after fifty. He was fifty-four so he'd better quit. The shorts were a different matter. Often when I watched them being filmed with Roy Rowland directing, I thought they were merely rehearsing."

But if the acting was easy, Benchley found it ultimately meaningless. He did it strictly to pay his debts.

Bob's entanglement with Hollywood had started with his debts. A Worcester, Massachusetts, patroness, Lillian Duryea—who had been engaged to his older brother Edmund, who died—had put him through college. It cost her five thousand dollars, which is what you would have to pay in one year now for higher education. When he was successful in Hollywood, she felt entitled to be repaid. Bob told Albert Hackett, "I'm paying my way through college."

Bob disliked many of the people with whom he had to act. I was on the set when Bob had a small role in a Betty Hutton film at Paramount. As usual he was reading in his dressing room between takes. He put his book down when I appeared, and he was glad to talk. Betty Hutton, who had never heard of him or his work, was treating him like an extra. It made him writhe, and he loathed her and despised himself for working with her at all. After cursing her to me, he made a joke. He had to or he could not have endured remaining in Hollywood.

Every incident was turned into a joke. In 1940 he had met a psychiatrist at a cocktail party who listened to him with great interest all evening. "I would like to psychoanalyze you," he told him. Bob was sure that the man was planning to use him for a series of histories for a Sunday supplement. He decided to have some fun with the doctor, so he agreed to an appointment. To the first question, "Is anything troubling you?" Bob said no, then, hesitatingly, yes, "but it's nothing." The psychiatrist, now very curious, repeatedly begged him to reveal what the matter was. Bob allowed himself to be persuaded to speak. He drew a deep breath and plunged. He lived in one of the bungalows at The Garden of Allah, he told him. His next door neighbor had a sheepdog—one of those great big wooly ones with blue eyes. The dog walked past his door every morning and their eyes met. "It gives me a kind of tingly feeling because of the recognition between us, and I am sure the dog feels the same way because of the way he looks at me with those great big blue eyes."

As Bob related to his son, "I told the analyst that it had reached a stage of tension where I could not go to the studio until the sheepdog had come by and looked meaningfully at me. Then I went to work and felt fine for the rest of the day."

"That's all there is to it," he concluded. The psychiatrist's eyes were glazed. "I warned you it wouldn't interest you," said Bob. The doctor looked thoughtfully at him and asked, "Are you married?"

"Certainly," Bob replied with some asperity. "I've not only been married for twenty-six years but I have two children." He pretended to be indignant at the insinuation.

The doctor suddenly remembered another appointment, "perhaps another time . . ." his voice trailed away. When Bob left him, choking back the laughter, the man was staring out of the window. Bob never heard from him again.

In the same year, I remember, Bob came down with pneumonia. I phoned him at the Garden and sent flowers. The doctor gave Bob some new miracle sulfa drugs, and cautioned him about how many to take because too many could have some bad side effects. Before the doctor's next visit, Bob and Butterworth tore open a pillow, removed the feathers and glued them to Bob's body from the waist down. The doctor arrived and examined Bob's chest and he seemed better. Had he suffered any side effects from the pills? Bob beamed and thought they had done him a great deal of good. But he didn't quite know what to make of this. He pulled back the covers.

I wish I could have seen the doctor's face. It was one of Bob's great after-dinner stories.

John Carradine remembers the parties Bob was always giving. "Something was always going on in his cottage. Once there was an especially big and noisy party on a night when I had gone to bed early because I had to work the next day. I dozed off but I was awakened into a sitting position by a strange metallic noise. I got up, looked out of the window, and there was Benchley shaking a porch swing which was mounted on a metal frame. Done with this, Bob raced up and down the paths, pulling an imaginary cord and letting go with his imitation of a Mississippi River steamboat whistle. At this point I hollered, 'Mark Twain!' Whereupon Bob called to Butterworth, 'Come on Charlie. We're going into Carradine's. He's having more fun than we are.' "

John's last—and saddest—recollection is of late in 1945. As Carradine was leaving "21," Benchley was coming in. John asked him, "How are you?" The reply, and nothing else, was, "I'm tired. I'm tired." This was two days before he died.

At another party in his bungalow, Bob's guests included Dorothy Parker, Scott Fitzgerald, myself, and the Robert Sherwoods. Suddenly backing away from Sherwood, Bob exclaimed, "Those eyes, I can't stand those eyes looking at me." Everyone thought he was joking, as he usually was, but he was frowning at Sherwood who had recently won another Pulitzer Prize. "He's looking at me," sighed Bob, "and thinking of how he knew me when I was going to be a great writer. And now he's thinking, Look what he became!"

Bob had this guilt with him always, even when he was roaring around like a small boy, seeming to have fun. His anger with himself escaped in odd unexpected moments. He was arguing with Butterworth about whether Gregory Ratoff had acting ability. Gregory, an actor from Russia who later became a director, had a thick accent. Butterworth said he could not act. Bob said he could. The argument went back and forth until finally Bob erupted, "Fuck you, I used to be a critic." He didn't want an actor telling him, a critic, what acting was.

"It couldn't have been too serious," Marc Connelly commented when I told him the story. "In the first place no one ever got into an argument with Charlie. And when Benchley turned on anyone it was usually a moral anger. He was used to morons and cretins and was tolerant of them. You don't argue with a jelly. Bob would get truly angry about such things as Sacco and Vanzetti." I remember hearing Bob and Dorothy Parker discussing the Sacco-Vanzetti case. They talked about it a good deal and were full of anger.

Mr. Benchley did not like Mr. Fitzgerald. He invited him to his bungalow when he lived at the Garden because he thought he might be lonely. He detested Scott's habit of whipping out a notebook and writing down something that Bob had just said. "It makes me uncomfortable," he complained to me. Bob knew it was going into one of Scott's books or short stories, and as a writer himself he resented this.

Like many people who drink a great deal, he—like Scott—was not amused when someone else became drunk. He disapproved of Scott's behavior when he was drunk. And while he considered his own pranks fun, he thought that Scott, when he was drunk, could be cruel.

He told me of the time Scott was in the south of France and there was this old woman with a tray of sweetmeats that she was trying to sell. When she asked Scott to buy, he stood back a pace and took a flying football kick and knocked the tray to kingdom come. Scott had told me this story before Benchley did, and I had no excuse for him. It *was* cruel.

Scott knew that Benchley didn't like him. He thought he was jealous of his early success. He told me of a cocktail party in the early days of the success of *This Side of Paradise*. "I was in the center of the group and they were making a fuss about me. I saw Bob on the far outside and caught his eye. There was absolute hatred on his face."

I doubt that. There might have been irritation at the cocky, beautiful young man taking it all as his just due.

It is a pity that Benchley's witticisms were not all written down. I always thought he was much funnier than Dorothy Parker, who was expected to make brilliant remarks all the time. If only Bennett Cerf had been around at the time. Whenever Bennett heard anything funny, he would write it down on his shirt cuff.

Unlike Dorothy Parker's jokes, Bob's were not at anyone else's expense, which is why people liked him so much. He had a particular gift of making everyone his friend. He was like Santa Claus giving out the goodies—he really would give you the shirt off his back if you asked for it. I resented him being the court jester for the rich. I thought they wasted the talents of people like Benchley, who exerted himself to the fullest to amuse them. He was better than they were, but apparently you had to be better to be popular with the rich, who are often so boring.

I remember when Bob went to Finlandia, a Finnish bath on the Strip, with a woman from San Francisco. When they returned to The Garden of Allah, the woman commented to Bob, "You smile so much that I've never seen your eyes before. They are pure white." She may have been right. I never saw his eyes wide open. They were usually behind the long crease of a smile.

Donald Ogden Stewart said to me recently, "It was hard not to be in love with Bobby. He made you feel warm and clever and funny. Charlie Butterworth was in love with Bobby, as we were all in love with him. If he had been a woman, I would have married him."

"Benchley was so soft and warm," said his Garden of Allah neighbor, Gloria Sheekman. "But Butterworth was a cold personality."

"Mr. Benchley was always kind to me," said her daughter, Sylvia. "Charlie Butterworth, on the other hand, was grumpy and ignored me totally." One day Bob came out of his bungalow. It had been raining. Sylvia was sitting by the side of the pool. The little girl was feeling lonely. The sun came out suddenly, forming a huge rainbow. Bob stopped and they talked about the rainbow at great length. The sun, Sylvia remembers, was "a silvery yellow mystical orb. We were sitting on the steps of the pool, he in his swimming trunks. I noticed he had red marks on his body. Like blood blisters. I don't know what caused them." I never saw Bob in swimming trunks. He must have swum during the day when no one but a child was around.

Gloria Sheekman also remembers Bob's gentleness. One late afternoon when he came home to the Garden after playing a role in *County Fair,* she asked him, "How did it go?" Bob was depressed and Gloria was surprised. Usually he took out his frustrations in drinking.

"I don't know what I'm doing out here," he replied, "country dancing!" Gloria tried to console him. "You are making people happy. Please, I want you to be saturnine about this." A slight frown creased Benchley's forehead, but he said nothing. Later Gloria looked up the word "saturnine" and realized she had used the wrong word. She called Bob, and before she could explain he said, "Yes, I know, dear. You meant sanguine."

Walter O'Keefe, who was a great entertainer in radio and in person, recalls the evening Bob and Butterworth came into his villa at the Garden to have a drink before they all went out to dinner. Benchley was sitting in an overstuffed chair. It was about six P.M. and the usual drink was in his hand. Every few minutes his whole body contorted into a convulsive shudder. Walter tried not to notice it—a hangover, he thought. But after five shudders, he asked solicitously, "Is there anything the matter?" Walter investigated the chair. His son Michael had concealed an electric battery under the cushion and was operating it long distance from the swimming pool. It was typical of Benchley that although he was being practically electrocuted, he was too polite to say anything.

Somewhere in a lost trunk, Muriel King has a photograph of Benchley, Butterworth, and Eddie Mayer taken at the Garden. Benchley is dressed in a shirt and green Swiss apron. From the front he looks very respectable. From the back, she told me, the view was of his little round cheeks. Musician Woody Herman remembers the apron was leather, like that worn by a butcher or a wine steward. "He would wear it either over his shorts or with a bare behind." It wasn't meant to be shocking, just funny.

Bob's bar was made for him by Dave Chasen, whose restaurant had been financed by Harold Ross. "Two box crates supporting a board," Dave recalls.

Corey Ford, in his book, *The Time of Laughter,* describes Bob's bungalow: "The Benchley apartment was small and had only one entrance, and delivery boys were forever elbowing guests aside as they crossed the living room on their way to the kitchen. The most prominent furnishing was a bar made of two upended cartons, well stocked. Promptly on our arrival Benchley would busy himself mixing drinks. Scott Fitzgerald, who had recently gone on the wagon, shook his head in mock disapproval. 'Don't you know that drinking is slow death?'

" 'So who's in a hurry,' Benchley demanded, stirring a martini contentedly."

I met Corey with Scott at the Garden in 1937. He was one of the best of the humorists, Scott informed me. He had gone to Hollywood to write *Sports Page* for Joel McCrea. It was a grim exposé of the professional-wrestling racket. Naturally the story was totally bereft of comedy. Just as illogically, Benchley had been given the assignment of making a film of the newspaper strip *Little Orphan Annie*. "Fortunately," stated Mr. Ford, "it was never produced."

Bob's "cell" at RKO was at the far end of the writer's block, and each morning Corey and he exchanged greetings as Bob passed his window on his way to work.

"One morning he showed up suffering from what I could see was the granddaddy of all hangovers. His hands were shaking, his face ghastly gray." Corey asked him solicitously whether he had had breakfast. "Had it?" Bob shuddered. "I've thrown it up." There was a garden hose on the grass, parallel to the walk. As Bob was staggering towards his office, the gardener accidentally flicked it, "sending a snakelike ripple down its length past Bob, who gave it one horrified look, turned on his heel, and rushed back to the Garden and went to bed for the rest of the day." He did not stir until cocktail time.

The next day Marc Connelly was working outside his villa at the Garden. He was typing on the patio protected by a small whitewashed wall from the wind, if any. (In Hollywood there is either nothing or a violent windstorm.) A shadow fell on his typewriter and it belonged to Benchley. "What are you doing here?" asked Marc. "I thought you were supposed to be working on *China Seas* at the studio?" "I've been dismissed for drunkenness," said Bob. "Were you drunk?" Marc asked. "No," said Bob. "It's one of the biggest lies in history." He was full of righteous indignation. "Oh, what a wonderful explosion there'll be when I introduce my proof that I was sober." The next day Benchley came to Marc's bungalow with some photographs. He was triumphant. "I'll make them shoot bacon now," he snorted. In the photographs he was shown standing on the set. In his extended right hand there was a highball glass. "Look at that right hand," he exploded. "Steady as a rock." The liquid in the glass was totally smooth. Where Benchley's face should have been, there was an obscuring cloud. It might not have been him at all, and actually he had not been dismissed. He had invented the dramatic buildup as an excuse for showing Marc the photographs. Nat Benchley feels that all the talk of drinking was a pose. Well, perhaps Bob talked more about drinking than he actually drank. But I often saw him drunk, all the same.

Nat insists, "Drinking is in the eye of the beholder. How much did they drink really? No one was ever a disaster. No one was ever arrested or in a drunken auto accident. No one was ill-behaved. No one got into any fights."

Bob made sure they would not when his sons were around. It did not take much to make him drunk. Bob boasted to me once that he had not had a drink or a cigarette until he was thirty-one. He certainly made up for lost time.

Some of the epigrams attributed to Bob belonged to someone else. He did not say, "Let's get out of these wet clothes and into a dry martini," although it sounds like him. The remark was supposedly made by Bob when he was acting in *China Seas*. He spent one whole day in a tank, the scene being one in which he had fallen off a ship. A press agent culled the famous quip from someone—probably Billy Wilder—and sent it out in a press release, attributing it to Benchley coming home from his day in the tank. Bob tried to disclaim the remark—he was an honest man and would not ever take credit for something he had not said. But it is still attributed to him.

There were enough bon mots without inventing them for the spirit of the Garden. One evening Bob left the Players and said to the man in uniform, "Get me a cab."

"I'm sorry," said the man haughtily. "I happen to be a rear admiral in the United States Navy."

"In that case," quipped Bob, "get me a destroyer." In his son's version, his father was sober and asked for a battleship.

"Traveling with children by car," he told me when I had my baby daughter along, "is like traveling third class in Bulgaria."

Al Wright of *Time* and Dick Pollard of *Life* came into Romanoff's shortly after Pearl Harbor. Al was in his green navy flier's uniform. Benchley arrived very tight. He always fancied himself as a strong man.

He used to take on his sons at wrestling, and the uniform of Lieutenant Wright inspired him to a feat of derring-do.

"I'll take you both on at Indian wrestling at the same time," he boasted at the bar, adding, "one with each hand." They smiled over his head, and let him win. In high spirits they went back to The Garden of Allah.

Bob decided they should all have a "treatment" from Doc, who came over with her little black leather valise and her Salvation Army costume. No one was ever going to question her in *that* outfit. After the treatment they all went to bed, Al and Dick in the double bed in the spare room.

Bob usually got up at 8:00 in the morning no matter how late he had gone to bed. He went into the living room, and, as usual, remembered nothing of what had happened the night before when he was drunk. He saw the green uniform and shrieked, "My God, the Japs have landed."

Bob was a bad sleeper. It was better when he drank, then he would fall asleep without knowing it. Otherwise he would be awake long into the night. Sometimes when Woody Herman returned late from playing with his orchestra and turned on the light in his villa, there would be a little scratching on the window and it was Bob Benchley asking apologetically if he could come in. "Sure," said Woody, and Bob would stay sometimes until six in the morning. Then start drinking again after an hour or two of sleep.

One night Bob picked up his friend Monty Woolley, the bad-tempered actor with the beard. He found him down the road at the bar owned by Mickey Outwaite. Monty returned home with Benchley and soon disappeared into the bathroom. He was there a long time, and Bob became worried. He went in and found Monty sitting straight up in the empty bathtub, naked. Bob fled.

Harry Ruby, the songwriter who lived there for a while, wonders why these great wits, underneath the epigrams and the laughter, were such unhappy people. He believes they had a Freudian death wish.

"I went over to the Garden one morning at eleven to see Woody Herman. As I was walking out, a voice from the next bungalow called, 'Harry!' It's Benchley and he says, 'Come in, have a drink.'

" 'Drink of what? I ask him. He had a big jar of martinis on the table.

"He said, 'Sing me one of your crazy songs.'

" 'At eleven in the morning?'

" 'I'll get you a piano.' I left. It was so sad. These wonderful guys, so intelligent. I'm not a sentimentalist, but something hits you."

"Benchley and Butterworth," said Frances Marion, "always had an open door. As people they liked passed, they called, 'Come in for a drink.' This bar had no closing time."

Muriel King had a dinner date with Bob in the spring of 1945. They went to several nightclubs, where acquaintances kept asking Bob to tell them a story that was going the rounds. Bob never kept a good joke to himself. He told it to everyone: "A man went sobbing to his psychiatrist.

" 'I'm goinng mad,' he told him. 'I have all these decisions to make.'

" 'Yes?' encouraged the doctor.

" 'Well,' sobbed the man, 'I work in an orange factory (sob) and I have to pick the big oranges and put them in one pile (sob, sob). I put the medium in another pile, and the small oranges in another. And (sob, sob, sob), I can't stand all the decisions.' " Bob roared with laughter. He thought it was a fine joke, one he had invented but told as though it had really happened.

"He wasn't holding his liquor too well that evening," Muriel relates, "and things got vague. He took me home and started the wrong way to the Garden." Muriel, pretending she was afraid to stay in her Holloway Drive home with just her sleeping son, called Bob back and asked him to spend the night on her couch. Bob stretched out on the sofa beneath a ledge full of sea shells. Muriel was an avid collector.

The next morning Bob entered her room, leaning against the open doorway, the lace curtains and the poinsettias behind him. "I've had the most awful time," he groaned. "How on earth did I get into the Natural History Museum?"

One of the pianists in The Garden of Allah bar was a young man, Felix de Cola. "My recollection of the whole place was that there was a continuous party going on. They would come for a party and stay for days. You never knew who was a guest and who was living there. Everyone just sort of flitted about. They were talented people who resented anyone who wasn't creative in some way."

De Cola had come to Hollywood from London in 1936 and played the piano at the Bar of Music on Beverly Boulevard, where many of the Garden crowd came in the evenings. "They had to behave there. It was a strict place and even Dietrich was kicked out for wearing slacks in 1937. My time at the The Garden of Allah was fascinating. No one knew day from night . . . they didn't care . . . and they were especially belligerent with no-talent studio heads. Why they kept falling into the pool, I don't know, but Benchley was the worst offender. I'd be there sometimes in the daytime in the thirties and saw Garbo joining in much of the activity. Perhaps she wanted to be alone in her cottage, otherwise she was part of the fun. When I was there in 1936 it was as though they were still celebrating the repeal of Prohibition three years earlier. I'd see them roaming from cottage to cottage, subletting or buying from each other, and the next day they had forgotten the deal. Some honored their commitments, others just chalked it up to another good evening. As the years went by, no matter how shoddy or cheap the atmosphere, the Garden was always brought back into glamorous focus by the residents. I was amazed one afternoon hearing some lovely music coming out of a cottage with an open door. I looked in and was invited inside by Rachmaninov who was rehearsing for a concert—his last. He died shortly after, in 1940.

"One night in the bar I heard them talking about John Barrymore's funeral. Errol Flynn, they said, had propped him up for one last drink with the boys. Maxie Rosenbloom was always around Barrymore, and I'll never forget Dana Andrews. He got stoned there one night but wanted to talk. So I took him home to my studio and let him talk until dawn. When I was taking him to the taxi, he picked up a bottle of my wine on the way out and gulped it down before he got to the taxi."

Dana has long since given up the bottle, which at one time threatened to ruin his career.

In the early forties, the traffic in the bar, which had been almost nonexistent, was fairly heavy. The war was on, and it was hard to get your own liquor. The most regular patrons of the bar, Mr. de Cola remembers, were Robert Benchley, Gene Fowler, Leo McCarey, and John Barrymore. One night, McCarey, well remembered for his direction of *Love Affair* and *Going My Way,* insisted on helping de Cola at the piano, running his fingers all over the keyboard.

There was no tipping, but the customers expected de Cola to keep

George Kaufman was always ready to play "The Game" at the
Garden. *Springer/Bettmann Archive*

up with the drinking. "I'd have the bartender mix me a long drink with very little scotch, and I'd nurse it along all evening. It was an almost constant state of alcoholic euphoria or melancholia, and inhibited or uninhibited behavior. My main impression of the bar was that it was like a private club, a feeling of never-never land. Time stood still there and nothing at all mattered."

The bar was mostly for men. De Cola cannot remember ever seeing a woman there.

Benchley, the New Englander, would rarely have taken a lady there. He was a courtly protector of women. I remember John McNulty coming to Bob's bungalow from the studio where he was writing the script for *The Stork Club*, starring Barry Fitzgerald, who complained, "These lines are so terrible I can't remember them." And McNulty on the set was playing the piano and singing:

> Keep your dreams within reason
> Life is terribly harsh
> You start out on the mountain
> And end up in the marsh.

McNulty was very proper in a tweed suit and button-up sweater, and people drifted in and out of Bob's bungalow, as they always did. McNulty, sitting on the couch with Mrs. Woody Herman, unbuttoned his sweater and relaxed. "You're very attractive," he said and placed his hand on her knee, a gesture she did not appreciate.

Robert, coming over with a drink in each hand, realized the situation, and leaning over Mrs. Herman asked quietly, "Is my friend becoming offensive?" McNulty buttoned up his sweater and left. But not angrily. Bob had softened the reproof by referring to him as "my friend." But it was effective, and McNulty did not bother her further.

During the war, Bob was going east by train from California—it was extremely hard to get a seat on a plane because top officials and ferry pilots had priority—and, in any case, Bob preferred the train. The long journey gave him time to catch up on his reading. He never traveled without a large book box. It was almost as difficult to travel by train during the war. I had to wait two weeks for a seat when I returned to Hollywood from New York after I had been in England in 1943.

Bob settled into his compartment with his books and looked forward to a peaceful trip, reading, drinking, and sleeping. Shortly after the train pulled out of Pasadena, Bob beelined for the bar. On the way, he found a woman who was very pregnant. She was unhappy and explained she did not have a berth. Bob, always gallant to a lady in distress, offered her his compartment. The conductor, who was passing through, interrupted them, saying that the ticket was not transferable.

"Yes, it is," snapped Bob.

"No, it isn't," snapped the conductor. This went on for some time with Bob getting more and more angry.

The train stopped at Needles, Arizona, and Bob descended in high dudgeon. As the train pulled out he realized he had left all his baggage behind. It took him some time to find a taxi and an even longer wait at the airport before he could get a seat on a plane that would take him east—with several stops before reaching Chicago where he could board the express train for New York.

He was unshaven, his nose was bleeding, and he had no baggage. The Sherman Hotel at first refused to take him. He finally found the owner, who knew him, and was given a room.

"This," said Bob when telling the story, "is my last adventure in gallantry."

There were always girls around the Benchley bungalow, and people sometimes wondered about his wife. Where was she? But it was her choice to stay in Scarsdale. She enjoyed playing bridge with the ladies of Scarsdale, and her husband had convinced her that it was a healthier place for her and the boys. A close friend of Benchley assured me that he telephoned her every morning and night, no matter where and in what condition he was. He admired her, but apparently he preferred the life of a bachelor. Her name before she married was Gertrude Darling, and I remember Bob's smile when he told me this.

Among the girls in villa 16, or 17, or 10, or wherever Bob was in residence at the Garden, I recall a baroness from Berlin; Carol Goodner, an actress; willowy Betty Starbuck, whose acting career he had nurtured; "Mugsie," his secretary; Louise Macy; and the present Mrs. Winston Guest, who was then Lucy Cochran from Boston. Bob liked being with women more than seducing them. The red haired wife of an actor who lived at the Garden often came over when her husband was on the road. She would take off her clothes and dance wildly. "The Flaming Bush" they called her.

Bob said to Al Wright, "There are two girls in town, one is blond, the other a brunet. Either would be great for you, although I think you'd like the blond best. They're too young for me," explaining his generosity.

The blond was from a well-known eastern family. Her freewheeling mother had advised her to enjoy life to the fullest and this included having affairs with men if she fancied them. Bob would never even try with a young girl. He did not want the responsibility.

Al liked the blond, and they had an affair. Today, when I read about the lady's exclusive parties and her homes in elite locations along the East Coast, it is hard to believe that the dignified society matron is the same girl Al met in Bob's bungalow at The Garden of Allah.

She adored Bob platonically. She warmed his bed for him when he was out late and was sleeping tranquilly when he returned home. Then she went to her own nearby apartment which she shared with the brunet, who was also to marry one of the top rich society names in America.

The two girls had come to Hollywood to try their luck in films. The brunet was doing a bit better than the blond. She had a better apartment and the blond envied her and longed to move in with her. The blond lady, who is now slender and petite, was big and beefy then. She weighed one hundred fifty pounds and was very athletic, which is now hard to imagine.

While her mother had social position in the East she had no money to spend on clothes for her daughter, who had been friendly at one time with A. C. Blumenthal, the financial promoter. He had a nude photograph of her at his nightclub in Mexico City. While she was at Fox, she had an affair with the president, Joe Schenck, who liked them blond and blue-eyed. It was generally believed that Joe also had an affair with Marilyn Monroe, who was his protégée.

Bob spoke German very well and he read pornographic books to the blond in German, which made them sound dirtier. She did not understand the language, but she got the drift of it. Bob had a library of pornographic books that he had received from a rich friend who loved pornography. Bob showed me a book of fiction stories about Clark Gable having all sorts of sexual adventures with all sorts of women. The rich man read his books on his flights east, and when he finished, he opened the window—this was when you could open windows on planes —and threw them out. I often wondered whether they were still intact on reaching the ground and what the people who found them thought.

Bob and the blond discussed necrophilia by the hour. She attended the funeral of Lupe Velez (Lupe had committed suicide), and returned to Bob full of gleeful details. "She [the blond] was just a little tramp," one of Bob's friends told me. "I remember her saying, 'I've slept with the best—Errol Flynn.' "

She once complained, "I don't know why people say I'm such an easy lay. After all, I don't know that many people." She was beautiful and dumb. When a friend of Benchley's was discussing a well-known piece of knowledge—that the sun is further from the earth than the moon—she was in rapture. "That's fascinating," she said. "You ought to write a book about it." She was told politely that he was not the only person in possession of this knowledge. "Well, *I* didn't know it," she declared, "and I'm brighter than a lot of people who are stupider than me."

She was not really stupid. One day she produced a published list of the most eligible bachelors in America, pointed to the man who was the richest and most attractive among them and said, "I'll marry him!" Two years later, she did.

Benchley's girl "Louie" Macy had been a salesgirl at Hattie Carnegie's fashionable shop in New York, living in what she called the condemned wing of The New Weston Hotel. She returned to Pasadena in 1935. After Harry Hopkins died, Louie married again, and later committed suicide some years after Benchley's death. It would have distressed him enormously. He liked to think that his girls would be happy, and that after they left him they would live rich and glorious lives. When Miss Macy died, John McClain held a wake for her at "21."

I don't know whether he paid for Louie to return to California. He might have because he was generous and always doing things like that. When his secretary-valet MacGregor died, Bob paid for the education of his daughter.

He brought Mugsie to California after meeting her in New York in 1938, when she was a hat-check girl at The Barclay Hotel. "I had a musician boyfriend," she told me from The Hague in Holland where she lives with her husband, Adrian Van Der Deen, the literary editor of a Dutch newspaper. "He was working on a short for Mr. Benchley." (Like Dorothy Parker, she always called him Mr. Benchley, although Dorothy sometimes called him Fred). "He asked me if I would like to meet him. Would I! He was one of my heroes. I had read everything he had written, and I was overwhelmed when he said, 'Why don't you work for me? I have a secretary, but . . .' and his voice trailed off. When he said to me, 'Will you go to Hollywood?' it was like opening up the Arabian Nights dream."

Mugsie went to Hollywood in 1939 to be his secretary, and I have been told by several of Bob's friends that she could not type. But this did not matter to Bob. She was a pretty brunet and he liked having her around. He treated her like a much-loved daughter until she left him to get married a few years later.

"I had a vacation coming in 1942," Mugsie told me. (Her real name was Jeannette Le Mesurier.) "I wanted to go to Canada to ski. But Bob said, 'Why don't you go to Maine?'" He thought New England was better than Canada. He arranged for me to stay at a big old-fashioned hotel. There was a handsome young man in the dining room. We were the only two young people there. When I came back I told Mr. Benchley that Adrian and I were going to be married. He said, 'Isn't that rather quick?' Then he said with a smile, 'I was saving you for him.'" The marriage of Mugsie and Adrian has lasted twenty-seven years. Bob was the godfather of her son, whom she named Robert.

"He needed all kinds of people," Mugsie recollected. "And yet he was lonely. He was a serious man. He felt his talents were being wasted. His life in Hollywood was society and films, Dorothy Earle of Santa Barbara, Louise Macy of Pasadena. When it all became too much he would say, 'Mugsie, lock the door and pull down the blinds and get out the file on Queen Anne.'"

Bob's bookshelves at the Royalton in New York were filled with works about the Queen Anne period. He had originally intended to write a book on the humorists of that period. "He read everything he could get hold of, then filed his notes in a card file, with a secret coding system," Nat Benchley relates. But after an enormous amount of work on the humorists, he sadly came to the conclusion that not one of them was funny. Then he thought he would do a general history of the time, in the form of a play. He continued with his research and collected a great deal of material.

But like so many overresearchers, he never got around to the

writing. In his biography of his father, *Robert Benchley: A Biography,*
Nat wrote "Perhaps he was overmeticulous about checking out sources
and footnotes. Perhaps he was afraid of the project. At any rate, it was
one of those things that became ephemeral, a white whale."

After his death, all the research and notes on Queen Anne were
given to Exeter, his old school.

"He was always saying," said Mugsie, " 'We'll work on Queen
Anne.' At those times if anyone knocked or the doorbell rang, he pretended he wasn't there. He was sweet and gentle and seemed to have
an aura of sadness about him. I always felt sorry for him. Sometimes
he called me at three o'clock in the morning to say, 'I've just ordered
a limousine, to take us to the Samarkand Hotel in Santa Barbara."
Queen Anne was forgotten while he walked alone on the beach.

Mugsie had an apartment down the street from the Garden, and
when Bob thought that unexpected visitors might be dropping in on
him at the Garden, he slipped out the side gate and came with a book
and sat in her living room until Ben called him to say that it was all
clear. "Sometimes he would get fed up with 'the whole fucking rat
race' and simply take off to the ocean. He loved the sea, and if he
couldn't have Nantucket, the Pacific would do for the time being. He
gave me books to read about the sea—*Moby Dick,* the works of Conrad, *High Wind in Jamaica, The Ocean,* by James Hanley."

Bob seemed to need Queen Anne as a steadying influence, a
stern reminder that there was more to his life than the illusionary film
world and the sun worshiping moneyed existence of his rich society
friends. Mugsie always carried a pack of filing cards in her bag and
when he said, "Take a card, Mugsie," she had the feeling he found it
comforting and reassuring.

While he was working on a picture, he was told that the schedule
had been changed and that he would not have to go to the studio the
following day. He was delighted and told Mugsie to be at his bungalow
at 8:30 A.M., sharp. "We'll work all day on Queen Anne. We'll lock
the door, draw the curtains, and take no calls." They would have
crackers and milk for lunch and no drinking before 6:00 P.M. He was
happy at the thought. By nine o'clock, they were at work, Bob dictating, Mugsie busy with the card file, when they heard a key being turned
in the lock.

"Mr. Benchley swore, jumped up, grabbed me, and pulled me with
him into the coat closet. We heard the valet—I had forgotten to cancel

him—going from room to room, opening and shutting doors and then deciding apparently to leave." On the way out, he stopped by the closet in which they were hiding. Benchley, determined to save his day, grabbed the door handle just as the valet was trying to open it, and there ensued a grim, silent tug-of-war. The valet was stronger and won. It was like an old silent comedy to see the valet's surprised face as he fell backward while Mr. Benchley was propelled forward at great speed into the patio, only barely missing the pool. He helped the valet to his feet and explained sheepishly that neither of them had to work that day.

Bob was a premature anti-Fascist—a government euphemism for people who opposed fascism before it became the national attitude. He was a supporter of Loyalist Spain, with his friends Ernest Hemingway, Lillian Hellman, and Dashiell Hammett, and he organized a group at the Garden to make Mussolini unwelcome in Hollywood, in the unlikely event that he would come there. Bob was not politically opposed, however, to the government of the United States. He was a liberal and a Roosevelt supporter.

Nat Benchley was at the Garden waiting for his father, who was at the studio, when he heard about Roosevelt's death. "I learned the news from the cleaning woman. She said, 'Isn't it terrible.' The studios closed down and father came home early. It seemed that the whole Garden was sitting around moping."

Libby Holman sat on the steps of her villa muttering, "Oh, my God! Truman! Anything, anybody but Truman!" Little Ingrid Herman, Woody's daughter, her hair in two little pigtails, went around telling people, "My best friend died today."

Bob, groping for something good to say about the change of leadership, told them that Truman had headed a Senate committee investigating the corruption in defense contracts. "It takes guts," he said vehemently, "to say to someone, 'You're crooked.' " And with halfhearted conviction, "That's *something.*"

Bob called himself a confused liberal. He supported every good cause and voted the Democrat ticket, although he was a registered Republican. Every anti-Nazi and anti-Fascist group knew they could count on Benchley for money and support. He believed in the unions and belonged to as many as he could, the Writers, the Actors, any one that would take him.

But most of his friends in California, apart from those who lived at the Garden or who wrote in the studios, were horse-racing, polo-playing millionaires. Perhaps this is one reason he was for Roosevelt. The President was a millionaire, but he was a Democrat who cared about the people.

Bob loathed Hitler and Mussolini. When Nat Benchley was en route to the war in the Pacific in May of 1945, he saw in his father's bungalow a Disney toy similar to monkeys on a stick. It featured Hitler doing obscene things to Mussolini. Bob had painted the moustache on one face and the tight jutting lips on the other.

When sleeping pills kept him awake and benzedrine merely made him drowsy on the set, Bob gave up on benzedrine. In any case, he could think of no particular reason for wanting to stay awake. The pills combined with the drinking didn't help anything. He was tired of everything he was doing, he felt he had done it all before.

On New Year's Eve of 1944, Reginald Gardner, the British comedian, and Benchley were on the town, separately. They bumped into each other at seven different parties, the last at Greer Garson's Bel Air home on Stone Canyon Road.

They went into a corner of the elegant playroom and agreed that they had had it. They were both very drunk. Said Reggie, "Lesh go to the pub,"—the name for his home in Beverly Hills at 444 North Bedford Drive. It is now a dentists building where they are pulling teeth, not corks. Flopping into the pub, Reggie fixed some drinks for his guest and himself. They sat for some time drinking and laughing uproariously at each other's guips.

"Go on," urged Bob, "be wallpaper." Reggie had an act in which he managed to convey that he was a piece of wallpaper. I've forgotten how he did it, but it was most realistic, and at parties everyone laughed when he did his wallpaper act.

Then they sat quietly. Perhaps they were thinking, but they were more likely in an alcoholic stupor. After a while, Reggie put a blank acetate record on the Victrola. They each had a hand mike and they talked. One side of the record consists of lewd drunken conversation, with Bob's laughter all through it. Nonsensical talk between two men.

It was 8:45 in the morning when Reginald opened the blind a few inches and the sun streamed in. Bob, who was allergic to the sun, winced and covered his face and said, "There's such a thing as drinking yourself completely sober."

"At this point we had actually talked ourselves into sobriety," Reggie told me. The giggles were gone, and they looked gray in the morning light that managed to get through the blinds Reggie had hastily closed in response to Bob's anguished plea.

Reggie looked at the record on the Victrola. Only one side had been used. "Bob," he said quietly, "I'd love to have a recording of something you really love." Bob thought a minute, then said, "Do you have a Bible?" "I have three," Reggie replied. Bob opened a Bible to the Ecclesiastes, Chapter 13. Reggie set the record, and Bob read, "The Prophet sayeth . . ." up to "Vanity of Vanities, All is Vanity."

"He read it," said Gardner, "as though it had never been read before," to the accompaniment of a Debussy string quartet that Reggie had put on another record player. Afterwards, Bob said, "This is the greatest piece of writing ever done." Another remark that is on the record: "This is going to be the greatest year for us all, so will you all clap, or have clap!" It was 1945, and Bob would never celebrate another New Year.

His son Nat was extremely moved when he heard the record. "It contained the greatest weariness I ever heard in my life," he told me on the Cape last summer. He remembered a line on the record. "If there is going to be a 1945. Only kidding, God. Only kidding."

"It was a hard time," said Nat, "in which to be funny."

Muriel King believes that Benchley was killed by his own good nature. "People whom he had never seen would call and say, 'Can I come over?' and he didn't know how to refuse them if he thought they would be amusing, and even if he didn't. He was so outgoing and so polite. He was kind, and strangers came and used up his energy." Muriel never saw Bob cross or impolite until the last year, when he became so ill. "He had cirrhosis of the liver," she told me, "an ailment which acts on your disposition."

Muriel had a dinner date in New York with Bob the night he became ill. It started as a nosebleed that would not stop. He had had them before and no one was too alarmed, but he thought he should go to the hospital. It was the weekend of November 17, 1945.

Roland Young called Muriel to say that Bob had been taken to the Regent Hospital, but they would all meet later at "21." Shortly afterward Roland telephoned to say that Bob was seriously ill. When he was dying of a cerebral hemorrhage in the hospital, Gerald Murphy, one of his closest friends, remained outside his door, waiting for news. He died four days later on November 21.

They held a wake for Mr. Benchley at "21." And a more private wake at the New Weston Hotel for his closest relatives and friends, his wife and two sons, Bea Stewart, Roland Young, Jock Whitney, Deems Taylor, Quentin Reynolds, John McClain.

Mike Romanoff held a wake in Hollywood, and all the people who had loved Bob came and told stories, and laughed as he would have laughed if he could have listened. Five weeks later, on Christmas Eve, my son was born. And I named him Robert for Benchley, who had wanted to be his godfather.

[VIII]

the golden age at the garden

THE DECADE BETWEEN 1935 AND 1945 was an exciting time in Hollywood. It was like Florence during the Renaissance. The artists in every field came to Hollywood. Fred Allen, at the height of his fame on radio, signed for a film at Fox and brought his troupe of gagmen with him from New York to Hollywood. They included Herman Wouk, Arnold Auerbach, Harry Von Zell, and Herman Huppfeld, who wrote "As Time Goes By" for *Casablanca*. Allen quartered his group at The Garden of Allah. Wouk called the Garden Rainbow's End in *Youngblood Hawke,* his novel about a successful writer who goes to Hollywood. Rainbow's End featured drab hotel furnishings. Hawke's living room was "beige and tan," and he always breakfasted by the side of the pool. "The sky was clear blue, the sun beat white and hard on the cottage walls, and the breeze smelled of flowers. Hibiscus and bougainvillea splashed raw color all around the courtyard."

"I was a happy gagman," Wouk (who achieved fame in 1950 with his novel *The Caine Mutiny*) told me from his home in Washington, D.C. "The Garden was a paradise, a Rainbow's End. I remember Stoopnagel and Budd jumping over each other in the pool. Sometimes I saw Nazimova in the evening, a wraithlike creature in black. I was shattered when I returned in later years to the Garden. It was desolate and so different."

But in the golden decade at the Garden it was an exciting place to live, reflecting the activity and prosperity of the studios.

127

One night during the war, Kay Thompson saw Benchley and Butterworth going to the bar together. "They were acting up and giggling like a couple of pansies. After that there was a rule that no man could be in the bar without a woman. Imagine them being suspicious of Benchley and Butterworth!"

They put a Pinkerton detective at the door to enforce the rule. Benchley and Butterworth were halted the next time, and yelled bloody murder about their constitutional rights. "Would you rather we went out and picked up a woman on the streets?" Bob demanded. The detective grudgingly allowed them in. After that, when the Damon and Pythias of the Garden went together to the bar, they circumvented the ruling by Charlie dressing as a woman.

Kay, still paper thin in profile, remembers that the fun at the Garden was mostly on the surface, although you could swear that Benchley was enjoying himself. "The whole thing about these writers in Hollywood," she mused, "they were incarcerated and frustrated, and they were there for years. They knew they weren't going to leave and they had to find an out so they drank and played games."

The Garden of Allah was the Algonquin Round Table gone west and childish. When a night spot closed, they put the band in the car and went to the Garden. It was the original jet set, although the planes to New York took anything from eighteen to twenty-one hours with four stops en route. "Those lonely little airports" that Scott Fitzgerald wrote about in *The Last Tycoon*—You would land in Kansas City at four in the morning, as I did on the Christmas Day that I first flew to Hollywood—a waiting room like a railroad station in a small town. Most of the people at the Garden preferred the Chief and later the Super Chief. You were sure of meeting several of the people to whom you had just said good-bye.

Next to Robert Benchley, his shadow, Charlie Butterworth, was the most conspicuous resident of The Garden of Allah. Charlie came from South Bend, Indiana, where he was born in 1897. He slipped into Hollywood early in the 1930s and played balding, shy, bachelor roles in films like *Love Me Tonight* (1932) and *Road Show* (1941). Muriel King found him "a real funny, original, deadpan, adored guy." Like Bob, he was always immaculately dressed. He lived at the Garden following his divorce from his petite wife, Ethel, who has been Mrs. Ernest Heyn for a long while now.

Margaret Roach and Charlie Butterworth in *Road Show*. Charlie worshiped Bobby. Did he commit suicide after Benchley's death?

Walter O'Keefe, who also started life in South Bend, Indiana, worked with Charlie in Hollywood, and Charlie was difficult to work with. "I could never get a sober performance out of him," Walter reflected. "He told me, 'I went on sober once, and I was lousy,' and, 'I never ever went to bed sober with a woman.'" In view of this, it is remarkable that beautiful Dusty Anderson—who is now Mrs. Jean Negulesco—and Natalie Schafer were both in love with him during their respective residences at the Garden.

Those who knew Charlie before he came to Hollywood are sure he was not a drinker until he met Bob Benchley. Benchley had a protective attitude toward Charlie, who was usually even more drunk than Bob was. He fluttered over him like a mother hen. One time he even tried to straighten him out.

"Look Charlie," Bob said somberly, "we can't have martinis forever. We must have something to sober up with." Then his face creased in a grin. "Let's have three vodkas to sober up with."

Benchley and Butterworth were talking and drinking one night in the bungalow they shared at one time, above the Hacketts. The husband-and-wife writing team could hear their upstairs neighbors through the thin ceiling. Albert and Frances finally went to bed leaving a message with the telephone operator to be called at 7:30 in the morning. When they awakened they could hear Benchley and Butterworth still talking and drinking. They were still at it when the Hacketts took off for the studio at 8:30.

When the inseparable B. and B. were being noisier than usual, Elliott Nugent who could make his own noise, sent them a note: "When I hear laughter coming from Bungalow 16, I know it's coming from comedian Butterworth and literary wit Benchley, and I appreciate it very much. But my children, who have never heard of you, regard you as a couple of drunks." Bob and Charlie were highly amused and showed the note all over the Garden.

Al Newman, who arranged the music at 20th Century-Fox, told me he went to Charlie's villa at the Garden and asked him to do him a favor. "'How much do you want?' he said. 'No, I don't want money,' I told him. 'I just want to borrow a couch from your bungalow.'" Charlie saw nothing wrong with this, and they called Marc Connelly and Harry Ruby from their villas, and the four of them carried the couch across Sunset Boulevard. They were caught by the traffic in the middle of the road. "We all sat down on the couch and waited for the cars to pass. We had a kind of crazy thing."

"I was single when I was living at the Garden," Mr. Ruby recalls. "I invited ten people for dinner, including Oscar Hammerstein, Charlie and Bob, Roland Young, Marc Connelly, and Alexander Woollcott. Dave Chasen was to send the dinner from his restaurant. 'What kind of soup shall we have?' I asked. Charlie said, 'I don't like soup.' The others didn't want soup either. I went through each course and they didn't like anything. It ended with practically no food at all. At the end, Dave's waiter brought out an expensive bottle of brandy. Oscar Hammerstein turned to me very seriously and said, 'Is brandy good on an empty stomach?' All during the aborted dinner, Woollcott had been staring at Harry. Finally the songwriter asked him, 'Why are you staring?' Woollcott replied, 'Because you look like a dishonest Abe Lincoln.' "

Corey Ford remembers that Butterworth, like Benchley, had a particular aversion to the songbirds that abounded in the shrubbery around the cottage. "They shrilled incessantly when he was trying to sleep. Returning from a party in the darkness before dawn, he roamed the grounds in a mood of dire revenge, shaking the palm trees one after another to disturb any roosting occupants. "Wake me up would you, you feathered bastards," I could hear him muttering outside my window. "All right, now it's *my* turn!"

Dusty Negulesco, who was Charlie's girl in the early 1940s, had come to Hollywood from New York where she was a top Conover model. She was a lovely tall brunet with a gorgeous figure. She had come with fifteen other models to appear in *Cover Girl,* which starred Rita Hayworth and Gene Kelly.

"Harry Cohn, the head of Columbia, the studio making *Cover Girl,* decided on a publicity stunt and also our protection. He knew the Hollywood wolves would be howling around the door, so—," Dusty laughed when she told me this, "—he decided to make us inaccessible. He rented a large house that had formerly been the annex to Marion Davies's house in Beverly Hills."

I knew the house later, when oil millionaire Arthur Cameron owned it. There were acres of lawn, an enormous Spanish-style house on the slopes of the hill, a championship tennis court, and an Olympic-size pool. I used to take my children there in the fifties to swim and play tennis. Quite an annex!

The Cover Girls with Rita Hayworth in *Cover Girl*. They preferred the freedom of life at the Garden. *Copyright © 1944 by
Columbia Pictures Corporation*

Mr. Cohn hired Anita Colby, the most beautiful model of her day in the early thirties, to be a sort of housemother to chaperon the fifteen lovely ladies. He wanted it all to be pure and protected. Guards were stationed at the gates on Benedict Canyon to keep the men out.

In New York the models earned about a thousand dollars a week. They were the cream of the crop. But Mr. Cohn thought he was doing them a favor putting them in pictures, and paying them a meager hundred dollars a week, out of which they had to pay twenty dollars a week toward the rent.

"After a month," Dusty told me, "we became angry. Not so much at the salary, but at the confinement. Eight of us decided to leave the house and find a place that would be more congenial. We were in Hollywood and wanted to have some fun."

They had heard of The Garden of Allah, and rented two of the bigger villas, each with two bedrooms. They were somewhat fearful of Mr. Cohn's reaction to their rebellion and expected to be sent back to New York in disgrace. "But when we said to Mr. Cohn, 'We are a majority,' he knew he was licked, and he allowed us to stay." In any case, he had received full measure of publicity from the stunt. "We were supposed to stay six weeks for the film, but the job lasted six months."

Dusty met Charlie at the Garden. "He was my beau," she stated, and I could see she was still unhappy over his tragic death. "He was so amusing. You never knew how he would react to a situation. One evening we were dining at Romanoff's. We had two drinks before dinner and not much to eat. The bill came to fifty dollars. Charlie was horrified. He asked the waiter to review the bill because he was sure there had been a mistake. [Food was cheaper then.] The waiter came back and said, 'Yes, Mr. Butterworth, there *is* a mistake—it's sixty-five dollars.' "Charlie, without blinking, replied, 'Ah, that's better.' "

It reminds me of when Marc Connelly had a box at the roller-skating derby. He took Garson Kanin and Charlie—the sophisticated intellectuals had unsophisticated pastimes. The radio announcer stuck the mike in front of Charlie's face: "How do you like the roller derby this year?" he asked him.

Without a pause, Charlie said, "It's much dustier than last year." The announcer was left hanging.

"Charlie introduced me to Hollywood," Dusty continued, "so that meant I saw a great deal of his idol, Bob Benchley. They served dry martinis in a glass teapot, and asked Dorothy Parker to come 'to tea.' Charlie gave Dorothy a black fluffy dog which he had named Dusty."

One evening they were sitting around at the Garden—Charlie, Benchley, Dorothy, and Dusty. The two men and Dorothy were lamenting their fate in Hollywood. Bob was then appearing in *County Fair*. "Here I am," he said, "the man who was going to write the life of Queen Anne, doing square dancing and walking between sandwich boards." (In one scene he had to advertise the fair with a board harnessed to his body.) Said Miss Parker, "Here I am taking instruction in writing from Gregory Ratoff." Butterworth said soberly, "And me, if I don't step over the white mark [to keep the actor stationary for the camera], it's considered a good performance."

Charlie was paying seven hundred fifty dollars a month for his villa. During the war he took out all the kitchen equipment and most of the furniture in the living room. He filled the place with dilapidated chairs, and tables that he had found in a secondhand store. When he was asked, "How can you live in a place like this?" he replied, "I guess it's because it reminds me so much of Hollywood."

They could have left any time they liked. But it was as if there were a spell chaining them to Hollywood. It would have required too much effort to leave, and where else could they have been paid so much money for so little effort? And where else would their behavior have been tolerated?

One evening Charlie drove his small car right into Chasen's restaurant. Dusty thinks it was an MG; Dave was sure it was a Fiat. Whatever it was, it was the car in which he later killed himself. He also had a Lincoln Continental, but he liked the small open car because people could see him in it, and he thought they were saying, "There goes Charlie Butterworth."

Walter O'Keefe made a macabre prophecy: that Charlie would kill himself in his sports car. Charlie's friends give two slightly different versions of how it happened. Some say he wrapped himself and the car around a telegraph pole, others say he drove into a wall. It was near the dangerous crossing on Sunset Boulevard. Most of them are sure he was drunk when the tragedy occurred. But Dusty, who knew him well, told me he was sober. "The more he drank, the slower he

drove. I believe he deliberately drove his car into the wall. He had been
so depressed after Benchley's death. The night before he died, he took
me to Romanoff's for a drink. I had become engaged to Jean Negulesco. He held my hand and said, 'No matter what happens, I want you
to know that I'm happy about your happiness.' He wanted to be with
Bob and that is why he deliberately drove into the wall. He was sober
that night."

Charlie had been at a party on the night he died. Nat Benchley
thought it might have been suicide because, according to some of those
at the party, he had not had enough to drink to make the accident
plausible. This would make Dusty right, that he was not drunk.

But Leon Shamroy, the top cameraman at 20th Century-Fox, who
was living at the Garden with his family at the time Butterworth was
killed, believes he was drunk. "That night, he had tried to get into
John McClain's villa." Charlie was very drunk and noisy, according
to Leon. "When there was no answer—McClain might have been there
but, seeing Charlie in that state, didn't answer—Charlie went away in
a huff."

Natalie Schafer, who was engaged to Charlie, told me that he
came to her bungalow at the Garden. "He had been drinking with
John McClain all evening, and he had finally sent him away. He wanted
to sleep on my couch, but I wouldn't let him in. 'No, no,' I told him
at the door, 'go on home.' He got into his MG and drove to Sunset
and had the accident."

Walter O'Keefe received the news at seven in the morning. He
called McClain and told him, "Charlie is dead." They went to the
morgue and took charge of the funeral arrangements. After the funeral, Charlie's friends adjourned to Mike Romanoff's house and lamented the passing of their friend.

"Howard Reinheimer, the show-business lawyer, was a close friend
of Butterworth," Walter informed me. "He came to my house in 1961,
and we started reminiscing about Charlie. Howard almost knocked me
off my chair when he said, 'Did I ever tell you about Charlie's affair
with a nun?' "

Walter is a Catholic and he retorted, "Cool it. I'm not interested in
jokes like that."

"No," Howard persisted, "you'll like this story. On his last trip to
New York, we had to get Charlie off the streets, he was so drunk. We
moved him into a hospital run by Franciscan nuns. One day, after they

sobered him up, he said, 'You know, Sister, that I'm not a Catholic anymore?'

"The old, old nun smiled and said, 'Don't worry, we'll pray for you.' "

Charlie saw Howard soon after he left the hospital. "I've no chick, I've no child, and Bobby is dead. You'd better change my will." After he died, the old nun received a letter from his lawyer. She opened it and found a certified check for $389,000.

the grim weeper

DOROTHY PARKER USED TO AN-nounce that she was half Jewish, so if anyone said anything against the Jews, only half of her would walk out. She was the most unpredictable woman I ever met in The Garden of Allah, or anywhere else.

I had met her in New York be-fore I came to Hollywood. She had been tattooed in the Bowery, and the New York *Mirror,* which I was working for in 1934, sent me to get an interview with her. She was staying at The Lowell Hotel, and when she could not pay her bill there, she ordered an ambulance and was carried out on a stretcher. Who would dun a dying woman?

Her husband, Alan Campbell, John O'Hara, and John McClain were with her when I arrived. They were hanging on her every word. O'Hara had recently made a hit in literary circles and with the public with his first novel, *Appointment in Samarra.* McClain was writing the ship-news column for an afternoon newspaper. The interesting people traveled by ship in those days, and the reporters and photographers boarded the boat in quarantine to interview and take pictures of the celebrities.

Dorothy was apologetic. The tattoo, she said with shy embarrass-ment, was only on her arm. The newspaper had expected it to be somewhere more exciting. She gave me tea, and she offered me her undying friendship. "Call me up any time," she begged. "I want to see you again. Please remember to call me. Promise you will." I left feel-ing pleased with myself. I had made an impression on one of the great wits of the day.

Dorothy Parker, the bitchiest resident at the Garden. *Wide World Photos*

In a few days I telephoned her. She was out, I was told after giving my name to the operator. I phoned the next day and the next, and then realized she hadn't meant anything at all, that not only had I made no impression on her, but that she probably loathed me. With Dottie you could never be sure, as I was to learn when I knew her better in Hollywood.

It was rather embarrassing for me to meet her again in Robert Benchley's bungalow at the Garden. But she was friendly, and said she was delighted to see me again. I was to see a lot of Dorothy, mostly with Bob, whom she surprised me by calling Mr. Benchley. They didn't know each other very well, I assumed. Actually they knew each other very well. Eddie Chodorov, the playwright, is convinced that she was always in love with Bob Benchley. She had met him while working with him on *Vanity Fair* between 1917 and 1920. He was the only person I did not hear her malign as soon as he left the room. I can well imagine what she said about me after I had left the Lowell. I was always uncomfortable with her even when I got to know her very well at the Garden with Benchley and Scott Fitzgerald.

Dorothy wore her rather sparse black hair in sticky-looking bangs on her forehead, over round smudges of black doleful eyes. When I knew more about art under Scott's tutelage, I thought she looked like a tired Renoir. She wore the weirdest clothes. Once I saw her going to dinner at the Sheekmans' wearing tennis shoes and black stockings with a blouse and skirt.

When ever she saw me she would take my hand and hold it tensely, and sometimes tears rolled down her white cheeks, and she would say how glad she was to see me, behaving just as she had done at the hotel in New York. But now I knew her, and I said as little as possible when we met at the various bungalows at the Garden and at the dinners in the homes in Beverly Hills, including the one she gave during the last year of Scott's life.

When he died, a few days before Christmas 1940, she and Alan came to see me from the funeral parlor. I was in bed with cramps, clutching a hot-water bottle, and they were very kind and sympathetic when I cried, "I hope I meet someone just like Scott." "That had class," she told Gerold Frank, who collaborated with me on *Beloved Infidel,* which dealt mostly with my time with Scott.

But when she reviewed the book, she was murderous. "They not only dug up his bones," she wrote, "but they gnawed on them," which I have to admit is pretty funny, although at the time the stab was excruciating. But this was Dottie—nice to your face, cruel behind your back. I realize that she was a very unhappy woman. She inhabited a vale of tears, and the only way she could live with herself was to murder everyone else with her biting words. Everyone except Mr. Benchley. "Everyone else was an abstraction," Mr. Chodorov believes. "She was in love with Bob and that was all she knew."

I'm not as sure, although I realized from their closeness that at some time they had had a serious affair.

She had been born Dorothy Rothschild in August 1893 in West End, New Jersey. She married Edward Pont Parker in 1917 and divorced him in 1928. She was very beautiful when she was young, Eddie Mayer used to tell me. It was hard for me to believe. Her face was too white and dissipated when I met her. She had married Alan Campbell in 1933. They divorced in 1947 and remarried in 1950.

After the second ceremony, she sobbed dramatically, "I've been given a second chance. How many people are given a second chance?" But she never stopped maligning Alan during their first and second try at matrimony. She told people how he gypped his agent, never paying him his commission. But I knew Alan, and I am sure he was an honest man. Why did he put up with his cruel wife, who was always telling lies about him? When she fell down and bruised herself she told sympathizers, "Alan hit me."

Dorothy became quite lachrymose when Alan went off to the war, and talked about him all the time, saying a few nice things and weeping, as usual. She asked some friends, "Would you like to have a photograph of Alan? I have two in my bungalow." The friends chose the one in which he was not smiling. "Oh," whimpered Dotty, "you don't like the other one?" It was simpler to take the two pictures of Alan.

Dorothy frequently put her head in the oven, making sure that she had called someone first. I doubt whether she even turned on the gas. She often slashed her wrists. She wore bracelets to hide the scars. Natalie Schafer was seeing McClain, who had had a romance with Dorothy. One evening he rang Natalie's bell at the Garden. There was an ambulance outside, and when Natalie opened the door, John exclaimed, "Oh, thank God, that was too quick. The last time the ambulance was for Dottie Parker."

Benchley once said to her, "Oh Dottie, if you keep on committing suicide you're going to injure your health permanently!"

There were certain people she despised more than others although she used them as needed. She met a writer who also had a bungalow at the Garden. His option was picked up, and he decided to rent a house. Dorothy asked if she could live at his home, platonically, for six months. This was after the first breakup of her marriage to Alan Campbell. When they remarried and she took a house of her own, she gave a housewarming. She did not invite the man who had put her up—and put up with her. He couldn't imagine what he had done to annoy her. He had done nothing, except give her shelter for six months.

The Hacketts spent one Christmas at the Garden, and they remember Gloria Sheekman cooking for days and preparing a beautiful meal. When they arrived, Dorothy was holding a tray of mouth-watering hors d'oeuvres. She said to Frances, "Will you hold this shit for me?" This was especially nasty because Dorothy had invited herself to the party.

Gloria had come home early from the studio. It was Christmas Eve, and the actors could go home or attend the office parties where everyone got drunk and the secretaries told their bosses what they really thought of them. The gatherings became so acrimonious, sometimes ending in fights, that they were abolished about ten years ago. Gloria was in a hurry because she was giving a Christmas Eve dinner party, and while she had been preparing for it for several days in her meticulous way, there was still a great deal to do. She smiled when she stopped at the window of Benchley's bungalow and saw his Christmas decoration, a small pink candle made of clay, resting on a red crocheted doily. Bob looked up and came to the door. They chatted for a while. "It suddenly occurred to me," Gloria told me, "that he had nowhere to go that evening."

"What are you doing tonight?" she asked him. "Nothing," he replied, a bit embarrassed. "Would you like to join us for dinner?" she asked him. Bob was not a man you could feel visibly sorry for. "I'd love to," he replied with alacrity. Half an hour later Gloria's phone rang. It was Bob. "Are you having a big party?" he inquired. "No, only family and a few friends." Bob continued diffidently, "Well, Dorothy and Charlie don't have any place to go. Can they come too?"

During dinner Gloria asked her guests about their plans for the next day. These famous wits had not been invited anywhere for Christmas Day. They dined again with the Sheekmans. "For three years," Gloria told me happily, "I cooked for the three of them, Benchley, Butterworth, and Dottie Parker."

I wonder, was Marc Connelly being sarcastic when he said to me, "Because Dorothy Parker knew so much about the human heart, she was given *Madame X* to write for the screen"?

She was just as bitchy when the party was her own. She telephoned Harry Ruby and said, "Harry, this is Dorothy Parker. I'm giving a party on Wednesday. Can you come? Everyone will be here—Hammerstein, Benchley, Butterworth."

Harry arrived at the party to be greeted by his hostess who gushed, "It's so nice of you to come, isn't this a lot of shit."

Nat Benchley has rather strong sentiments about Miss Parker. "I didn't trust Dottie. Lovable she wasn't. Hers was the lashback usually given after the person she was lashing had left the room." People were afraid to leave the room, for fear of inspiring one of her vicious remarks.

Her staunch principles about the Screen Writers Guild, the anti-Nazi and anti-Fascist organizations did not extend to her private life. When young Benchley, the son of her greatest friend, wanted to talk to her about the biography he was writing on his father, she twice agreed to an appointment and twice stood him up. Then she proudly told an acquaintance, "I refused to see the little shit."

"Being friends with Dottie," said George Oppenheimer, "was like living on a volcano. She eviscerated you when your back was turned. Nonetheless, I remained close friends with her through all the ups and downs."

George knew Dorothy well. As co-founder of Viking Press (with Harry Guinzburg) he was her publisher. He knew her in New York and also in Hollywood when they were both writing for the screen. "On one occasion when Dottie and Alan came to Hollywood," he told me, "they stayed with me in my Brentwood house. Then they lived on Canon Drive and gave terrific parties."

Dorothy had rugs on each side of her bed with raised chenille letters that spelled Welcome.

I attended one of her parties with Scott Fitzgerald. It was Friday the thirteenth. Three of the people at the party were dead by Sunday morning: Scott, Nat West and his wife, Eileen, who were killed on Ventura Boulevard in a car crash. Everyone then remembered that it had been Friday the thirteenth at Dottie's.

Muriel King had met Dorothy in 1925 when they both lived in New York at The Leonori Hotel and joined the Algonquin crowd for lunch.

"Dorothy," says Muriel, "was charming, darling, and loathsome. No, not really loathsome, disappointing. When you thought you were friends, you didn't expect her to slap you down. She'd come in and ask, 'What did you do yesterday?' You'd tell her. Then she would say in a flat, bored voice, 'That is a very interesting story.' One felt totally deflated. But I never had so much fun in my life as with Benchley and Dottie together."

Miss Parker's writing partnership with her husband Alan Campbell was always rather a mystery. Alan once had a piece in the *New Yorker,* but no one can remember anything else that he had done on his own. During the time they were in Hollywood they were a writing team.

Garson Kanin remembers them writing *Passport for Life* for him. They came punctually to his bungalow at The Garden of Allah for conferences. But the film was never made. Dorothy's first Hollywood screen credit was *Here Is My Heart* for Paramount. She and Alan were two of the sixteen writers on *A Star Is Born,* the 1937 version with Fredric March. William Wellman wrote the original *Star Is Born.* Under cover of darkness, Budd Schulberg and Ring Lardner were brought in by Selznick to write another version. "One day we sent a section to Selznick," said Budd. "The mail boy inadvertently took it to Dorothy and Alan. They sent it back to us with one scene underlined. 'We think this is good and should be in the master script.' " Dorothy's last screen credit was based on a story called *Horsie* for United Artists in 1950. After that she spent more time drinking, and she found it impossible to pick up the writing assignments they still wanted her for.

Alan's great value to his wife was that he could remember everything she said. She was lazy and hated writing and above all hated writing in Hollywood where she had to work under supervision. This almost drove her insane. She disliked all the producers she had to write for and vilified them whenever anyone mentioned their names.

When Alan repeated something witty Dorothy had said, she denied it and made him look foolish. She might have actually forgotten be-

cause she had no memory for what she said. She hated to hear her remarks repeated, and once she said to me, "Everyone expects me to be
witty. I'm not, you know." Years later, when the Garden was gone, she
reminisced sadly, "All those things seemed so funny. Were they really?"

While Dottie and Alan worked together during their marriage, he
never received personal credit for his contribution. Everyone believed
that Dorothy was carrying him. But he was quite a good writer—and an
industrious one, which his wife was not. He was the one who always
kept going at the typewriter.

When the Hacketts were working at MGM in "the Thalberg"
bungalow—the huge new building outside the studio facing the parking
lot—their office was next to Dorothy's and Alan's. Alan's desk was
against the wall, on the other side of which was Albert's desk. Albert
could hear Alan ask Dorothy, "Now what does she say?" Dorothy was
sitting by the door knitting and looking to see who was coming up the
stairs. (They were working on *Sweethearts* for Jeanette MacDonald
and Nelson Eddy—the combined factors, she said, were enough to turn
her stomach.) The next thing Albert heard Alan say was, "Don't use
that word!"

Then: "What does he say?"

Then: "DON'T USE THAT WORD!" Whatever he asked her, he
always received the same answer: "Shit."

This reminds me of the evening with the Campbells and Reginald
Gardner. An American girl who had been in England for two years had
returned to Hollywood with a super-British accent. She kept saying that
everything was on *sh*edule. "Oh shid!" interrupted Dorothy.

There was an evening with Eddie Mayer, Dottie, and George
Oppenheimer at the Garden when she was working on a Cecil B. De
Mille picture, *Dynamite*. Dottie told us she wanted to call it *Dynamite,
I Love You*. But C. B. had absolutely no sense of humor. He had said,
"This is a very serious picture." I don't know how long she lasted on
the project, but I doubt if it was very long.

Artie Shaw met Miss Parker when he lived at the Garden and
thought she was a sad, strange lady. "These people who are supposed
to be enormous wits, they have constantly to live up to their reputa-
tions. I found many of Dottie's remarks quite lame, but of course one
only remembers the good ones. I think she outlived her period."

I am sure Dorothy would have agreed with him. She was seventy-
four years old when she died. So many of her friends had already died.

The Garden of Allah, where she had been so active, was no longer in existence. But there was still some of the old vinegar left when she attended the funeral of Alan, who died in 1963. A solicitous friend approached her and asked, "Is there anything I can do for you?" "Yes," Dorothy moaned. "You can get me another husband." The other was shocked and exclaimed, "You can't mean that!" Dorothy, dabbing her eyes, replied, "Then get me a ham sandwich and hold the mustard."

In the early days wherever you saw Dorothy Parker, in New York or in Hollywood, you would find her two shadows, John O'Hara and John McClain. The two young men were not very popular with the other worshipers who hung around, although McClain seemed to fit into the group with more ease than O'Hara.

I had a few dates with John O'Hara, who died recently, before I met Scott Fitzgerald, and I could see he was making an effort at conversation, but it was laconic and uncomfortable. I never saw him drinking much, but I knew that at times he did. He had a fight with Dave Chasen, and Dave, always quiet and good tempered, is just about the hardest man to have a fight with. It was something that happened at Dave's restaurant, and he asked John to leave. "He wrote to Harold Ross, who was financing me," Dave told me, "and he intimated that I was padding the bills of the customers." After that, Dave barred him, and I don't blame him.

One evening, after taking me to dinner, O'Hara deposited me at the door of my home. He left his engine running. I wondered if he thought I was going to rape him and that this was his way of informing me that he was not planning to stay. Later I heard he was saying all over town that he had had a dose of clap. I thanked God he hadn't come in.

I can see him standing against the wall in Benchley's villa, a glass in his hand, listening intently to the conversation but not joining in. Benchley did not love O'Hara, although he did not object to him hanging around. He always seemed ill at ease. He never smiled. He never laughed. He admired Scott Fitzgerald and Benchley and treated them with deference when the prevailing tone at the Garden certainly was not deferential. He would sometimes say shocking things.

Muriel King remembers him in the early forties calling his wife from the Garden, and through the thin walls she heard him screaming endearments consisting solely of four-letter words. One didn't really need a phone to hear him in New York, let alone in the next room.

John O'Hara, part of "the Group." *Phyllis Cerf*

O'Hara was a self-conscious man, according to Marc Connelly. "He was not a graceful steward of his talent. I think he was extremely gauche, and was disturbed by him. I don't like being disturbed by people. I resent being stimulated unpleasantly."

O'Hara had wanted to join the National Institute, to which Connelly belongs. His name was constantly rejected, although the rejection had nothing to do with his talent. O'Hara's revenge, according to Marc, was to tell people, "Connelly wears his Institute button with his tweeds."

Joel Sayre, a writer I met with Eddie Mayer, referred to O'Hara as "the master of the fancied slight."

John idolized Scott, and it is interesting that his *Pal Joey,* book and play, was reminiscent of Scott's *Pat Hobby Stories.* Both were antiheroes, and you liked them in spite of their dreadful behavior. When the late producer Jerry Wald told him he wanted to do a film biography of Scott, O'Hara advised him to see me. "What has Sheilah Graham got to do with Fitzgerald?" Jerry was astonished when John said, "She was his girl."

Roland Young was nicer, but I never knew what to say to him, either. Roland, after I had met him in Hollywood with Deems Taylor, visited me in New York when I lived there for a year after Scott's death. I dreaded his visits. If he telephoned beforehand, I pretended to have a date. Sometimes he came without letting me know, and there we'd be, sitting or standing in my living room while I desperately tried to make conversation to which he replied in monosyllables. He was British, and I always trotted out the tea things if he came in the afternoon. Anything to have some action.

In *The Time of Laughter,* Corey Ford describes Roland as "the very pattern of a gentleman, slight of build, erect and poised, with an aristocratic beaked nose and a long upper lip which terminated in a pencil moustache, as carefully clipped as his enunciation." His mouth, stated Corey, "barely moved when he spoke." W. C. Fields called the actor Stingy Lips. His voice always tailed off in an unhappy whisper.

Muriel King remembers him as a short dapper man with a flower in his lapel when he took her six-foot son and herself to lunch in New York. "Roland Young," she affirmed, "was a consummate actor. He acted not only with his hands but with his feet." She must have seen a different Roland than I did. He was a good actor. But I don't remember any activity with the feet or hands. I don't remember any activity, period.

O'Hara, on the other hand, said what he had to say, which wasn't much, then closed his lips and did not speak for a considerable time. Perhaps he was shy. In the years before his recent death I saw only him at the funerals of mutual friends. He worshiped his first wife, Belle, and I never saw him at the Garden after he was married. Roland also married after leaving the Garden.

Muriel King felt, as others did, that John McClain was a hanger-on, someone who likes to be where it's happening but who does not belong. But he hung on as though it were his birthright, to be where Dottie and Benchley were. Nasty people said he climbed to attention on Dottie's shoulders.

McClain fitted into the world of Pasadena and Santa Barbara and also into the bohemian world of Benchley, Parker, and Butterworth. Unlike O'Hara, he never treated his friends with a self-conscious deference. McClain seemed to be a long-term bachelor, but after the war he married twice. With the plenitude of women and the popularity of being an extra man, he saw no reason to be married while he lived in Hollywood, and especially at the Garden where there were girls around the pool just waiting to be plucked. He served in the navy during World War II and married when he came back to New York. By that time his friend Benchley was dead. He was surprised and pleased to find that Bob had willed him all his clothes. Donald Ogden Stewart saw McClain, who died a few years ago, during the war when he was wearing a lieutenant commander's uniform. Don, at that time a constant drinker like everyone else at the Garden, declaimed, "John, I have alcohol just where I want it," then he fell on the floor and knew nothing until he woke up next morning.

McClain was a kiss-and-tell man. When he had an affair, he would brag about it all over the Garden. One afternoon he said to Natalie Schafer, "We're going to have a lot of girls around tonight. I'll leave the shade up a little bit and you can come and peek if you like." Natalie admits she did not have the nerve or the desire to peek, and she missed the orgy.

McClain was proud of his friendship with important people. Natalie recalls him describing a marvelous letter he had received from Anita Colby, whom he met because of her friendship with his closest friend, "Quent," Quentin Reynolds. "He asked me to get something from his bungalow and there, propped up on the table, was the letter from Anita. He very obviously had left it there for me to read."

I found McClain easy to be with, as everyone did. Except the time I was to have dinner with him after Scott's death, and he called for me at my home and lunged at me after we had talked about Scott and I had burst into tears. The lunge was while he was presumably comforting me. I wrote him off for a long while after that, but we bumped into each other at first nights in New York when he was the drama critic for the *New York Journal*. And sometimes we stopped and chatted on Park Avenue. In spite of the incident and because of the past at the Garden with all those dead friends, it was interesting to talk to him.

Eddie Mayer. It is hard to write about Eddie. I did not see much of him after the war, and he died in 1960. I loved Eddie for his gentleness and sensitivity. He could be angry with producers, but he was never unkind to his friends.

Eddie lived at The Garden of Allah for most of the time I knew him, except for the brief time that he rented a house in Beverly Hills when his small son, Paul, was staying with him.

I can see Paul, nine or ten, with one leg of his trousers rolled up to midcalf and the other clipped at the ankle with a bicycle peg. Eddie had a deep love for Paul, and they were good together. He was an indulgent parent and an indulgent person. He had a passionate fondness for Gilbert and Sullivan, and at his home in Beverly Hills, he constantly played the records and hummed to the music, and I, like him, learned the words.

I met Eddie at the home of the Frank Morgans on Chevy Chase Drive in Beverly Hills. There were about thirty people there—actors, writers, and some directors. I had been taken there by Jonah Ruddy, the Hollywood correspondent for the *London Daily Mail*. Jonah had received a letter about me from R. J. Minney, a mutual friend, and he met me at the airport when I arrived and constituted himself my guardian. He seemed to know everyone, and the Morgans were special friends.

Frank and Alma. He was the same in real life as he was on the screen—charming, with a deprecating giggle after his sentences. Alma was German and warm and gemütlich. I enjoyed my evening and stayed longer than I usually do. The party was in the playroom downstairs, and when I was waiting for my coat on the ground floor, I executed a little tap dance on the black-and-white squares of the entrance hall. Eddie, whom I had not noticed at all until then, came up and saw me dancing, and he stood there, watching and smiling. He asked me to dine with him when Jonah had introduced us. After that, the Morgans always invited me to their home whenever they gave a party, and I always had a good time.

Frank had starred in Eddie's first play on Broadway, *The Firebrand.* His role was secondary, but he stole all the reviews, and MGM brought him to Hollywood where he was about the most popular person at the studio. His last big film was *The Wizard of Oz,* with Frank as the Wizard and Judy Garland as Dorothy.

I saw a great deal of Eddie, who was also to introduce me to Scott Fitzgerald. Dorothy Parker thought Eddie was in love with me, and she told people that I treated him badly. I didn't know this at the time. I liked having dinner with him and going to the Garden, where he had a bungalow and where I met the other people who lived there. Sometimes we stopped at Benchley's bungalow, or Dorothy's, or Sam Hoffenstein's, the poet, who always seemed unhappy. I met Oliver Garrett, another writer, there with Eddie, and Marion Spitzer, and Natalie Schafer, and Ernst Lubitsch, and many others.

Eddie always said, "You know what I mean?" at the end of every sentence. He was blind in one eye. It had been injured when he was a small boy. "It was useful," he laughed when he told me the story. "When the other kids ganged up on me, I'd say, 'Be careful, I have a bad eye.' And they would be careful."

He also suffered from diabetes and had to inject himself with insulin, I don't know how many times a day, but it seemed to be often. Sometimes he felt ill and would disappear into his bedroom and inject himself.

It was Eddie who told me the story of Scott Fitzgerald, at the height of his success, brushing past him on the way to see Eddie's publisher, Horace Liveright. "He was so successful," Eddie said, "that he made me feel dirty."

Eddie had attended Columbia University with Howard Dietz and a few others who became famous writers and composers. My lack of interest in him as a lover exasperated him. I have always loved food, and after gorging myself at Romanoff's, Eddie often sighed, "If you would only look at me the way you were looking at that steak!"

He always drove a big Buick. After Scott died, and I was going to England to write about the woman's effort in the war for my syndicate, a moth flew into the car. I am terrified, or was, of moths and I crouched and cried, "Get it out! Get it out!"

Eddie smiled in telling this, "Here she is going to England where there's a war on, and she's afraid of moths!"

He was a very successful screenwriter. In the time that I knew him in the late thirties, and after Scott died in the late forties, he seemed to be working mostly for Paramount and on films for Marlene Dietrich and Gary Cooper. When Scott died, Eddie had a house in Bucks County where he was trying to do some serious writing. I still have the telegram of condolence that he sent me. He knew how much Scott Fitzgerald had meant to me.

Eddie earned about two thousand dollars a week, which to me was the same as being as rich as Rockefeller. But he was always hard up. He told me it was his family who kept him poor and kept his nose to the grindstone of Hollywood. "I have to make thirty-four thousand dollars before I can eat," Eddie said to me dolefully.

He was separated or divorced from his wife, but they saw each other when she came to Hollywood. At the end, when he had no money at all and was very ill, he was looked after by a sister, who cared for him until his death. I was sad reading the account, remembering how much I had liked him.

Eddie was always hoping that lovely women would fall in love with him. But he was rather fat and his blind eye bulged and didn't help with the girls he coveted. He wanted desperately to have an affair with Hedy Lamarr, and he wrote her a sonnet that he recited to me with great enthusiasm. I was a bit jealous. He had never written a sonnet for me. He sent her the poem with flowers, and, to his delight, she wrote thanking him. The night he had planned for her seduction was ruined by a producer who wanted him to report to his home at 10:00 P.M. to discuss a script. His date with Hedy was for 8:00 P.M. He was terribly nervous during dinner, he told me the next day. He had to get Hedy into bed and done by 9:45. He rushed her through the meal and was ready to go by 9:15, by which time he was almost hysterical with nerves and knew he wouldn't be any good; so he asked her to stay for a liqueur and never did get to first base.

Eddie was probably the most highly educated person I had ever met. Certainly he knew more about English history than anyone I knew.

I listened with amazement to this man who knew so much more than I did about the Whigs and Tories of old England where I had been born and presumably educated. Pitt the Elder and Pitt the Younger— Eddie could talk about them by the hour. As late as 1947, he was still working in Hollywood. He was called in to smarten the dialogue of *The Foxes of Harrow,* which starred Rex Harrison.

Eddie had started in Hollywood as a press agent for Sam Goldwyn. Oh, the dozens of Goldwyn stories he told me, and I can't remember' any of them except those that are well known. He wrote some of the subtitles for silent films, as Benchley and Donald Ogden Stewart had done. He had worked at MGM on the scripts of *Romance, Blushing Brides,* and *Never the Twain Shall Meet.* At Paramount, in addition to *Morocco,* he also wrote *Desire* for Marlene Dietrich.

His play *Firebrand* was made into a film under the title *The Affairs of Cellini.* I remember his film *The Buccaneer* for De Mille in 1938 and *To Be or Not to Be,* in 1942. In that year my daughter Wendy was born, and when I brought her to The Garden of Allah in October while I looked for a house, Eddie bought a silver frame for her photograph, which I still have.

He was very amusing and always had a good story to tell. He told me of his friendship with Joel Sayre, who was an enormous man and much stronger than Eddie. They went to various functions and homes together. On one of their excursions, Joel patted Eddie on the back. A pat from Joel was like a blow from someone else. "I don't want your friendship," Eddie howled. "It hurts too much. I'd prefer your enmity— you know what I mean?"

[X]

Scott

ON JULY 26, 1937, THOMAS WOLFE wrote to F. Scott Fitzgerald from Oteen, North Carolina: "I don't know where you are living, and I'll be damned if I'll believe anyone lives in a place called The Garden of Allah which was what the address on your envelope said. I am sending this on to the old address we both know so well." "The old address" was Asheville, North Carolina—Wolfe's home town—where Scott had lived to be near his wife, Zelda, who was mentally ill in a sanitarium. The letter was forwarded to Scott at The Garden of Allah.

Scott had come to Hollywood for the third time hoping he would finally succeed at writing for motion pictures. The first time had been in 1927 when he had been drinking and quarreling with Zelda, whom he was punishing for her affair with a French flier, by having a flirtation with Lois Moran, a beautiful young film actress. The Fitzgeralds stayed at the Ambassador, a very correct hotel, and raised holy hell.

Scott was then at the height of his fame—*The Great Gatsby* had been published to critical acclaim in 1926. John Considine of United Artists had hired him to write *Lipstick,* a modern college story for Constance Talmadge.

At first, Scott and Zelda were treated like the visiting royalty who usually managed a detour to wicked Hollywood on visits to this country. The Fitzgeralds were given the signal honor of a luncheon party at Pickfair. They met Lillian Gish and were the center of a congenial group that included Carl Van Vechten, John Barrymore, Richard

F. Scott Fitzgerald and Sheilah Graham in 1939. They met at the Garden.

Barthelmess, and Miss Moran. Scott was thirty, Lois twenty. He was flattered that she would be interested in an "old" man.

Scott took over everyone at the parties then, as I saw him do later. When he was drinking, even mildly, he was imbued with love of his fellow man and wanted to direct them in games with him. At one party on this first visit he took all the guests' watches and boiled them, which the owners did not find amusing.

He had received a down payment of thirty-five hundred dollars, and, if the story was accepted, another eighty-five hundred dollars. It was not. This was a blow for the bright young man of American letters, and the night before he and Zelda left Hollywood, Zelda, angry at his attentions to Miss Moran, had tried to burn their bed. They then piled all the furniture in their suite at the Ambassador into the center of the living room and considered burning the lot. But they thought better of it and merely left the unpaid bill on top of the stack and left.

Scott may have been inventing when he described to me their getaway from the hotel. Fearful of being caught up with by the law, they crawled on their stomachs until they reached their compartment. "We pulled down the blinds and kept them down until we arrived in Chicago," where they would change for the train to New York.

At the end of 1931, MGM brought him to Hollywood again to work on a script from the Katharine Brush novel *Red-Headed Woman*. Zelda had had her first breakdown and hospitalization, but she was feeling better, and he had left her with her parents in Montgomery, Alabama. He saw his old movie-star friends who had survived the talkies, and Carmel Myers, who gave a party for him. On arriving at Carmel's some of the old mischief stirred in him. He was glad to be back in Hollywood and glad that Zelda—in time, they had told him— would recover. He went upstairs to Carmel's bedroom, took a bath, and refused to come out until all the guests had visited him in the bathtub.

But it was a repetition of the previous time. The producer changed the script, and the result, Scott told me, was an awful one hundred twenty pages. He was drunk at the Irving Thalberg home, and the invitations and his popularity dropped off. He vowed he would never return to Hollywood. But he extracted something from the stay—his fine short story *Crazy Sunday*. I am sure he told me this was based on an incident at the home of King Vidor. Since Scott's death I have read other versions.

Three Comrades, Fitzgerald's only sole screen credit, with Franchot Tone, Robert Taylor, Margaret Sullavan, and Robert Young. Margaret Sullavan found life at The Garden of Allah noisy and frightening. *Springer/Bettmann Archive*

Zelda's father died in 1931 while Scott was in Hollywood, and she had fallen apart again and had to be rehospitalized. His drinking and lack of disciplined writing before he completed *Tender Is the Night* had contributed to his mountain of debts.

His mother left him some money when she died and it was a godsend, but he still owed forty thousand dollars. His agent, Harold Ober, managed to get him a contract at MGM for six months at one thousand dollars a week with an option for another twelve months at twelve hundred fifty dollars a week.

Scott agreed that Ober should receive his salary, allowing him four hundred dollars a month to support himself and pay Scottie's school bills. (She was at the expensive Ethel Walker School in Connecticut.) He would also pay for Zelda's stay in the hospital. Four hundred dollars wasn't much for all this, but I never had the feeling that he was hard up. He took me to the best restaurants, got front-row seats for the Broadway plays—Maurice Evans's *Hamlet* among them—when they came to Los Angeles, and always sent flowers accompanied by small notes and humorous drawings.

Eddie Knopf, the story editor at Metro, thought the sea air would be good for Scott—as I did later, disastrously—and he rented an apartment for him at the Miramar, facing the Pacific Ocean at Santa Monica. But he was lonely out there, and someone (I don't know who, although it might have been Carmel Myers, whom I had met with Scott) suggested The Garden of Allah. It would be private, and yet he could, at a moment's notice, be with the people he knew—Ogden Nash, S. J. Perelman, Nat West (Sid's brother-in-law), Donald Ogden Stewart, Robert Benchley, Dorothy Parker, and Eddie Mayer.

It was Eddie who introduced me officially to Scott, although I had first met him in Benchley's bungalow on July 14, 1937. Mr. Benchley had decided to give a party to celebrate Bastille Day and my engagement to the Marquess of Donegall, who adored Bob and had asked him to be best man at our wedding. "He is the most civilized American I have ever met," Donegall pronounced. I realized later why Bob was irritated when I told him what was meant to be a compliment.

The party had started earlier at my house up the hill at 1530 Kings Road, from where I could see the Garden if I stood on my balcony outside the Spanish living room and squinted to the left. I was giving a party for Donegall and had invited Bob, Dorothy, Eddie Mayer, Lew Ayres, Jonah Ruddy, and the Frank Morgans. These are the only names I can remember, but there were more.

It was a big house with three floors, each floor was up one floor around the winding hill. I had brought my maid, Christine, from New York, and her husband had followed her and was living with us. But Bob thought I needed more help to impress my titled fiancé, so he loaned me Albin.

We had a table outside on the patio, with cheese and crackers, nuts and German sausage. The party was such a howling success that one of the neighbors shouted, "Be quiet!"

"Let's go to my place," Bob said when there was a slight lull. We piled into the cars and drove to the Garden, where Bob telephoned some of his friends to come over, he was having a party. They rarely refused.

Looking back and knowing that Scott did not like Bob too much, I am surprised that he came and that Bob invited him. But Bob was a kind man and thought Scott might be lonely. Also Bob was something of a snob and liked to pepper his parties with well-known people. Even though Scott's fame had declined, people were still curious about him.

I did not notice Scott come in. He simply materialized through the thin walls. One moment he was not there and then he was, and then he was gone.

There was a lot of drinking and laughing, and I was happy because I was going to be a marchioness. I hadn't thought it was really possible, but that night I believed it was true. I liked Don and I thought I was in love with him. I bloomed in that murky room. Glancing around I saw this man, his pale face illuminated by the lamp on the table next to him. He seemed to be all shades of blue. His face, his hair, his shirt, his suit. He was sitting quietly, holding a cigarette, and the gray smoke was a restless cloud around his face.

When I looked again, he was gone. He had seemed so detached, so apart from the others, and I wondered who he was and how he came there. He was F. Scott Fitzgerald, Bob told me. He had not noticed his departure either. "I'll get him back," he said.

"No, no, don't bother." I was only faintly interested. I had heard of the Roaring Twenties and that Fitzgerald had written books and short stories about them, but like so many nonreaders of that time, I confused him with the author of *Flaming Youth*. It would have been a paragraph for my column if I had talked to him.

But no matter, soon I'd be giving up the column, and my days would be spent in London drawing rooms or in country mansions and giving birth to a son who would be the Earl of Belfast and a daughter whose title would be Lady Wendy Chichester. My lingerie and stationery would have a coronet, and I would attend the crownings of future kings and queens of England in Westminster Abbey. Don had been a page boy at the coronation of George V. I was sure I would soon be as much in love with him as I was excited at the thought of the fine life I was going to live.

Don and I left the party and Scott came back, and, as he relates in *The Last Tycoon,* he was disappointed to find "Kathleen" was not there. When Benchley had phoned him to return, he had cautiously asked, "Who is still there?" and Bob had said, "Tala Birel," among other names. He thought my face fitted the name. "Is she wearing a silver belt with cut-out stars?" he asked Bob, who looked over at Tala. "Yes, she is, come back and meet her," Bob insisted. It was the right belt but the wrong girl, and Scott, never one to throw out a good incident, used this in *The Last Tycoon* when Stahr mistakes Edna for Kathleen because of the silver belt with the stars.

It was the height of the anti-Fascist and anti-Nazi fever among the Hollywood writers who were liberals. And I was to see Scott again at a dinner at The Biltmore Hotel to raise money for the Anti-Nazi League. Dorothy Parker and Marc Connelly, both very active in the group, had taken tickets for two tables, each with twelve guests. I was at the Connelly table. Scott was with Dorothy.

Jock Whitney, who was at Dorothy's table, came over and whispered that I looked beautiful. I showed him the engagement ring Don had given me before returning to London to inform his mother of the impending marriage. Don wasn't sure how she would react. I was nobody she had ever heard of. Twenty years later, after the publication of *Beloved Infidel,* I asked Don what he had believed my background was, and he replied, "I imagined you were the daughter of a country doctor."

When Don met me in the winter of 1932 after a squash racquets match at the International Sportsmen's Club in London, he did not ask any questions. But later he was glad I had been presented at Court, and he told me he would bring that up when he talked with his mother. She would become the Dowager Marchioness after our marriage. I wasn't sure she would like that.

I don't know how it happened, but there was a moment when Scott was alone at his table, and I was the only one at Marc's table. We were facing each other. I recognized him—Scott Fitzgerald, the man who had vanished in Benchley's apartment. His face seemed even more pale against the black and white of his tuxedo. I was wearing my best evening gown, a light gray soft check silk, caught at the waist with a broad band of crimson velvet. When Scott smiled at me, I smiled back from sheer exuberance, knowing I was looking so well. Then he spoke, his head slightly on the side, "I like you." It was a good opening, and wanting to include him in my excitement, I said "I like *you*." It was only half meant. I wanted to be kind, and he *was* attractive. Why aren't I dancing, I thought. Why am I wasting my excitement? And why not dance with him? "Shall we dance?" I said. He could not dance he replied, now smiling only faintly. "I promised the next dance to Dottie." The band stopped playing, and they all came back and we left soon after, without our dance, which in any case I had forgotten.

I did not think about him at all until a week later when Eddie Mayer called me from the Garden. It was a Saturday night, and I was going to the concert at the Hollywood Bowl with Jonah Ruddy, who had difficulty getting the tickets. It was about seven thirty and I said to Eddie when he invited me to dinner, "I can't. I'm going to the Hollywood Bowl with Jonah." "Oh, what a pity," he said, but he made another bid. "Scott Fitzgerald is here, and he wants to meet you." Ah, that was different. I would like to talk to him. He looked nice and he must be interesting from all I had heard of the goings-on in the twenties.

"But Jonah . . ." my voice trailed helplessly. "Bring him along too," Eddie persisted. When Jonah arrived, I told him that I had half promised Eddie we would go to the Garden. He grumbled at the waste of tickets, but he too was anxious to meet the once-famous author. We dropped off the tickets to someone on the way to the Garden.

I don't remember what Scott said when we met (why don't we write things down at the time, as Scott always did?), but soon Eddie suggested we all go to The Clover Club on the Strip for dinner. We went in his big Buick. Humphrey Bogart and Mary Phillips were downstairs in the bar. Bogart said hello to Scott, and his voice was deferential. I was surprised because I assumed that when you were a failure in America, no one remembered you, as opposed to England where they love the old failures for evermore.

We had a table on the far side of the band, and I was enjoying myself, one girl with three attentive men. I believe I danced with Jonah first, but Eddie did not have a chance to ask me. I had never danced with him and perhaps he did not dance. We had been to the Trocadero, where people danced, but we had merely watched.

Scott stood up while we were waiting for the first course, and we danced. We stayed on the floor for at least half an hour, talking to each other when the music stopped and dancing again when it started up. He was flirting with me, and I was flirting back. I remember my shoulder-length hair was brushing his face. "Is it getting in your mouth?" I asked coquettishly, which was no way for an engaged girl to be carrying on.

Yes, he had heard I was engaged to a lord. And he asked me whether a lord was higher than a duke, and I laughed and explained the order of the titles: a duke, a marquess, an earl, a viscount, a plain, ordinary lord, and the difference between a baronet and a knight. He listened with rapt and amused attention, holding me at arm's length then drawing me in closely so that we danced cheek to cheek with our rears jutting at an angle in the fashion of the day.

I was having a lovely time. Now and then I glanced at our table and caught Eddie's eye, and he raised his shoulders questioningly, as if to say, What *is* going on? "We must get back to Eddie and Jonah," I said regretfully. Jonah looked at me suspiciously. He knew me for a flirt, and I was supposed to be engaged, wasn't I? But I didn't care. I liked this man, and while we were dancing he made a date with me for dinner on Tuesday.

The depth of my disappointment when he sent me a telegram canceling the dinner surprised and alarmed me. Why should I care so much? It was as though my body had dropped to my shoes. The telegram said that his daughter was coming to Hollywood, and he regretfully had to break the date. But we could all have dinner together, I said when I phoned him. The telegram had not suggested another time, and I had to see him again. He seemed reluctant to include me in the time with his daughter, but he finally said, well, all right, and arranged to pick me up at my house, then we would go to The Beverly Hills Hotel to get Scottie. She was staying in a suite with Helen Hayes, who had brought her to Hollywood.

We went to the Trocadero. You could see the lights of Los Angeles from the wide windows. Scottie was a plump, pretty little blond of fifteen. "I'm glad she is overweight, it will hold off the boys a bit longer," Scott said later. But now he was a different man. He was the critical father, asking which boys she had seen in the East, telling her she was slouching, asking her to sit up straight. So many questions and commands. Her "yes, daddy" did not conceal her exasperation. I didn't like him at all, and my sympathy was for Scottie. What had made me think he was attractive? What on earth was I doing with a middle-aged tired-looking father who I thought was treating his daughter unfairly?

I was relieved when it was time to drop her at the hotel, and I was silent as Scott drove me cautiously—twenty miles an hour when he was not drinking—to my house on the hill. I wanted to say good-bye quickly and go inside and forget him. We stood by the door in the half light from the sky and the hills, his beautiful face in the shadow, very sad. I couldn't let whatever this was end, and I asked him to come inside. That was the beginning of the three and a half years we would know each other very well. There would be no marriage to the Marquess of Donegall. Scott was the only man I cared about until he died in my living room in Hollywood at three in the afternoon on Saturday, December 21, 1940.

Whenever anyone writes about The Garden of Allah and the famous celebrities who stayed there, they always mention Scott Fitzgerald first. Actually, he lived at the Garden for only nine months, from July 1937 to October 1938. But it was a hectic nine months, and it was possibly the worst place for him. It was the wrong atmosphere for a man who was trying to give up liquor and whose future in Hollywood depended on it. There was always the sound of merriment coming from Benchley's bungalow, and it must have been hard for Scott to refuse the drinks that were pressed on one by an eager host who could not imagine anyone not wanting a drink.

When I met Scott he had been on the wagon for some months. The drinking started again when he went up to see Ginevra King in Santa Barbara. He had to fortify himself to make a good impression on the woman who had been his first love when he was at Princeton, and later the heroine of *This Side of Paradise*. She had written to him at the Garden asking to see him. He told Scottie about it in a letter, wondering if it was a good idea to see a woman he had been in love with so long ago. After twenty-one years he thought it might be disillusioning. But he went, and Ginevra believes that the effort made him drink again.

When he came with me to Chicago a few days later to help me with my radio sponsor who did not like my English accent, I realized he was on a bender. Until then he had seemed sober and serious. He had been so quiet when we dined at the Beverly Hills home of Gladys Swarthout and her husband Frank Chapman. He was withdrawn from everyone, sitting by himself and barely interested when John McCormick, the Irish singer, sang a duet with our opera-star hostess. I glanced at him every now and then, and I knew he was restless and bored.

"My social life is in definite slow motion," he wrote Scottie. "I had dinner at Gladys Swarthout's last week [the end of October] with John McCormack and some of the musical crowd. I have taken in some football games with Sheilah Graham and have met the love of my youth, Ginevra King (Mitchell). She is still a charming woman, and I'm sorry I didn't see more of her." He also mentioned that he was living at The Garden of Allah but had done nothing about looking for a house because there seemed no chance of "your mother coming out here at present." The letter was dated November 4, 1937.

By this time we were very much in love, but at the beginning he did not want his daughter to know, and he never wished his wife to be aware that he had found another woman to love. But as he confided to his friend Norah Phipps he hoped that if Zelda recovered, he could marry again and have a good life again. But if she did not, he would never abandon his poor lost Zelda.

I thought he would stop drinking if he were at the ocean, so the following spring I found him a house in the Malibu colony that belonged to Frank Case who owned the Algonquin in New York. In the summer he invited Scottie and her best friend from Baltimore, "Peaches" Finney, to stay with him at Malibu. With some embarrassment he asked me to take my clothes out—although I only came there for weekends. He did not want Scottie or her friend to know about us. I knew he was right, but I was terribly hurt because by now we had settled into a sort of domesticity. He stayed at my house in town, and we went together in his rattling Ford to the beach on Friday, after I had loaded the car with flowers. It was only much later that he told me he detested cut flowers.

I sat brooding for a long while that afternoon, wondering why I had ever let myself in for such a situation and vowing to get out of it. But during this visit, even though Scott made elaborate pretenses of asking me to the beach to swim, Scottie realized the situation as I saw when she glanced from one of us to the other with an objective look in her gray blue eyes that duplicated Scott's. She was glad that he had someone who cared for him, as she wrote me after his death.

But it was still the fall of 1937 and Scott was paying three hundred dollars a month for his apartment at the Garden. He could not afford it from his four hundred dollars a month, but it was convenient to MGM—and for seeing me, just a few minutes away. He honked the horn as he rounded the bend to the back of the house where the garage was, and once, when he was ill, he stayed in the spare room one entered from the garage.

Sometimes I drove my bright blue Ford sedan to the Garden and parked it there. He always made fun of my car. It *was* an awful color. "But it is so easy to find in a parking lot," I protested. It never let me down, as his Ford did sometimes. He was always getting it fixed at the garage near Metro where he went to listen to my weekly appearance on a radio show that emanated from Chicago.

I learned to know Scott during those nine months at the Garden. The disastrous flight to Chicago had shaken me. Instead of helping me with my sponsor, Scott had punched him in the nose. This was my first experience of being with a man who was drunk beyond recall. I'd seen Benchley drunk but that was nursery stuff compared to this. In Chicago, I watched helplessly while Scott poured anything that contained liquor down his throat. Gin, whiskey, bourbon—it didn't matter. He did not nurse a drink. As soon as it was in his glass, it went down his throat.

With my radio career in Chicago now very doubtful, I went into my bedroom and closed the door. We had two bedrooms with a sitting room between us. I heard him ask the bellboy to get him a bottle of gin. The boy hesitated and Scott chased him out the door. It was awful. It was like being with a madman.

He was thrown out of the rehearsal. It was a variety show, and I gave four or five minutes of Hollywood news when it was an important place for news. Scott found the film editor of the *Chicago Daily News,* which ran my column, and they went on the wildest spree. It is all rather vague now, but one of them called me and asked me to meet them at a bar. The bar was dingy and smelly. Scott told filthy stories, which he could never do when he was sober. I was more amazed than angry. This was a stranger, flushed and greasy, and I remember how filthy his handkerchief was.

The important thing was to get him back to The Garden of Allah where he was due for a meeting with Joe Mankiewicz the next morning to discuss *Three Comrades,* Scott's first important assignment at MGM.

The steps leading to Scott Fitzgerald's upstairs apartment at The Garden of Allah. *Courtesy of R. L. Samsell*

Arnold Gingrich of *Esquire* had visited us earlier in the day, and he realized Scott's condition. He asked me to call him if I needed help. He had seen Scott like this before. The people at the airport refused to take him aboard. I watched our plane fly off, and I was desperate. "What shall I do?" I wailed, calling Arnold at his home.

It was midnight and the next flight to Los Angeles was at five in the morning. Scott was flopping all over the airport counter and in a loud, irate voice insisting on a private plane to fly us back to California. He was cursing everyone and itching to get into a fight with someone, anyone.

"Put him in a taxi and cruise around until the next flight," Arnold advised me. For five hours; "I'll call all the bars nearby," he promised, "and if he wants liquor I'll tell them to give him beer only."

How I got him into the taxi I still don't know. He fell asleep on my shoulder at once. I had a cramp from not moving. He must stay asleep. But every now and then he awakened and slurped, "Where are we?" "Going home," I told him, and he was asleep again.

He managed to get on the plane, but somewhere he had found a small bottle of gin, and drank it on the way. When a man across the aisle stared at him, he demanded who he was staring at, then shouted, "Do you know who I am? I am F. Scott Fitzgerald." The man recognized the name and looked at Scott curiously. I felt ashamed for him. He was better than any man I knew, and the man across the aisle was feeling superior to him.

"I'm going on the wagon," he announced, suddenly sober, when I dropped him off at the Garden. "I'll get a doctor and a nurse and please don't come here until I'm well again."

When he drank he referred to it as being ill. Afterwards he told me of the agony of withdrawal from liquor. When he stopped drinking he threw up whatever he ate. By the third or fourth day he was able to keep something down, but it took another day before he could face me.

When I saw him he said he had told Joe Mankiewicz that he was ill and therefore unable to work. He was paler than ever and looked very worn and delicate. "How can you drink when it makes you so ill?" I asked him. But he sternly forbade me to discuss the matter.

It was about ten days after I had deposited him at the Garden. I had gone back to Chicago the following Monday in a futile effort to retain my spot on the radio show. Shortly before I was to leave for Hollywood, a former beau in New York—I had originally gone to

Hollywood to get away from him—called me and said, "Why don't you come here. You could see some shows, and I'd love to see you."

I remembered how drunk Scott had been, and I thought, why not? I telephoned Scott and told him I was going to New York for a few days. I didn't mention the man, but Fitzgerald had extraordinary intuition. He knew there was a man in New York waiting to pick up the pieces.

"If you go to New York," he said quietly—he was quite sober—"I won't be here when you come back. I shall leave Hollywood."

I paused. Was he bluffing? "I'll think about it," I said. I knew how important it was for him to work and make money in Hollywood. I had thought I was in love with him, but he had given me a dreadful time, and now I wasn't sure that I didn't hate him. I lay on my bed and thought. But not for long. I *was* in love with Scott, and from his voice it was hard to believe that he had ever taken a drink in his life. He was so marvelous, and I had been so lost before I met him. I phoned and said I would be there in the morning.

Scott went east in January of 1938 to see his daughter, and asked me to come with him. We stayed at the Ambassador Hotel on Park Avenue and that was the first time I realized the quantity of sleeping pills he took.

Through the wall I could hear him pacing up and down in his bedroom every time I awakened. I called to him once, and he came in and told me he had taken five strong sleeping pills. When he closed the door between us, I telephoned his doctor in Los Angeles to ask if this was safe. Five strong sleeping pills! I spoke in a whisper, as he hated to be fussed over or for me to talk to doctors behind his back. The doctor assured me it was all right. "He has built up such immunity, he could take eight Nembutals and they wouldn't hurt him." This was the doctor who gave him heavy doses of digitalis which I believe weakened his heart and caused the fatal attack.

The Garden. I always went there with Scott on Saturday after lunch at the Hollywood or Beverly Hills Brown Derby. There was the time I took a bath in his apartment, and he came in and put a pillow under my head. That small gesture bound me to him forever.

I read while he worked on his script, and sometimes we played Ping-Pong by the pool or walked to Schwab's for the papers or a chocolate malt, or to a delicatessen on Hollywood Boulevard for a sandwich before or after going to see a movie. He loved films and always came with me to the previews. Afterwards we invariably stopped at the Pickwick Book Shop to browse. His own books were out of print.

There was the time he burst in on John O'Hara at the Garden and asked him to be his second in a duel with Billy Wilkerson. The owner of the *Hollywood Reporter* had maligned me in an editorial, misreporting the lecture Scott had written for me, and which I delivered in five cities. Scott had been drinking, or he would have found a better way to inform the editor of his error.

O'Hara refused point-blank to have anything to do with such a foolish venture. "Okay, baby," Scott said angrily. "I'll ask Eddie." Eddie Mayer spent the next hours composing arguments to deter Scott from getting himself killed. But he never called, and it was just as well. In his condition a baby could have knocked him out.

There was the terrible time Scott broke a porcelain tap in his bathroom at the Garden and ran the jagged edge across his wrist. The spurting blood frightened him. He called the doctor. I didn't see him for a week.

By the end of January 1938, Scott had completed the script of *Three Comrades*. He was happy when Joe Mankiewicz told him it was the best he had ever read. Then he discovered that Joe, who was producing the picture and was originally a scriptwriter in Hollywood, was going over it and making clumsy changes. Scott was shocked when he read the final script, and wrote him a heartbreaking letter. "Oh, Joe, can't producers ever be wrong? I'm a good writer, honest. I thought you were going to play fair."

"We were all in the know that Joe Mankiewicz was rewriting the script," Sid Perelman told me. "But none of us could tell Scott. We knew it would break his heart. We were all used to such things. We were numb from being rewritten. But Scott's dream wasn't yet jaded. It was to write something so brilliant that it would securely establish his reputation in Hollywood." Unfortunately for Scott, Joe Mankiewicz had been a writer. He wrote all the early Jack Oakie pictures, also *Skippy* for Jackie Cooper and Jackie Coogan at Paramount. He believed he knew more about a screenplay than Scott did. "We all knew how unhappy Scott would be when he found out."

Unhappy! He went on a grade A bender.

Sid Perelman had gone to Hollywood originally to write scripts for the Marx Brothers and, like them, had stayed at The Garden of Allah. Now he had his own house with his wife Laura. He lunched every day at the crowded writers' table at Metro with Dorothy Parker, Herman Mankiewicz, Benchley, Butterworth, Hammerstein, Donald Ogden Stewart, Eddie Chodorov, and Scott Fitzgerald. They played a dice game to see who would pick up the entire check. Mankiewicz offered to insure anyone for five dollars against being stuck with the bill. One week a "client" lost consistently, and it cost Mankiewicz two hundred dollars.

Scott was sober at the beach until we drove to the Academy Theatre in Hollywood for the preview of *Three Comrades.* He was now reconciled to the rewrite, mostly because it would give him the screen credit he sorely needed for future assignments. "At least," he consoled me—and himself—"they've kept my beginning." But they had changed that, too. I could not find him for three days.

He hated working at the studio. It was hard for this free soul to check in and check out and be interrupted by fellow writers dropping into his office for a chat. He was not used to working under these conditions. But he did not complain because he was anxious to earn a good reputation.

After the mutilation of his script for *Three Comrades,* he told me he had no further desire to revolutionize the attitude of the producers toward the writer. In a letter near the end of 1938, he wrote that Hollywood was a strange conglomeration of a few excellent, overtired men making the pictures, and as dismal a crowd of fakes and hacks at the bottom as you can imagine.

While he was at the Garden, he conceived the Pat Hobby character for a series of stories about a class D writer faking his way through Hollywood. The expression used in so many films of the time, "Get hot water, lots of it," choked him with laughter, and this was the basis for one of the Hobby stories. It is a good thing he found them humorous, because he was only paid two hundred dollars by *Esquire* for each one. But toward the end it was the only money coming in.

After *Three Comrades,* Scott worked on *Infidelity* for Joan Crawford. He told me he had seen her on a street at MGM—he had known her on his previous visits to Hollywood. When he said he was writing the script for her, she took his hand earnestly and said, "Write hard." This amused him very much, as it did when they changed the title to *Fidelity.* They had run into censorship trouble; the things they censored are a joke now. Scott was less amused when, having written what they all considered a good script, he was dropped from the film, which was never made.

He worked on *The Women* with Donald Ogden Stewart, and it revived a friendship that had started when they were both young and living in Saint Paul, Minnesota. Scott had showed him a box filled with pages for a book he was calling *The Romantic Egotist,* which later became *This Side of Paradise.* Donald confided that he wanted to be a writer too. He was then working in an office. Scott advised him to go to New York and try his luck, and it changed the course of Donald's life.

After two months on *Madame Curie* for Greer Garson, he was replaced, as was the custom in Hollywood, but Scott thought it was because he was who he was. He had two weeks with *Gone With the Wind* and resented David Selznick's reverence for the Margaret Mitchell words. He sat in at a long conference with David Selznick, the producer, and George Cukor, the director, while George complained, "How do we get Aunt Pitty to bustle quaintly across the room, as it says in the book?"

At the end of his contract at MGM, Scott had only the one screen credit, and his drinking bouts were known to the studios. When Walter Wanger offered him fifteen hundred dollars a week to guide a young writer, Budd Schulberg, through the maze of *Winter Carnival,* a Dartmouth College story, Scott accepted eagerly. But he was ill and tired of Hollywood, and the assignment was just for the money like the rest of them. Wanger brought him east to plow through the snows of Dartmouth to get the real feel of a winter carnival, and Scott collapsed. He was handed back to me in New York by the anxious Mr. Schulberg, who made the incident the cornerstone for his best-selling novel, *The Disenchanted.* The disenchantment for Scott had begun while he was living at the Garden, when he wrote himself a postcard. "Dear Scott. How are you? Have been meaning to come in and see you. I have (been) living at The Garden of Allah . . . Yours, Scott Fitzgerald." The postcard is at Princeton with Scott's other papers and books.

Like everyone else who visited or lived at the Garden, I rarely went through the main house to get to the bungalows. I walked through the gate on the Havenhurst side. Scott's apartment was upstairs on the right-hand side of the pool, up some outside Spanish-tiled steps. I don't know who was living underneath, but many people claimed that they either lived in Scott's apartment or underneath him. It was quiet during the times that he was sober. But I would have hated to be below when he was drinking and rampaging around.

Artie Shaw met Scott at the Garden and remembers that no one was paying him any attention at this time. When Artie asked Scott, "What are you doing out here?" Scott replied, "I'm trying to get a job."

Later Scott gave the bandleader a copy of the script *Babylon Revisited,* which he had written for Lester Cowan. "I still have it," Artie told me. So does Mr. Cowan, who brought in the Epstein brothers to do another script after Scott died. He sold that one to MGM for one hundred thousand dollars, and it came out *The Last Time I Saw Paris,* —the title taken from Elliot Paul's best-selling book—with Elizabeth Taylor and Van Johnson. I forget who played the little girl, if there was one. She was the center of Scott's excellent short story and of the script for which Cowan paid Scott $6,000, including ten weeks of his time. Cowan did very well from the deal. He still has Scott's original scenario, and one of these days he will sell it and make another fortune.

George Oppenheimer, who worked in Hollywood on and off for eighteen years, met Scott when he lived at the Garden in the early months of his final stay in Hollywood. "We were at Metro at the same time. I followed Scott on *A Yank at Oxford,* and fought to keep in one of his scenes, the scene on the river between Robert Taylor and Maureen O'Sullivan."

George's book, *A View from the Sixties,* gives a clear picture of the frustrations suffered by writers working in Hollywood. They were constantly having their assignments changed, yanked off one project, and put to rewriting someone else's. Pictures were shelved without a reason after being given to a hack. The original writer might have spent six months trying to turn it into an epic. Writers were always being suddenly taken off the job. They came to work in the morning with a good idea, only to be told that they were through on the story. No wonder they drank. They should have left, but the inertia and the debts kept them chained to what looked like paradise from the outside.

"It's impossible to do creative work here," Scott used to say. "The climate is against you." But he wrote *The Last Tycoon* in Hollywood, although it was difficult for him and he worked slowly. He sometimes visited Corey Ford who lived on a top-floor apartment with a balcony at the Chateau Marmont.

In his *Time of Laughter,* Corey writes, "I seldom stepped out on it [the balcony]. There was nothing to see but a bare hillside where bulldozers were gouging out new building sites, one drab excavation below another. Sandy rubble had spilled down from the successive terraces, and was grown over with coarse trailing weeds. One night Scott wandered out onto the balcony. I joined him, prepared to apologize for the view. He pointed to the vine-covered terraces bathed in moonlight. 'The hanging gardens of Babylon,' he said, and from then on my view was enchanted, and I could not wait to get home each night to look at it again."

Scott had a way of making everything seem enchanted, even the drab villas at the Garden. When he was there I did not see the hideous furniture. We never ate at the Garden, except for the watery soup in the dining room. He made himself strong coffee in the tiled kitchen, and sometimes sent Ben across the road to Greenblatt's delicatessen for a sandwich and cigarettes, and oceans of Coca-Colas when he was not drinking. I never saw him in the pool, or sitting in the sun there or at the beach or at the house I rented for him at Encino, on Edward Everett Horton's estate. He thought the sun was bad for his tuberculosis, which had been serious enough to keep him out of Princeton for a year.

While the parties were swinging at the Garden, he rarely visited the bungalows except Eddie Mayer's and Nat West's. He admired West and advised me to read *Miss Lonelyhearts* and *The Day of the Locust.* The latter was the best book on Hollywood, Scott informed me. He hoped *his book* on Hollywood would be good, too, but he was now so shaken that he considered writing *The Last Tycoon* under a different name.

He was proved right with his title. There are no film tycoons left in Hollywood, and Irving Thalberg might well have been the last of the tycoons in charge of film creativity. Most of the writers disliked Thalberg. But Scott admired him. I interviewed Thalberg before he died. He was courteous and gave me all the time I needed. Scott wanted my impressions of the man who would be the central character of his book.

Scott had a sense of humor, but when he was trying to be funny he usually failed. I winced when he tried to talk cockney. It was all wrong. He was good at getting people to play his games, but he was not a wit in the way that Benchley or Sid Perelman or Donald Ogden Stewart or Dorothy Parker could be.

Donald told me that Scott could not understand why he and Benchley always made people laugh. "In Paris at the Quatorze [the July 14 holiday], Scott asked me at a party, 'What is funny about that?' It made him angry when no one laughed when he was trying to be funny. He said, 'Why are you laughing at Bob and not at me?' What he lacked, said Donald, "was the *key* of humor."

"It was a funny group of people," the first Mrs. Stewart recalls. "Get Dorothy Parker, Robert Benchley, Roland Young, Deems Taylor, and Don Stewart together in the same room, and something funny is bound to happen." Roland and Deems, who rolled around town in Deems's little car, were known as the Bobbsey Twins.

The Garden was like a club, a club difficult to get into. And Scott Fitzgerald, who was never a joiner, was a member. But he kept aloof from the group and the gay doings. He simply lived there and was full of hope there, and he suffered there and he drank there, but he never really belonged there.

[XI]

the war years

WORLD WAR II BROUGHT NEW faces to the Garden, and some disappeared, and some of those who had left returned. Robert Montgomery had been a constant visitor to Benchley's bungalow, but now he was in the navy, somewhere in the Atlantic. Every bungalow was filled, and even the eight drab rooms in the main building were occupied for the first time since Nazimova had turned her home into a hotel.

Food was in short supply, but one could usually get a fair steak in the nearby restaurants. When Eddie Mayer took me to the Players for dinner, I asked for two raw eggs to take home for my baby daughter who was born in September of 1942. I had come back to Hollywood as Mrs. Trevor Westbrook. I stayed at the Garden until I could find a home for us and the nurse I had brought from New York. Errol Flynn was in the next bungalow, and my nurse, a gray-haired nanny of the old school who avidly read all the scandals, was worried at the proximity of Mr. Flynn to my six-week-old daughter. When I told this to Artie Shaw, he agreed, "She might have been safe at four weeks, but not six!"

The maid service was worse than ever. Most of the former help for the rich and medium rich of Los Angeles were working in defense plants. The parties were wilder and more frequent, and everything seemed noisier and more hysterical.

But the Garden, the oasis for the intellectuals of Hollywood, was also concerned with what was going on in the world outside. The

175

majority of the writers were left wing, as were some of he actors such as John Garfield, Edward G. Robinson, Freddie March, and Ronald Reagan. Before he married Nancy Davis of Chicago, Ronnie was a strong liberal. Then he became just as staunch a Republican. Previously Ronnie had lived at the Garden after his divorce from Jane Wyman, and he was often in the bar talking politics by the hour.

During the war, André Malraux was in and out of Hollywood. I had first met him at the Garden in 1936 when he had been flying for the Loyalists in Spain. He wanted the well-paid writers and actors of Hollywood to donate money to build up the air force for the Spanish Loyalists, which was taking a beating from the Republicans. Most of those I knew at the Garden were very much involved and gave whatever they could spare from their everyday comfortable living.

Malraux had the dramatic and romantic aura of a man who was actually flying for the Loyalists, and he made several visits to Hollywood in 1936 and 1938. He had already written *Man's Fate,* but had not yet written *Man's Hope.* In addition to a speech at the home of Lillian Hellman, he took over the Philharmonic Auditorium, paid for by his liberal friends in Hollywood. The Garden of Allah was well represented.

I found Ernest Hemingway in Benchley's bungalow one Sunday morning. He was sitting quietly having coffee. He seemed well fed and confident. His moustache was heavier than Bob's, but not his beard. He was polite to me but continued his conversation with Bob. It concerned the documentary *The Spanish Earth.*

He had made it in Spain with Joris Ivins and Lillian Hellman. Joris was in Hollywood with Hemingway. Fredric March had a party at his home for twelve people and showed the film. The idea was that each of the twelve would give one thousand dollars. The money was to buy ambulances. Benchley, Dashiell Hammett, Lillian Hellman, Donald Ogden Stewart, John Garfield, Melvyn Douglas, Dorothy Parker, and Eddie Mayer were there.

Also Errol Flynn, who had given interviews about his involvement in Spain with the Loyalists. But when it came time to collect the money, Errol disappeared. He had pressing business in the toilet. Actually, Hemingway said, Errol had traveled only a few yards over the Spanish border, then prudently turned back. He found it safer to limit his fighting to his films.

I first met Hemingway (here shown with Gary Cooper and Y. Frank Freeman) in Robert Benchley's villa at The Garden of Allah in 1936. *Springer/Bettmann Archive*

In the First World War, it had been the actors who were actively patriotic—the war-bond tours of Mary Pickford and Douglas Fairbanks. With the rise of Hitlerism, the Italians bombing Ethiopia, and the war in Spain, the well-paid writers were imbued with the desire to help the oppressed.

The Hollywood Anti-Nazi League included Rupert Hughes, Eddie Cantor, Dudley Nichols, Gloria Stuart, Donald Ogden Stewart, Marc Connelly, Dorothy Parker, and Marion Spitzer. It had five thousand members. After the Hitler-Stalin Pact, Melvyn Douglas, Chairman of the Motion Picture Democratic Committee, presented a resolution which denounced Nazi aggression and Soviet perfidy. Douglas was maligned, the resolution came to nothing, and he resigned. The pact had thrown the Hollywood Anti-Nazi League into confusion. The pro-Stalin faction suddenly de-emphasized their antinazism. When Russia invaded Finland, the league didn't know whether it was coming or going. Donald Stewart and Herbert Biberman made speeches about boycotting Nazi goods. They published a weekly paper, had a weekly radio show, and held mass meetings with speakers of the caliber of Thomas Mann and Dr. John R. Lechner, Chairman of the American Legion's Americanism Committee.

Most of the writers in Hollywood, including those who lived at the Garden, had been young men during the Depression of the early 1930s. This had caused them to veer sharply to the left. They had lived through the terrible time when there were fifty million unemployed. They were appalled at the stories from Germany. I remember Eddie Mayer saying to me, "It's ironic. Of all the Jews in the world, the German Jews are the most integrated. They are Germans as much as they are Jews. Perhaps more so."

I met Hemingway again with Benchley while Scott was living at the Garden. "Don't you want to see him?" I asked. Scott did not, and yet he wanted every detail of the conversation when I reported back to him. Scott had not forgiven Hemingway for the slighting "Poor Scott" reference to him in his story *The Snows of Kilimanjaro*. "It sounds as though I'm dead," he complained.

At Scott's insistence, the Poor Scott was changed in future editions to Poor Julian, to whose romantic notion that the rich are different from you and me, someone says, "Yes, they have more money." Hemingway despised Hollywood, and while he avidly sold his stories to the studios, he swore he would never work for them. He made a tentative deal with Darryl Zanuck to work on the script of *The Snows of Kilimanjaro,* but he went to Sun Valley instead. However, he did become involved later with the filming of *The Old Man and the Sea.*

I met Peter Viertel with some of the writers at The Garden of Allah and later at his mother's—Salka Viertel, who wrote Garbo's films. Peter asked Hemingway why he was breaking his rule. The famous author replied to the eager neophyte, "Did I ever tell you my stock answer for 'How to write for the movies'? First you write it, then you get into a Stutz Bearcat and drive west. When you get to Arizona, you stop the car and throw the script out. No, you wait until they throw the money in, then you throw it out. Then you head north, south or east but for chrissakes don't go west to Hollywood."

He was involved with *The Old Man and the Sea,* he explained, because he liked two of the people connected with it—Spencer Tracy and Leland Hayward. "No, on second thought, only Spencer. Leland still has agent's blood in his veins."

The film had every kind of problem. Spencer had promised to lose weight and did not. He was drunk and could not report for shooting until they flew Katharine Hepburn to Cuba to straighten him out. The directors were changed. The picture was postponed and started and postponed and started again. It was an all-around mess, and when it was finished and released, it failed.

Robert Parrish who started his career in Hollywood as a child actor in *Our Gang* for Hal Roach, and had become a director, was present when Hemingway talked to young Viertel. Two years later, Mr. Parrish saw Hemingway at Saint-Jean-de-Luz on the Basque coast near Spain. He was shaking an orange tree in which Bob's son was clinging, and saying to the boy: "Here's a chance to show if you're a man. If you can stay in the tree, you're a man. If you fall out, you're a monkey." Later Mrs. Parrish said to her husband, "For God's sake don't mention *The Old Man and the Sea* to him. It must have been an unhappy experience."

"We went to the bullfights with him," Bob told me, "and Mary Hemingway was charming. I heard someone, and it must have been me, saying to Ernest, 'How did *The Old Man and the Sea* turn out? The last time I saw you, you were speaking of it.'

"Hemingway replied,'Weren't you there when I was giving advice to Peter Viertel? I should have listened.' "

He never again was concerned with his stories after they were bought for films, although previously he had helped Ingrid Bergman get the role of Maria in *For Whom the Bell Tolls*. His book *To Have and Have Not* was filmed three times, the last version in 1944 was written by William Faulkner and starred Humphrey Bogart and Lauren Bacall. "If you want me, whistle," she said in the film. She whistled and Bogey came. It meant his breaking up with Mayo Methot at tremendous emotional and financial cost. Miss Bacall was installed at this time in the Garden with her mother, with Bogey in the next bungalow.

I first remember Bogart at the Garden with his second wife, Mary Phillips, when he came to Hollywood in 1936 to play Duke Mantee in the film version of *The Petrified Forest*. He owed his film repeat of the stage role to Leslie Howard, who refused to accept anyone else. Leslie played the gentle poet. Bogart was paid four hundred dollars a week, but he had heard of actors being dropped after the first film, and The Garden of Allah was a convenient place to leave in a hurry should the option be dropped. The Bogarts were soon at home in their surroundings and floated happily from bungalow to bungalow in the eternal round of parties.

Miss Phillips, a good actress, returned to New York to star on the stage in *The Postman Always Rings Twice*. While she was away, Bogey met Mayo Methot, whom he invited to go sailing with him on weekends. She soon sailed into his bungalow at the Garden.

When Mary Bogart returned to Hollywood, she gave her husband a stern ultimatum. He must choose between her and Mayo. He chose Mayo, and it was a good thing for Mary. She married Kenneth McKenna, the story editor at MGM, and lived happily with him until his recent death.

During Miss Bacall's time at the Garden, Bogart employed a guard to protect them from the tempestuously physical Miss Methot. When Bob Benchley heard of this he quipped, "You would need a Marine Corps to keep Mayo away." The guard proved ineffectual. The Garden was famous for its battles, but there was never anything like the fights between Bogart and Methot while he was trying to get rid of her. When she discovered Bogey with Baby, as her adoring Humphrey called her, the dialogue was as good as the toughest Bogart film. Bottles flew, furniture crashed, and while Baby escaped out the back door, the man who loved her was being chased out front by his irate wife, who was armed with a kitchen knife and brandished it while she tried to catch up with her terrified mate.

Humphrey Bogart and his second wife, Mary Phillips, in the late 1930s at The Garden of Allah. *Culver Pictures, Inc.*

Bogey and Baby cutting their wedding cake at Louis Bromfield's
"dream" farm in Ohio. He met them while living at the Garden.
Wide World Photos

Everyone came out to get a ringside seat at the battle. It is re-called by those who witnessed it as the noisiest and fiercest of all the husband-and-wife scraps. Lauren was young and determined and Bogey got his divorce and married her.

Louis Bromfield was then at the Garden on a writing assignment. His longing to buy a farm was well known. He argued about it with his secretary-manager, a nice man called Hawkins. Bromfield had a passion for a certain model farm in the Midwest. William Randolph Hearst used to say, "I wish my writers wouldn't buy farms, it's very expensive for me."

Hawkins and Bromfield were heard all over the Garden fighting over the advisability of the farm.

"You can't afford it," Hawkins lamented. Then Louis went into a long, brilliant, ecstatic speech about how the farm would support him so he could be "free to write." "I'm going to do it all scientifically," he shouted in exasperation. "It will be a showplace, and I can live there happily and *write!*" Hawkins said angrily that only farmers could farm and that all of Louis's talk was a snare and a delusion.

Day after day the great debate continued, and they made book at the Garden on who would win. Ben held the betting money. Humphrey Bogart was betting on Bromfield. In the end, Hawkins lost and Louis bought Malabar in Ohio about which he wrote a book. Perhaps he should have listened to his secretary-manager. The farm killed him because he had to work so hard to support it. It took everything he could make from his novels and film scripts to buy the expensive machinery. But apart from the happiness it gave him, the farm served one useful purpose. Bogart and his intended, Miss Bacall, went there to be married.

Betty Bacall, as she was known to her friends, was a good wife to Bogart. She did not stand for too much drinking. He never fought with her, and he certainly never struck her, as he had tried to strike Mayo, who always whacked him first. Bogey was a naturally timid man. When he was drinking he started fights with people, but someone always stepped in to stop them. There was always an eager crony to protect Bogey.

"By midnight when he had a few drinks under his belt," said the gentle Dave Chasen, "he became the Bogart of the screen. One night Bogart, Gable, and Brod Crawford got into an argument at the bar, and they started wrestling on the floor. Bogey wouldn't let up, and I had to throw him out bodily." Dave is a small man, but Bogey didn't resist. Besides, it was almost a habit with him to be thrown out of places.

When an "in" member of The Garden of Allah died, there was usually a party for the departing spirit. The party for Bogey lasted three days. Mike Romanoff contributed the drinks, Dave Chasen supplied the food.

John Howard Lawson, one of the "Unfriendly Ten," was one of the founders of the Screen Writers Guild, with Dashiell Hammett, Lillian Hellman, Frances and Albert Hackett, and Donald Ogden Stewart. From the time I arrived in Hollywood in 1936 until it was settled late in 1938, all I heard at the Garden was the fight between the Left and the Right to gain control of all the writers at the studios. The announced aim of the Screen Writers Guild was to better the working conditions for them all, and especially for the hacks who were poorly paid. To combat this dangerous idea, the producers organized the Screen Playwrights under the presidency of Rupert Hughes. The studio bosses were determined their side should win. They put in anyone who could spell his name to vote for the Playwrights. Jean Harlow's mother was down as a writer. Louis B. Mayer put her in. (She was supposed to have scripted a story for her platinum-blond daughter, The Baby, at Metro.)

Bob Benchley was legitimately down for the Screen Writers, although his chief job at that time was appearing in film shorts. When Bob went to vote, Howard Emmett Rogers of the Screen Playwrights challenged him for his registration. Bob silenced the opposition by declaiming, "Get away from me, you Knickerbocker Gray!"

The Screen Writers won the election and consequently the right to establish all the conditions of work, minimum salaries, contract obligations, and so on.

Frances and Albert Hackett were very active in the 1938 election, and when they explained the justness of their cause, I promised I would deliver Scott Fitzgerald to vote "if I have to carry him there." I was swept along with all the talk at The Garden. Scott was recovering from a drinking bout and was weak. He went on his own feet, rather shakily.

Herman Mankiewicz refused to vote for either side. "You just don't care," they stormed at him. "You don't care what happens to the little people. But that is perhaps because you don't know any little people earning fifty dollars a week." "Oh yes, I do," he replied. "I know them all. They are all getting fifty dollars a week."

The film *Pasteur* was a factor accelerating the founding of the Screen Writers Guild. Darryl Zanuck had left Warners to take over production at 20th Century-Fox. Hal Wallis, who had begun at the studio in the publicity department, was now in charge of filmmaking. Eddie Chodorov, a young playwright from the New York theatre, had read Paul de Kruif's book *The Microbe Hunters*. He extracted the chapter on Pasteur and wrote an original screenplay. Jack Warner hated it from the start.

"I told him this was going to be about a great man, Pasteur," Eddie told me, "but he said, 'It's no good. It's full of disease, it has no sex, and a man with a beard! I asked someone in the Green Room who Pasteur was, and he didn't know. Forget it.' "

"You should get Muni to play Pasteur. He is important at the studio and perhaps he can swing it for you," Eddie was told by another writer, Abem Finkel, who was Muni's brother-in-law. Abem was a rare, sweet, compassionate person who later committed suicide.

Muni, whose real name was Paul Weisenfreund, had an unusual contract at Warners. If they gave him three properties which he did not like, he could refuse them, and he would not be suspended. Then the studio had to do a film of Paul's choice.

When Mr. Finkel took Chodorov's script to Paul, he shouted, "I don't want to play a character with germs in his beard!" Eddie explained why this would be a great film for him. Eddie finally turned the scales when he said, "Can't you see. It isn't about who sleeps with who, it's about saving millions of lives. It will make *you* a great man." Muni found this irresistible, and he took the script to Jack Warner and said, "I want to do *Pasteur*."

Mr. Warner screamed that if he caught that double-crossing son-of-a-bitch Eddie Chodorov, what he would do to him, etc. etc. Warner sent for Eddie, who received a torrent of abuse.

"There was no Screen Writers Guild then," said Eddie, "and he threw me out of the studio, retaining my script. With the Guild this would not have been possible."

Warner took Chodorov's name off the film as writer and producer. The new producer, Henry Blanke, hired two new writers, Sheridan Gibney and Pierre Collinge. Both hocked the Oscars they won for *Pasteur,* and, three weeks after winning the award, Pierre Collinge committed suicide. Jack Warner was strutting proudly at the Awards. He knew now that he had a winner, and he had a big party afterwards with Oscars flashing everywhere.

Chodorov did not attend the Awards. On the big night he was at home working on a play, *Decision,* for Broadway. At that time he was getting seven hundred and fifty dollars a week. It was doubled when he worked for Sam Goldwyn. Eddie's brother Jerry came in and said,

"I don't want to play a man with germs in his beard." Paul Muni, in *Pasteur*.

"What a crime. You, who thought it through, and you are not there." The next morning Eddie received one telegram: "My first thought last night was of you. I remember how hard you wished for this to be made. Signed, Herman Politz." He was the tailor who had been around at the time measuring Eddie for suits. It was the only acknowledgment he received that he had had anything to do with the writing of *Pasteur*.

When forming the Screen Writers Guild, they used the example of Stephen Foster, the great writer of American folk songs, who died penniless in the Bowery after cutting his wrists. With a guild to protect him, he would have been rich all his life.

The Hacketts were justly proud of their victory, and there was a party in Benchley's bungalow to celebrate. This was the most important thing that had happened to all these writers since they had succumbed to the fancy salaries of Hollywood. They had done something for their less successful colleagues, and they were happier in their own bondage.

Albert Hackett began his career as a child actor. He married Frances Goodrich, who had been educated at Vassar, in 1931 when he was thirty-one years old. They had a good career in Hollywood. Among the films for which they received credit, some before the victory for the Screen Writers Guild, were *The Thin Man* pictures with William Powell and Myrna Loy, beginning in 1934; *Naughty Marietta,* 1935; *Ah Wilderness,* and *Rose Marie* in 1936; *The Father of the Bride* in 1950; *Seven Brides for Seven Brothers, Easter Parade,* and *The Diary of Anne Frank,* for which their play won the Pulitzer Prize in 1960.

The Hacketts lived at The Garden of Allah for various brief periods when they were in Hollywood. If the stay was longer, they rented a house in Beverly Hills. I went with Scott to one of their dinner parties. Scott was working on *Marie Antoinette* for Norma Shearer. I remember Joan Blondell, Dick Powell, and the Nat Wests were there. Albert told us he had gone duck shooting with Nat up north. They got into barrels and shot down ducks. "But he didn't come when we ate them." The Hacketts liked Nat, "but it is hard to know him," said Frances, "although I am sure he had a good time in Hollywood."

In the middle of dinner, Scott received a call from his producer, Hunt Stromberg, to come to his house to discuss the film. Afterward he sent a few lines of verse in apology to the Hacketts: "Stromberg sent for Poppa, though Poppa hadn't et, to do what Jesus couldn't, save Marie Antoinette." Before he left, Scott had everyone on the staircase, which rose from the side of the living room. They were playing a game, mesmerized by Scott. I don't remember the game, only the laughter, and Scott at the top of the stairs, flushed with alcohol, but also with his magic that they were responding to.

"While we were living at the Garden," Frances Hackett recalled, "we were working on a picture called *The Hitler Gang.*"

"It was one of the worst pictures ever made," said Albert Hackett, who is an honest man. "It was one of the three that lost money during the war."

The other two were *Wilson,* Zanuck's pride—and he still insists it was a good picture—and *Orlando and the Thief.* Everything else in the war years was a gold mine. The public didn't care what they saw as long as it distracted them. War pictures are usually made after the war is over and won, or war comedies during the war.

The Hacketts were given a two-week vacation during the writing of the Hitler film. Their holiday in Mexico City was terminated by a telegram, "We have Hitler. Come back." It took a long time to finish the war, and to finish the film. These were some of the problems plaguing the Hacketts and Johnny Farrow, who was the director. *The Hitler Gang* was released in 1944.

Unlike some of the complainers I heard at the Garden, the Hacketts enjoyed their time in Hollywood. They were normal, intelligent people who liked a drink but did not get drunk. They gave good dinner parties, and invited interesting writers and directors to them, and they respected their producer, Hunt Stromberg.

"He fought for the writer, even against Louis B. Mayer [sometimes known as Louis B. Merde] who had been against our project of *Naughty Marietta* all the way. Mayer hated the story, the whole idea. At the preview it was obvious that the picture was an enormous success. Mayer gave a banquet for it on the opening night and took all the credit for its conception."

Stromberg had courage and experience, and he was one of the top producers at MGM for a long time. Scott worked on *Madame Curie* with him and also liked him.

The Hacketts had first gone to Hollywood in 1932. In 1939 they left for three years. They were living in New York when Scott died, and I took them the little verse he had written about their dinner.

Albert had been on the verge of a breakdown from overwork. They had quickly written three *Thin Man* movies, *The Firefly,* and *Rose Marie.* When Stromberg told them that next year there would be another *Thin Man* and another *Naughty Marietta,* Albert started to throw up and cry.

After the war, when they came back to the Garden, they found that Hollywood had changed. The spiraling cost of each production had a stultifying effect, and they were no longer given the free rein they had enjoyed with Stromberg. "Now we wouldn't go back for anything," Frances assured me. "But it was a wonderful life while it lasted."

Donald Ogden Stewart was not a Communist, although he left Hollywood and went to England to avoid being called to testify against

Donald Ogden Stewart, the most highly paid scriptwriter in Hollywood, with his first wife, Beatrice, were among the first residents at The Garden of Allah. *Springer/Bettmann Archive*

writers who were Communists during the McCarthy and the House-Un-American Activities Committee investigations. John Ford believed Donald was a Communist and so testified. "But I lived with the man," the first Mrs. Ogden Stewart told me, "and," she assured me, "it wasn't true. He was an ardent Socialist, just like Bernard Shaw." When a lawyer, a right-winger, heard Ford's testimony, he called Stewart and told him to "breeze." Don thought it was a good idea. He went to England where he still lives with his second wife, Ella Winters, who had been married to the great liberal, Lincoln Steffens. When the State Department revoked his passport, thus preventing him from leaving England, Donald sued the State Department and won. They return to America from time to time but prefer the way of life in England.

A friend was talking recently to Bea Stewart about that frightening period and recollecting the people who had served time in prison, Ring Lardner, Jr., among others. She said, "How come Don missed the boat?" "What do you mean, missed the boat?" Bea demanded, "He caught it!"

"I was the first of the Algonquin 'gang' who came to Hollywood," Donald informed me in London last year. I had not seen him since the old days of the Garden. He had first gone to Hollywood in 1924 to lecture in women's clubs in Los Angeles, Beverly Hills, and Pasadena.

His first screenplay in Hollywood, *Brown of Harvard,* starred William Haines, the silent-film star who became just as famous as an interior decorator. "Two people had already worked on *Brown of Harvard,*" Donald recalled. "I was one of Irving Thalberg's stable of writers. He was one of the most brilliant men I had ever met. You took in your daily stint to Irving, and the most he said after reading it was, 'It's not bad,' but I liked him."

He was not so enthusiastic about Louis B. Mayer. "In 1931, during the depression, Mayer called in the writers at the studio one by one. As one of the better-paid writers, I was called in first. Louis began to cry and I began to cry. 'Don,' he said, wiping his tears, 'I'm going to have to ask you to take a cut.'" When things got better, Mr. Mayer forgot to restore the salary. It took the newly formed Screen Writers Guild to remind him.

Don wrote some of the big hits at MGM, and he was one of the seventeen writers on *Gone With the Wind.* But only a few received credit for their work. The final credits for the film read: Screenplay, Sidney Howard; Contributor to Treatment, Jo Swerling; Dialogue, Ben Hecht; Screenplay Construction, Oliver H. P. Garrett; Adapted from the novel by Margaret Mitchell.

"I started at two hundred and fifty dollars a week," Don told me. "This went up to twenty-five hundred dollars." Then to thirty-five hundred dollars on a fifty-two week-a-year basis. When he was working on *The Philadelphia Story,* he came down with pneumonia. His wife posted guards at his bedroom door with strict orders that he was not to be disturbed. Thalberg and Cukor somehow slipped past the guards into Donald's room. He had a temperature of 105 degrees but he got up, dressed, and they went to work on the script.

As president of the Anti-Nazi League, Stewart, with Dorothy Parker, rented a hall for Fredric March to recite Irwin Shaw's *Bury the*

Dead. "Everyone became terribly excited and wanted to march on MGM which became the Bastille," Donald recalled. "Until then, Hollywood had been a Graustark. Now all the liberals rallied to the cause against injustice."

When Lincoln Steffens died in 1936, the league of American Writers, the forerunner of the Screen Writers Guild, held a memorial service for him in San Francisco. His widow, Ella, was present. She made a speech. Mr. Stewart was in the audience. "She was a tiny woman, and I fell in love with her."

Bea divorced him in 1937 and he married Ella. Don and Ella were in Benchley's villa at the Garden during the Battle of Britain in September 1940. Germany had not yet attacked Russia, and the Hitler-Stalin Pact was still in effect. The Stewarts were in sandals and dirty blue jeans. (He had dressed elegantly when he was married to Beatrice, who was very social.) They kept harping on how England wanted to get us into this imperialist war. Ella, who still dresses with great originality, was the first hippie in her weird clothes. She was much farther to the left than her husband. There was a joke at the time that when Don was in the hospital after being hit by a car, Ella visited him, and he came out a Communist sympathizer. Anyone who was a liberal in those days was likely to be called a Communist or a fellow traveler.

Benchley, who was never involved with communism, only causes, took his son Nat and Donald to a party in Santa Barbara, where Bob's friends the Wright Luddingtons had a mansion that resembled a castle. There were Napoleonic flags over the beds and coats of arms everywhere. The living room, Nat remembers, was enormous.

Wright said to Benchley, "I think you ought to look at your friend." Mr. Stewart, completely naked, was seated on top of the mantelpiece spouting proletarian doctrine, while the rich people of Santa Barbara drank, and laughed, and had a right royal time.

[XII]

of cabbage and kings

DURING WORLD WAR II, THE GARden of Allah was filled with amusing people. Writers, artists, and musicians from Europe found refuge there. There were some shortages—gasoline, eggs, and bacon, in that order, but life at the Garden was about the same. It was a problem for me to get safety pins for my daughter's diapers, but it was never a problem to find a feast in progress at the Sheekmans'. In 1931, Arthur Sheekman had written the screenplay of *Monkey Business* for the Marx Brothers in collaboration with S. J. Perelman. Arthur is still a close friend of Groucho, who would not dare be grouchy with him or with Gloria, as he sometimes is with me. No one could be. Arthur is kind, and Gloria is still a lovely lady. She gave up her acting career a few years after she married Arthur in 1934.

I once asked Arthur to describe the plot of a Marx Brothers film. "Very simple," he replied. "I want you." "OK, you're on my gang." Answer: "You'll never get it." A typical joke. "May I ask what you're doing?" "You may ask." This is what Woody Allen meant when he said he wanted to make pictures like the Marx Brothers did because there was no plot.

It reminds me of the late brilliant film critic James Agee's description in *Agee on Film: Reviews and Comments* of a proposed scene in a Laurel and Hardy film: "It is simple enough—simple and real, in fact, as a nightmare. Laurel and Hardy are trying to move a piano across a narrow suspension bridge. The bridge is slung over a sickening chasm, between a couple of Alps. Midway they meet a gorilla."

193

In their few years at the Garden, Gloria and Arthur Sheekman provided the feasts for the intellectuals from the East. *Wide World Photos*

The Sheekmans were catalysts. They brought people together at their bountiful table. The beautiful Gloria was a beautiful cook. Arthur has always been the friendliest and most helpful of men.

Sam Hoffenstein, the poet of The Garden of Allah, wrote a paean of praise for Gloria:

On Hearing the Wings of All the Poets Brush Through Gloria's Kitchen

> Goose with Kirschwasser Aspic
> You Know the Story of Jason
> Who Hunted the Golden Fleece
> When the Goose with the Kirschwasser Aspic
> Rose from among the Geese
>
> The Hell with the Fleece and Jason
> We'll Roam and Hunt No More
> The Goose with the Kirschwasser Aspic
> Is What I've Been Hunting for

SAM HOFFENSTEIN

John McNulty was invited to one of Gloria's dinners. Afterwards he reviewed the dinner as though for *Variety*, the show-business weekly.

GLORIA'S DINNER DISTINGUÉ
BUT NEEDS SHOWMAN'S TOUCH

The twelve-point dinner [the points referred to rationing], elegantly tossed by Gloria Sheekman (Sheekman Productions, Inc.) last night, was the kind of dinner that calls for a review. It was not the fantastic concatenation of groceries designed to be tossed down the gullet and given no further thought to.

As a dinner it was, of course, superb. Sheekman Productions has truck with no less than superb. In all honesty, however, it could have been brought even closer to perfection by a more showmanly touch. The dinner was unpretentious, ca va sans dire, so we won't dire it. It was as simple as money can buy.

What happened! The glorious ineffable soup came first and it was past perfection. Mankind, including Gloria, could not hope to keep up the standard set by the soup.

What comes after that was mere excellent, unostensibly marvelous, but naturally not up to the soup. In a word, a dinner to remember. A plaintive cry for just one tiny bit of showmanship in the future.

Signed, SIME [SIME SILVERMAN founded *Variety*]
MCNULTY

I knew their daughter Sylvia when she was a baby. I was surprised when they woke her up at midnight to bring her into a party, the little girl rubbing her eyes, but otherwise quite happy to be the center of all the attention. They had a house on De Longpre Avenue before they moved into the Garden in 1943, where they stayed for three years.

Arthur wrote *Wonder Man* in 1945, and in 1946, *Blue Skies* for Bing Crosby, and *Welcome, Stranger* for Bing and Barry Fitzgerald. He has always had a great sense of humor and is spontaneously witty. I remember dinner being rather late at the Sheekmans' on my first visit to their home. Groucho was not eating the glorious food, and I asked him why. "Hollywood dinners are never served before ten o'clock," he explained. "I always eat at home first."

Gloria preserves her recipes and the following are sample menus from one of the great gourmet cooks of our day.

March 28, 1944. Party for Benchley, Butterworth, Lois Earl, Arthur Schwartz and wife Kay, Dore Schary, and Dorothy Peterson.

> Beef stew supreme
> Artichoke hearts stuffed with mushrooms
> Shell macaroni aux fines herbs
> Green salad
> Black walnut sponge cake

July 10, 1944. A buffet supper for Groucho, Benchley, Butterworth, and the Jerry Walds.

Egg plant	Stewed chicken
Caviar	Asparagus vinaigrette
Crab in aspic	Spanish rice with Greek olives
Tomatoes	Apple sauce
Melon and pastrami	Hot fruit dessert
Mustard beets	Cafe diable

No wonder everyone loved them and hankered for invitations to dinner. Remember this was during the war.

It was an exotic atmosphere for a little girl. "I was very lonely at The Garden of Allah," the grown-up Sylvia told me. "I was not pretty." Now—in her midthirties—she is attractive and successful as an author and the mother of four children. She lives at Malibu with her husband, Vaughn Thompson, and four children. She is not lonely.

"My mother worked and my father worked. It wasn't like being Eloise at the Plaza." But she had two good adult friends at the Garden, or thought she had. Kay Thompson, who proved her friendship by cutting a record for her small friend when Sylvia had her tonsils removed. She also gave her two female kittens called Roger and Wilco.

"I loved Louis Calhern, who took me to Schwab's for sodas and tried to teach me to swim. He was living in a bungalow with Dorothy

Gish, and I remember how shocked I was when I found out they weren't married. I was an extremely shy eight year old, wandering about with no one taking any notice of me except for Kay and Mr. Calhern, who was my very special friend. But he did something that ended our friendship. I didn't know how to swim yet, and the shallow steps of the pool were slippery—they were shaped like a moon. One Sunday morning, I was playing around and I slipped down the second step into the pool. Mr. Calhern was watching me. He was wearing a new pair of white pants with a white jacket and a white shirt with a bright blue tie. I was bobbing up and down screaming for help. Mr. Calhern just stood there. Then he walked away. He didn't want to wet his beautiful clothes. I managed to get out of the pool by myself. Mr. Calhern had been the closest friend I had, but I never went by his villa again."

Calhern adored children, and even Natalie Schafer, who divorced him, believes he could never have behaved so inhumanly toward a child. "It was the sadness of his life that he couldn't have children," she told me. "He must have thought she was play acting."

I go along with this.

Natalie learned to cook from Gloria Sheekman. She usually managed to set the kitchen on fire, as I usually do when I cook. After her separation from Calhern, and after her romance with George Kaufman, Natalie was still at the Garden and still trying to cook.

One hot summer day she attempted a crème brûlée. She wanted to impress Gloria, who made them so well. You have to be very careful with crème brûlées. If the brown sugar catches fire in the broiler, the whole kitchen can go up in smoke. Natalie was lying on the floor by the oven, quite naked, when her mother, visiting her from the East, entered, "What on earth are you doing?" she asked her daughter. It was hard to explain that she was watching the crème brûlée to see that it did not burn. It was hot enough even without the oven and that was why she was naked.

Natalie's bungalow had only one bedroom, and she rented a room for her mother in the main building overlooking her bungalow. "Any time the door is open it means I'm awake and you can come in," she informed her parent. The mother walked through the open door one morning to find John McClain sprawled on her daughter's bed. He had come over to say good morning. Natalie was still in bed. John offered to get some coffee for them all.

Louis Calhern (in background) and Natalie Schafer, who lived at the Garden during and after their marriage. Also at the table are Natalie's fiancé Charlie Butterworth (center), Joe E. Brown (left), and Spencer Tracy (right). *Wide World Photos*

When he left the room, her mother turned to Natalie and said, "I've never interfered with anything in your life. But now I absolutely must speak up. I don't think you should have a man in your room until you've put on lip rouge."

It had been convenient for Natalie with George Kaufman in the bungalow next to hers at the Garden. It made the romance less exhausting. One day when she was having some people in, the phone rang, and it was Kaufman saying in loud ringing tones that could be heard by all, "When you get rid of the people, come over and make fudge." The distinguished playwright's voice was so loud he might have been speaking through the thin walls.

George was not a handsome man, but like Scott he had the ability to make a woman feel attractive and needed. In a man as courted as George was then, Natalie found this a remarkable and appealing trait.

The Mary Astor diaries had hurt Kaufman's amour proper. At that time, 1936, he was living in a house off the Strip, and the reporters were trying to beat his door down. He was furious with Miss Astor for keeping a diary and for letting it be discovered by her husband. No man could be that good in bed, and far from being proud, George was embarrassed. The diary had been published in the Hearst chain of newspapers. After that, the first thing he asked a lady with whom he hoped to have an affair was: "Do you keep a diary?"

When Mr. Kaufman went on his way to another love, Natalie was consoled by a trio of sought-after men—Benchley, McClain, and Thornton Delehanty, who wrote for the New York *Herald Tribune*. They set up drinks for her to be ready when she got home from the studios and took her to dinner at the Players. On Sundays it was Natalie's turn to entertain, and she cooked a lunch of whiskey sours. To follow this main course she boiled some eggs.

Mr. Delehanty's bungalow was next to Natalie's. He did not quite have the talent or money to live the life he wanted to, but this was remedied when he married a rich woman and faded from the Garden and the Hollywood scene. I missed him. Thornton was everybody's friend, easygoing and popular.

There was a call girl who used to wander at will in and out of the open doors of the Garden. She became friendly with Natalie, who is open-minded about most things. The girl plied her trade down the road at La Maison Frances, the most popular call house in Hollywood. Some of the top stars tarried at Madam Frances' on the way for drinks at the Garden.

While Natalie was married to Louis Calhern, he was violently jealous of her friendship with a young attractive man, Michael Pearman, who now owns the Running Footman, a fashionable restaurant in New York. Calhern went on drinking binges that lasted several days. When he disappeared, Natalie was frantic. Once Pearman was in her bungalow keeping her company while she waited for Lou to return. The bungalow had an upstairs turret. When Calhern suddenly arrived,

Michael scurried upstairs into the turret where he spent the rest of the day hiding in a closet. Natalie had never known an alcoholic at close quarters before.

"I learned what being an alcoholic meant," Natalie told me. "We had to keep an emergency supply of oxygen in our bungalow. I once asked him who was the real Calhern, the drunk or the sober man. He replied that he didn't know."

She believed Calhern's drinking started when he had been unhappy with his second wife, Julia Hoyt, a society beauty. His first wife was Ilka Chase, the actress-authoress.

When Julia was married to Calhern, they lived in a cottage at the Garden close to those of Benchley, Butterworth, and Sid Perelman. She often appeared with a black eye. Sometimes two black eyes. She had fallen off a ladder arranging books, she explained. But she was always arm in arm with her husband when they appeared in public, and they seemed to be very much in love. When a writer at the Garden asked about the black eyes, Calhern explained Julia had fallen the night before and struck her head on a bird bath. Whenever she had a black eye, her devoted husband always volunteered the same explanation. When Louis was married to Natalie, and they were having a fight, she sobbingly reproached him, "You never even gave me a black eye!"

Natalie had been attracted to Calhern when she read about his romantic life at the Garden with Miss Hoyt, who was one of the first society beauties to go on the stage. Natalie read of Calhern jumping into the pool in full evening dress. It all sounded so glamorous. It was, until she lived with it.

Louis, Julia, and Natalie were in a play, *Rhapsody,* in New York, and Natalie and Lou fell in love. When he divorced Julia to marry her, Natalie insisted that they too should have a glamorous home. She gave up acting "because I played a wife so well." They went to Hollywood by boat and on arrival sped to The Garden of Allah.

During Calhern's time with Dorothy Gish, his villa at the Garden never had the lights on. The shades were always drawn. And there was a feeling of arsenic and old lace. This was when he was separated from Natalie, who was living next door. It was Dorothy's mood. She was very ethereal and fragile. "She smelled of violets," sniffed Natalie.

When Calhern married his fourth wife, Marianne Stewart, and moved with her into the Garden, Natalie was still living there. When she was introduced to her successor, she said, "I have something for you—some stationery with Mrs. Louis Calhern engraved on it." The wives could be changed, but the Garden and the stationery were always reliably the same.

Lillian Gish disliked Calhern. She felt that he was treating her sister Dorothy badly. After they starred together in Los Angeles, in *Life with Father,* Dorothy suffered with ulcers, and Lillian blamed her association with the suave actor. For a long time he used the excuse of still being married to their next-door neighbor for not being able to marry Dorothy. When I heard that he could not get a divorce because Natalie was refusing to give him his freedom, I mentioned this in my column. The next time I saw Natalie she said, "Thank you." And she meant it. She was damned if she was going to be the heavy in the triangle, and she promptly divorced Calhern. But he never married Dorothy.

Natalie was introduced to Nazimova in the last year of the veteran star's life. Natalie was swimming in the pool when Nazimova's companion-manager Glesca Marshall asked her, "Would you like to see Madame? She doesn't see many people nowadays." Natalie found a tired, wrinkled lady who was very ill, and Natalie made her excuses and left.

Calhern was sixty-four when he died in May 1956. His first film had been *The Blot* in 1921. His last, *High Society,* with Grace Kelly, Bing Crosby, and Frank Sinatra, was released in 1956, the year of his death. He would have enjoyed the title for an epitaph.

Frank Sinatra lived at the Garden in 1941, with his press agent George Evans, who had organized the kids in New York to scream and swoon for Frankie at the old Paramount Theatre on Broadway. RKO, for whom Sinatra made his first film, was so sure that it was all a press agent's stunt that the studio organized five hundred girls to scream for Frankie when his train came in at Pasadena. There were more than a thousand girls meeting the train. The skinny crooner owed Evans a great deal. Evans mothered him. He thought up great publicity angles, and he made sure that Frankie kept the dates with the Hollywood reporters.

As soon as Frankie had settled into his villa with his expensive suits, his records, record player, and the latest recording equipment, George walked over to Schwab's and told one of the brothers, "Frankie is staying at The Garden of Allah, but we don't want anyone to know.

If you keep still, we'll give you all our business," which was considerable.

"Frankie," comments Sidney Skolsky, "was a bewildered kid at that time."

Frankie led a quiet life at the Garden, preferring to stay home in the evenings rather than test Hollywood night life. He had an employee called Mike, who made the Italian spaghetti he loved. Mike was proud of his cooking, and often called at the back door of the cottage next door to show the big bowl of spaghetti to Kay Thompson and Bill Spier.

Until Bill gave Sinatra his first dramatic role in a *Suspense* episode on radio, no one had thought he could act. Bill, sensing the bursting ambition behind the tenseness, signed him to play a deranged killer who was threatening the life of Agnes Moorehead. Frank was excellent, and this led indirectly to *From Here to Eternity*. They might never have allowed him to test for it if Harry Cohn had not heard him on *Suspense*.

Sinatra's career had touched rock bottom in the early fifties, aided by the reporters with whom he had traded punches and given a hard time when he was riding the crest of the wave. With no films in sight, and his records not selling, he accompanied his wife Ava Gardner to Africa in 1952 where she was starring in *Mogambo,* with Clark Gable and Grace Kelly. Frank was bored sitting around, and he let everyone know it, including Ava, who was just as bored having him around. They had fought until they could not think of anything new to quarrel about.

Clark Gable, the star of *Mogambo,* was worried about Frankie and wanted to help him. He knew that Columbia owned the film rights to *From Here to Eternity,* and he gave his copy of the book to Sinatra. "There might be something in it for you," he said.

Frankie read the book and was sure that the role of Maggio was written for him. Ava, delighted to get him off her hands, bought him a ticket back to Hollywood. The film, released in 1953, reestablished him on a different level, as a dramatic actor.

Before Ava's first marriage, to Mickey Rooney, she lived in a tiny apartment on Fountain Avenue, which paralleled The Garden of Allah. She roomed with a young actress, Peggy Maley. But Ava always had ambitious ideas: One was to have a large family; the other was to be educated. She thought she could realize both dreams after she divorced Mickey and married Artie Shaw.

Ava and Artie lived at the Garden for a while. *The Barefoot*

Frank Sinatra, *From Here to Eternity*. "We will give you all our business," Frankie's press agent told the Schwab brothers, "if you keep it quiet that he is living at the Garden." *Copyright © 1953 by Columbia Pictures Corporation*

Contessa was aptly named. She loved to walk barefoot around the pool and through the parking lot over to Schwab's. The bare feet were a hangover from her life in North Carolina.

As Artie's wife, Ava was determined to improve her education. Artie had a reputation for knowing a great deal more than conducting a band and playing a clarinet. Ava hadn't read much, and when Artie said to her, "Why don't you read a book once in a while? You can't listen to Sinatra's records all the time," Ava sped to the nearest bookshop and bought the best seller of the day. When Artie came home, she made certain he would see her reading. When he saw the title, *Forever Amber,* he tore the book from her hands and threw it across the room. "How can you read such trash?" he shouted. Artie's next wife was Kathleen Winsor, who wrote *Forever Amber.*

When Ava was starring in *One Touch of Venus* I gasped as she passed me on the set. She was wearing an evening gown molded to her figure, and she was breathtaking. I was interested when she told me her husband was helping to turn her into an intellectual. With her face and body, it seemed rather a waste of time. She was reading some of the nineteenth-century poets, she confided. She finally learned that Mr. Shaw was not the man she wanted. He was too egotistical, and as a teacher he was unsympathetic.

Artie was staying at the Garden early in 1938 when he met Scott Fitzgerald. I remember Scott telling me about him, that he was surprised to find him so well read and so full of knowledge about so many things. Artie also stayed there in 1942 when he had given up being a band leader. He had enlisted and was in Hollywood for a few days en route to active duty in the Pacific. On this visit he met Betty Kern, the daughter of composer Jerome Kern. She became his fourth wife and lived with him at the Garden after the war. The last time Artie stayed at The Garden of Allah was in 1954, when it was spiraling down to the end. He was resting after an exhausting cross-country tour with the Gramercy Five. This time his stay was brief. "I succumbed to an irresistible amount of money to continue the tour to Australia."

John Carradine lived at Villa 15 during the war years. He was wedged between the Sheekmans in Villa 14 and Benchley in 16. Sinatra was in the inner block, not around the pool. The Garden was alive with the sound of music. Paul Whiteman had a bungalow facing Sunset Boulevard. The Woody Hermans were there, and Benny Goodman,

John Carradine and his wife Sonya. He spouted Shakespeare while she chased him around the pool. *Wide World Photos*

and you could hear Tito Guizar, the famed guitarist, practicing in the late afternoons. Resident Al James rehearsed his radio program there. His girl Friday was Betty White, who later became a television star with her own show, and is married to Allen Ludden, the popular host of various game shows on television.

Literature was represented, in addition to all the others, by Clifford Odets and his second wife, whom Benchley called Slats.

Richard Dix lived at the Garden, and John Carradine was there with his Sonya, whom he subsequently married. John was among the most picturesque people at the Garden. He moved in with Sonya in 1943. They were constantly fighting and chasing each other around the pool. Or rather, Sonya did the chasing. John believed in allowing the wife to be the boss. His charming boss sometimes came after him with a high-heeled shoe in her hand. Just being playful.

Carradine recited Shakespeare in a loud, flat voice, to impress Sonya. The recitals from the bard took place in their bungalow, but could be heard everywhere, even in the farthest corner of the Garden. The Sheekmans once heard him yelling to his wife, "The policeman asked me to move on. I said arrest me. And he did!" Sonya was a voluptuous blond with her long hair flowing free. She made terra-cotta sketches when she was not fighting with her tall, gaunt mate.

Sometimes at night Carradine saw Nazimova seated in front of the window of her second story apartment, smoking a cigarette. "I used to wonder what she was thinking about. She was a loner and never mingled with the guests. I never saw her in the bar or around the pool."

He made one picture with her, another remake of *Blood and Sand,* in 1941, with Tyrone Power in the role originally played by Valentino. Nazimova portrayed Tyrone's mother, a scrubwoman. Carradine was a bullfighter. He told Alla that he had admired her greatly ever since he saw her in Ibsen's *Ghosts* at the Biltmore Theatre in downtown Los Angeles. The theatre is now the parking lot for The Biltmore Hotel.

Carradine could be serious, but mostly he was eccentric. He had a bust made of himself and took it to the swimming pool while he swam. The bust was made of bronze and he believed it would get a nice patina in the sun.

There was the night that Carradine decided he was Jesus and tried to walk across the swimming pool. Marc Connelly, always a gambler, was betting on John to make it. He lost his bet.

Connelly, born in 1890, is best known for his successful play *Green Pastures.* In the very early twenties before he went to Hollywood, he had been quite broke. During a conference Jed Harris was having in New York with Ben Hecht and Charlie MacArthur about *The Front Page,* Harold Ross came in and said, "Marc Connelly is in a state of depression." They were going to Atlantic City to continue the conference, and Ross asked, "Can I bring him along as your guest?" "Okay," said Mr. Harris.

Marc Connelly commuted from New York to The Garden of Allah. He would stay in Hollywood "until my stomach revolted."
Wide World Photos

They had a card game at The Ritz Hotel in Atlantic City, and although Marc was hard up at the time, according to Jed, he played heavily and lost heavily. Jed told me he said to Ross, "Don't worry, I'll pay Marc's debt."

"I'd never met him before," Jed continued, "but when everyone went home, Marc stayed behind and lectured me on having sold out." Jed is still annoyed about it.

Marc had been living at the Garden for some years when I met him there in 1936. In 1937 he had a success with *Captains Courageous,* which starred Spencer Tracy and Freddie Bartholomew. In 1947, he was collaborating with George Kaufman on *Merton of the Movies.* His last screenplay, *Crowded Paradise,* was in 1957, a collaboration with Arthur Forrest.

Marc went to Hollywood for the first time in 1926 for Don Stewart's wedding. In 1927 he worked on Bea Lillie's film *Exit Smiling,* in which she played a stagestruck lady's maid. All he remembers of it is a subtitle he wished he had written, "She played the part of Nothing in *Much Ado About Nothing.*"

He returned to Hollywood in the midthirties, after receiving a telegram from his agent in Hollywood: "The situation is entirely changed. Now a playwright has an incentive to work for something besides money. The talkies depend on dialogue, not captions. Paramount wants you to make a film version of *The Cradle Song.*"

Marc moved into the Garden to be near his chums Benchley and Kaufman. He wrote the script in collaboration with a soft-spoken writer from Hungary, Frank Partos. Some months after he had returned to New York he received a wire from Frank, who had just seen the movie. "It will remind you in several places of our script." To accommodate the story of a Spanish nun to the acting ability of a German actress, the next writers had thoroughly mutilated the Connelly-Partos screenplay. But this happened all the time in Hollywood.

When Madeleine Hurlock divorced Marc in 1935 and later married Robert Sherwood, he was so sensitive about it he called people before going to a party to ask if the Sherwoods were coming. If they were, he apologized and did not go.

On the whole Marc enjoyed his time in Hollywood. His friends were there, and he could play badminton with Oscar Hammerstein. The Garden was two minutes from everything, and he liked Hollywood, in spite of the frustrations.

"Occasionally," Marc told me, "the work would be interesting. I enjoyed working on *Captains Courageous* with Buddy [Louis] Lighton, who was about to be fired from the studio, and Victor Fleming, who directed the picture. The three of us really worked well together, arguing, throwing it back and forth. It was a truly objective collaboration. It was a joy to see the picture come off."

The early thirties in Hollywood, he told me, were profitable for writers in every field, and they were imported by the bushel. "But those who proved inept as constructionists, or as writers of dialogue, did not stay long. It was said that if anyone could sign his name to a contract he was assured of an annual salary of one hundred thousand dollars— for two weeks. P. G. Wodehouse was able to write several Jeeves stories while he waited on salary for a whole year to get a studio assignment."

Like many of the writers from New York, Marc commuted between Hollywood and the East. Usually he would stay at the Garden, but sometimes when things were going better or longer than usual, he rented a house in Westwood, Bel Air, or on Doheny Drive. "I'd stay out west for two or three months, until my stomach revolted."

He was president of the Author's League at the time the Screen Writers Guild was established. He was on the side of the Hacketts, and the Left. He would have had to be. All his friends were members. One day Marc plans to write a book about the fierce fight for control of the Hollywood writers.

While Marc was in Hollywood, he preferred to work at the studio because of the advantage of having a secretary. But he hated the working conditions in what he refers to as that Thalberg Mausoleum. There is a cemetery next to the Thalberg Building, and Dorothy Parker sometimes could be seen looking out of her window in the direction of the cemetery and asking passing strangers, "What's it like down there?"

Connelly loathed Thalberg, as several of the other screen writers did, including Eddie Mayer, who resented his "paternalism." "Irving was a monstrously frustrating person," said Connelly. "Waiting endlessly to see him with the writing I had done nearly drove me out of my skin. I would finally leave the studio and go home, shouting as I left, 'If Thalberg wants to know where I am, I'll be at home!' "

Few writers received as much money or as many screen credits as Donald Ogden Stewart and Marc Connelly. "Thalberg would pay writers a fortune," Marc wrote in his autobiography, *Voices Off Stage,* "then he would spend all his days running away from them and in general running away from reality. He was the embodiment of the self-deluding influences of the world of the movies. He worked fourteen hours a day at MGM, completely insulated from the nonmovie world. At night he went home to his Santa Monica beach mansion that was air-conditioned to exclude the tangy smell of the ocean, and sound-proofed to keep out the roar of the surf."

He told me he considered Thalberg an essentially stupid man, "although he was clever in a superficial way."

"I was working on *The Good Earth*. I had been laboring over the screenplay for two or three months when Thalberg said to me, 'I don't think you have the right idea.' " Marc told the producer his concept for the script was to make it a tragedy—a vegetable personality unable to cope with circumstances. Said Mr. Thalberg, "There's nothing like love."

Marc was taken aback. He realized there was no communication. "I'm getting off this picture," he told the producer. "I'm of no use to you."

If Marc disliked anyone more than Thalberg, it was the MGM producer Sidney Franklin. "A poisonous little fellow who liked to portray himself as a supersensitive aesthetic person. At conferences on any picture he'd say, 'I see . . .' then give his dream about it. He was so lofty it was sometimes hard to see him up there in the clouds. He'd now and then throw you a tablet from Mount Sinai."

Marc started to write the script for *The Yearling* for Franklin, but soon asked to be relieved of the assignment. It was not often a writer wanted to leave. He was usually pushed out.

Marc was not alone in his dislike of Sidney Franklin. Franklin treated all writers badly, and his name was a byword among the well-paid boys and girls who ground out the scripts in Hollywood. Charlie Brackett and Billy Wilder, the famous writing team of the late thirties and forties, had been loaned by Paramount to work for Franklin at MGM. They were summoned to the office of the producer, who started the conversation, "Now, Mr. . . . ."

Charlie helped him out. "My name is Charlie Brackett and my collaborator's name is Billy Wilder. You know damn well what our names are, and the name of your little game is patronage. We are much nicer than you," said Charlie, working up steam, "and wouldn't work for a little squirt like you for anything, so good-bye!"

Marc stopped going to Hollywood shortly after we got into the war (during which he went around to the various training camps studying race relations). After the war he returned to Hollywood to write the script of *Hans Christian Andersen* for Walt Disney. "It could have been a lively, humane story. I wanted to show a sad semihomo pathetic young man, but Disney had the typical stereotype character a la Thalberg." Walt had wanted Andersen to be crushed because his serious plays failed to win popularity. Marc believed that Andersen knew that his fairy tales were his truly valuable contributions. After this disappointment, Connelly said, "To hell with Hollywood," and never worked there again.

Billy Wilder had come to the United States in 1934 and was signed as a writer at Paramount. He was born in Austria and was a newspaper reporter in Berlin, where he did some script writing.

When I saw him during the filming of his Sherlock Holmes picture in England last year, he said, "I was often at the Garden visiting Benchley. Hollywood was a good place for writers, although when you looked at the credits it didn't mean that these were the only people on the scripts. During my early period at Paramount there were 104 writers under contract. They worked on the famous fourth floor, facing Western Avenue. Every Thursday we all turned in eleven pages. MGM had 130 writers under contract. Warners had more." Among the writers at Paramount were Oliver H. Garrett, Eddie Mayer, and Scott Fitzgerald. "Scott, Charlie, and I would go over to Oblath's near Paramount and have tea. It was the only place in town where you could get greasy hamburgers."

Billy teamed with Charlie in 1935. "I had to learn English. I made $125 a week." They parted amicably in 1951. Charlie became a producer. Billy directs from his own scripts. His credits would fill a small book. Among his successful films—many with Charles Brackett—are *Ninotchka* for Garbo, *Double Indemnity* with Fred MacMurray and Barbara Stanwyck, *The Lost Weekend,* which won Ray Milland an Oscar, *Sunset Boulevard* with William Holden and Gloria Swanson, *The Apartment* for Jack Lemmon and Shirley MacLaine, and *Some Like It Hot* with Marilyn Monroe.

When Scott Fitzgerald told a group of young people in my North King's Road house in the fall of 1937 that the day must come when the writer would direct and produce from his own script, they expressed disbelief. Today it is more the rule than the exception. In fact, it had begun when Scott was alive, when Joe Mankiewicz rewrote Scott's *Three Comrades.* For years now, Joe has performed all three functions, writing, directing, and producing.

William Faulkner detested Hollywood, but loved the money. When he asked if he could work at home, he went all the way to Oxford, Mississippi. I did not meet Faulkner at the Garden or anywhere in Hollywood. He refused to be part of the scene, and was absolutely cold blooded about his writing for the studio. He had no interest in films as an art form. He never saw any of the films on which he worked. Few people in Hollywood knew him well. The Hacketts, who inherited his office at MGM found on the desk a yellow legal pad on which was written *Boy Meets Girl,* and a calendar with penciled circles around the paydays.

Thalberg asked Faulkner if he had seen any of the MGM films. The author decided to have some fun with the boy genius. He drawled that he didn't rightly know which pictures they made—was it the Mickey Mouse brand? Thalberg froze, and told him to study the important MGM pictures, to become familiar with the style of acting of the MGM stars. A projection room was set up for Faulkner's private use. After ten minutes he rushed out colliding with another writer who asked him solicitously, "Is anything the matter?"

With his pipe in his hand, Faulkner stuttered, "Jesus Christ, it ain't possible!"

If Faulkner was shocked by Hollywood films, the men who made them were just as disturbed by Faulkner. At that time he dressed like some of the characters he wrote about. At the story conferences, they were sometimes not sure if he was awake or asleep.

He spoke in the voice of a timid clerk. In spite of the mutual antipathy, Faulkner wrote or collaborated on about eight scripts, most of them for Howard Hawks, who had brought him to Hollywood in 1933 to write a screenplay for Joan Crawford. He wrote *Air Force* for Howard, *Road to Glory* in 1936, and *To Have and Have Not* in 1944. His last writing in Hollywood was *Land of the Pharoahs* in 1955.

Faulkner sometimes got drunk, but never on a job. When the script was finished he'd say, "Now I can get tight."

He went on a dove-shooting expedition with Hawks and Clark Gable. During a pause in the shooting, Gable asked Faulkner, "Who do you consider the five best authors of today?"

Faulkner replied, "Ernest Hemingway, Willa Cather, Thomas Mann, John Dos Passos, and myself."

"Oh," grinned Gable, "do you write for a living?"

"Yes," snapped Faulkner, "and what do *you* do?"

Eddie Chodorov came to Hollywood in 1932 when Kay Francis was the reigning queen at Warner Brothers. He was no sooner settled into a cottage at the Garden than he received an invitation to a Hollywood party. He was young and very excited about meeting some of the people he had read about in the scandal sheets of the day. He was overwhelmed by the house, and he thought, My mother would like to know about this. He went upstairs to make a call to New York. Entering a bedroom he stopped short seeing Miss Francis sprawled on the bed hanging on to an empty brandy bottle. He said apologetically, "I want to telephone my mother."

"Do it, for chrissakes," she said irritably and very drunkenly. Then, "Come here, kid," and she pulled him onto the bed beside her. Later he called his mother and when she asked, "How do you like Hollywood?" he assured her, "Very much!"

Eddie told me a story about a French director who lived at the Garden during the French influx. "He told the little starlet who was hoping for a role in his film, 'Come into my office. It won't be more than a few minutes.' To which she replied, 'Please, Mr. ———, for this little part I've been fucked three times. Thank you, no!' "

Chodorov had written *Wonder Boy* for Jed Harris in 1932 and the first act of *Kind Lady*. He worked on *Rasputin and the Empress* for MGM in 1933 and found the Garden a convenient place to relax between the strenuous assignments. The film cost MGM one million dollars in damages for Prince Youssoupoff, who instructed the brilliant American lawyer Fanny Holtzman to bring a law suit in London, where the libel laws are more stringent.

This was the time in Hollywood that Scott Fitzgerald wrote about in *The Last Tycoon*. Louis B. Mayer—Brady—was trying to eliminate Irving Thalberg—Stahr—the pilot of MGM productions.

"I found myself working on a project separately and secretly with five other writers, none of them knowing about the others," Eddie reminisced in London where he now lives. "A young lawyer, Charlie Feldman, had just started as an agent. He had one client, Gregory Ratoff, who had been in *Wonder Boy*. I left Leland Hayward because he could not get me out of my contract at Metro. Charlie could, and we became close friends. I was nineteen. It was Christmas Day and very hot. We were lying outside the beach house at Malibu that Charlie had given to Racquel Torres [a tempestuous Latin actress of the thirties]. Charlie said, 'I have a scheme. A package deal—the writer, director, producer, and star. I'll sell the package to the studios, and then I'll be in the driver's seat.' "

It took him ten years to do it. And he lived to regret it when he was the executive producer of *Casino Royale*. When Peter Sellers was signed as the star he insisted on including his own director, Joe Mc-Grath, in the package. It did not work out, and other directors were brought in to salvage the 16-million-dollar film. Charlie's packaged stars and directors aged him ten years in ten months. But the package system was useful for the writer. It gave him more protection. If the writer was fired, the star and the director would leave also.

Charlie took Chodorov to Warners and arranged for him to write the screenplay in 1933 for *Mayor in Hell,* one of Jimmy Cagney's first films in Hollywood. Hal Wallis was the producer, but whenever he made a suggestion, Zanuck, who was then running things at Warners, snapped, "Shut up." Eddie was embarrassed for Mr. Wallis and afterwards went to his office and said, "I'm sorry, there was no need for Darryl's outburst."

It was better at Columbia. "Even when Harry Cohn said to a writer, 'Come up and get forty pages out of this shit and get it out fast,' it meant he loved it!"

Thalberg, according to Eddie, was just as bad in a different way. "He was violently opposed to the forming of the Screen Writers Guild. He knew he would not be able to get away with his treatment of writers so easily. It was all right for Donald Ogden Stewart, who was very easygoing, and for Scott Fitzgerald, who had great respect for Thalberg, but most of the writers detested him. He took away their dignity, and he told them what to do and did not listen to them."

Louis B. Mayer said to Chodorov, "I don't understand you fellows. If I told Cedric Gibbons [the set designer] I wanted some armor, it would be there. You guys come in five months later with two scenes. You can't be controlled."

"Well," said Eddie, "no matter how you style it, Mr. Mayer, one is carpentry and the other is creative work. It might go quickly or it might go slowly."

Chodorov wrote fourteen plays and forty films: "It was phantas-magorical. I had to sit at the lunch table with Mayer twice a week. Usually he was not on speaking terms with Eddie Mannix [an executive] and he'd say, 'Mr. Chodorov, will you please tell Mr. Mannix. . . .' And Mannix replied, 'Mr. Chodorov, will you please tell Mr. Mayer . . .' "

The writers could be more vicious than the producers they hated. Gene Fowler was lunching at the Vendome, an excellent restaurant in Hollywood. Gene, a notorious drinker, was at the bar berating Jack Warner, to whom he was under contract. He was complaining to the top secretary of Warners. As Fowler heaped four-letter words on the company which employed him, the secretary informed him, "There's a conference this very moment about your contract at the studio." Mr. Fowler rose to the challenge. "A conference is just what I want."

He drove, rather erratically, to Warners in Burbank, took off his trousers, carried them into the conference room, and threw them on the table. "Look, Jack," he said haughtily, "I want these pressed and back in ten minutes."

The Warner boys had started as tailors. Fowler, one of the most highly paid writers in Hollywood, was fired on the spot.

Afterward Fowler went to the Garden to visit his diminutive friend Gladys Parker, the cartoonist, who was carrying a torch for Maxie Rosenbloom, the ex-boxer turned nightclub owner. Gladys, also inebriated, showed Gene a Nazi officer's overcoat that a newspaper correspondent had sent her from Germany. Gene asked if he might borrow the coat and put it on. On his way home, he stopped at The Beverly Hills Hotel and goose-stepped through the lobby, heiling Hitler, who had died recently in the Berlin bunker, and shouting that the Nazis were taking over Beverly Hills. People were frightened and some actually ran out of the lobby. It was lucky no one had a gun.

Sam Goldwyn was considered the most difficult of the producers. I was dining at his house when he said, "It was a toss-up whether I went into enchiladas or the film business. I flipped a coin, and it was motion pictures."

One of the guests laughed, "I'm glad it was motion pictures, otherwise we'd be eating enchiladas three times a day."

Every writer had a Goldwyn story. The system was not to give Goldwyn the script until the picture was almost ready to start. He became wise to it after a while and said to Eddie Chodorov, "Oh, no you don't. Another writer once tried that on me."

He had brought Maurice Maeterlinck from Europe without know-

Sam Goldwyn, the scourge of writers, with David Niven and
Ed Sullivan. *Springer/Bettmann Archive*

ing who he really was, only that he had written a famous book about bees. Maeterlinck's credit never appeared on any film.

When Goldwyn bought MacKinlay Kantor's poem *Glory for Me,* a novel in verse, which became *The Best Years of Our Lives,* he did not know it was a poem. All he knew was that MacKinlay was a writer in demand, and so Goldwyn bought it sight unseen for a lot of money.

He asked Chodorov to write the script. Eddie was doubtful: "It's an extremely important property. I think Robert Sherwood should do it because of the importance of his name."

Sherwood wrote the script, and he and Goldwyn wound up suing each other over the interpretation of their contract.

When Chodorov turned in his work on *Dodsworth,* he explained to Goldwyn he had made some bridges in the story so that when Dodsworth—Walter Huston—does not return to America for the birth of his daughter's baby, you don't hate him. "Are you mad?" said Goldwyn. "I didn't buy the book for this. I bought it to make a film about the automobile business." He raised such hell that Eddie asked Charlie Feldman to get him out of his contract. Goldwyn, a generous man, insisted on paying Eddie the fifty thousand dollars, according to their deal.

Willie Wyler, who directed *Dodsworth,* was naked in The Beverly Hills Hotel shower room when he groaned to Chodorov, "I'll give you another fifty thousand dollars if you find a way to get me out of my contract."

Eddie suggested that Goldwyn get Sidney Howard, who had adapted the successful play from the Sinclair Lewis novel, to redo the script. Goldwyn was never too angry to listen to a good suggestion. It cost him one hundred thousand dollars, but he brought Howard to Hollywood. Sidney wanted to share the credit with Eddie but he wouldn't hear of it.

Chodorov refused the assignment from Goldwyn to write the script of a Rachel Crothers story. Eddie thought it was terrible. Goldwyn was furious. He screamed in his high-pitched voice, "If you don't do it, you'll never work again!" Two years elapsed before he made the film, titled *Splendor.* Goldwyn usually took two years from the conception to the finish of a film. *Splendor* was a total disaster. Six months later when Feldman asked Goldwyn if Chodorov could write a certain film for him, Sam exploded, "Eddie Chodorov! I won't have him. He was associated with my worst flop!"

At the premiere of *The Night of the Generals* a few years ago, Chodorov saw Goldwyn and his wife Frances in the lobby. "People were pouring past. He had been nine feet high, and now no one knew him. I stopped and said, 'You look wonderful, Mr. Goldwyn.' He replied with a thin squeak, 'What good is it?' "

Thornton Wilder, who lived at the Garden during his film assignments, wrote a script for Goldwyn from Andreyev's *The Seven Who Were Hanged*. "Mr. Wilder," said Sam, "I read the script. It's not bad, but the baron . . ."

"Would you say, Mr. Goldwyn, that it lacks internal dynamism?" asked Wilder.

"Mr. Goldwyn said, "No. The baron . . ."

Wilder: "Would you say, Mr. Goldwyn, that the physical potential of the baron is not fully developed?"

"No, no, Mr. Wilder. The baron is a horse's ass."

At least you always knew where you were with Goldwyn. There was no polite horsing around.

Louis Bromfield had come to Hollywood and the Garden at the invitation of Goldwyn, who had kept him sitting around idly for two months. Finally Louis cornered Goldwyn and demanded, "I'd like something to do."

"Be patient," soothed Sam, "take your time."

"But why did you hire me?" the exasperated author asked.

"For your name, Mr. Bronstein, for your name."

Lillian Hellman liked the work in Hollywood. She enjoyed working for Goldwyn, perhaps because the scripts she wrote were mostly from her hit plays, except *Dead End* with Bogart and Sylvia Sidney. In 1936 she was writing *The Dark Angel* for Goldwyn, to star Merle Oberon. A little later she also wrote for him the script of her hit play *The Children's Hour*. It was called *These Three,* and was watered down to comply with the censorship of the day. The two girls, Merle Oberon and Miriam Hopkins, instead of being in love with each other, pursued Joel McCrea. Two decades later, Wyler directed the picture again under its original title and its original theme. It was a success the first time, a failure the second, with James Garner and Shirley MacLaine.

Ben Hecht and Charlie MacArthur scripted *The Barbary Coast* for Goldwyn. They also worked on several films for MGM. It took them a long time to recover from the experience. In 1942 they owned their own studio on Long Island where they made *The Spectre of the Rose* and *The Scoundrel*. They had a big sign over the studio entrance: If It's Better Than Metro Goldwyn Mayer It's Not Good Enough.

To express their hatred of conditions in Hollywood, they hired a madam from a call house, and sat her in the producer's chair on the set. When she began criticizing the production, they fired her. Charlie was a pixie. Hecht was more businesslike. He specialized in completing unfinished scripts. David Selznick used him as a troubleshooter. From the start they made up their minds to torment the brass who were as glad to see the back of them as they were to go.

Paul Jarrico told me, "I was doing a script at Universal for Bruce Manning, which Joe Pasternak was producing. My agent, Charlie Feldman, told me that Goldwyn wanted to see me, and that I should find out what he wanted. Goldwyn described the story of *Treasure Chest,* to star Bob Hope. It was funny in his accent and I laughed.

" 'Then you'll do it,' said Goldwyn.

" 'I can't,' I said. 'I am working with Mr. Pasternak.'

" 'Goldwyn said, 'Do the decent thing, Paul. Do this job for me and don't even tell him.' "

Mr. Jarrico wrote thirty screenplays, and fifteen were made into films, which was a high average. He started as a Hollywood writer fresh from college. He was a local product who had not written a book or a play and was happy with one hundred dollars a week. "I was twenty-two. Dore Schary recommended me to Nat Perrin, a producer at RKO. When he offered me one hundred dollars a week I gulped. 'You'd take seventy-five dollars, wouldn't you?' said Perrin. I said yes. 'Hell,' he said, 'it's not my money.' I slowly climbed to twenty-five hundred dollars a week, which was the most at that time, except for Donald Ogden Stewart's thirty-five hundred dollars. I worked on my original stories and other screenplays. They bought more originals in those days. The junior writers were usually born into the industry—Budd Schulberg, Maurice Rapf—their fathers were well-known producers. The producer would expect five pages a day from us. Someone like Dalton Trumbo (before he was blacklisted) would do nothing for weeks, then work round the clock and turn out the whole thing in a week."

Trumbo complained that the writers' working conditions would drain the energy out of Shakespeare. *Spartacus* and *Exodus* reinstated him, and now he earns more money than the stars for whom he writes.

In the early days the writers were important to the success of the scripts because the Hollywood directors had very little power. Except those at the top—De Mille, Ernst Lubitsch, Willie Wyler, Henry Hathaway, John Ford, Frank Capra, and a few others. The general attitude of the producer was, Here's a script; this is what I want on the screen. George Cukor always worked from a script that had been prepared for him in advance. Even Lubitsch's "Lubitsch touch" was written into the script.

Ludwig Bemelmans, a famous writer in Europe, succumbed to MGM money to write in Hollywood. After installing himself in a bungalow at The Garden of Allah, he went to the studio and waited for an assignment. And waited and waited. Becoming bored he decided to exercise one of his other talents, painting. He decorated the walls of his cubicle with animals, and on each side of the door, two giraffes with their necks intertwined at the top, and inscribed above their heads the MGM motto Ars Gratia Artis. Ludwig did not stay long.

Some of the more strong-minded among the famous writers resisted the efforts to lure them into the Hollywood gold mines. George Jean Nathan, to my knowledge, did not write for the movies. Neither did Henry Louis Mencken, nor Thomas Wolfe—although he was almost tempted at one low point. Alec Woollcott visited Hollywood but did not write for the studios.

And yet Hollywood producers were prepared to pay anything to lure the famous authors. As far back as 1919 Goldwyn had formed Eminent Authors Pictures, Inc. Among those who succumbed were Rupert Hughes, Mary Roberts Rinehart, Rex Beach, Somerset Maugham, and Gertrude Atherton, all well-known authors of the day. Sinclair Lewis tried and failed three times. Lewis was in Santa Barbara with his secretary. He said to her, "Never prostitute yourself by going to Hollywood. It's the most dreadful place in the world. Oh, by the way," he added, "pack my bag for me. I'm going to Hollywood tomorrow."

In 1939 Lewis spent a month in Hollywood, hoping to transform his *Angela Is 22* into a film for Lester Cowan. It was never made. Lewis returned to Hollywood to collaborate with Dore Schary on *Storm in the West,* but Louis B. Mayer would not sanction the film, supposedly a Western but actually a thinly veiled attack on Hitler and his men. In 1947 he came back for *Adam and Eve,* which Leo McCarey wanted for Ingrid Bergman and Jimmy Stewart, but it was never made.

There were nine writers on Walter Wanger's *Foreign Correspondent*—the film version of Vincent Sheeham's *Personal History*—
among them, Robert Benchley, James Hilton, and Ben Hecht. This was
made, but none of the writers listed cared about the credit.

Why did they do it? No one forced them to go to Hollywood and
write and suffer. No one put a gun to their heads. Most of those who
went had begged their agents to get them there. I saw them at the
Garden lolling around, enjoying the lazy life while hating the producers
who made it all possible and, meanwhile, despising themselves.

In his early days in Hollywood David Niven lived at the Garden
with Errol Flynn. David had met John McClain in New York in 1933
when David was a salesman for a champagne company. When McClain
heard David was trying his luck in Hollywood, he advised him to stay
at the Garden. David shared a bungalow with Errol and a writer, Bill
Lipscomb.

"Errol, Bill, and I were sitting around the pool, dangling our feet
in the water and bird watching," Niven told me recently. "We were
absolutely broke. Not quite. We had seventeen dollars between us. The
phone by the pool rang. It was for Errol. His agent, to say he had been
signed to star at Warners in *Captain Blood*." *Captain Blood* made him
an instant star.

"We rushed to the bar and spent the seventeen dollars," David
recalls. "The phone rang again. It was for Bill Lipscomb. His agent
informed him he had been signed to write the script for *Clive of India*.
Then my agent called. I landed my first role in a film, a bit in *Barbary
Coast* for Goldwyn. It called for me to be thrown out of a train
window."

This was the start of Niven's fifteen years with Goldwyn. There
was an interruption during World War II when David was starring for
Sam in *Raffles*. He was anxious to get back to England to fight. He had
been to Sandhurst, the military college, and was frustrated having to
stay in Hollywood making a picture when he wanted to fight for his
country. When Goldwyn was adamant, David had his brother in
England send him a cable, "Return to regiment at once. Signed, Adju-
tant." They must have finished the film with another actor in the long
shots, otherwise I doubt whether Goldwyn would have let him go without completing his role, not if the King of England had asked for him.

Niven had met Errol at a party in Lili Damita's bungalow at the

Garden. "Everyone there," Niven told me, "was a poop [a homosexual]. It was full of poops, and Errol and I each thought the other was a poop." A year later, Errol and Lili were married, but meanwhile he and David rented a house in Beverly Hills from Rosalind Russell. "When we left the house, the agent came with a list and went over everything and said, 'There were five hundred logs of wood when you came in, now there are only four hundred and sixty,' and made us pay for the forty logs."

When Flynn broke up with Lili after agreeing to pay her three hundred thousand dollars in alimony, David shared a house with him at the beach. "It was called 'Cirrhosis by the Sea.' " Today, Niven owns a villa in Saint-Jean-Cap-Ferrat, in the south of France, and a chalet in Switzerland. He is a millionaire.

Errol died broke, although his estate became solvent from the sales of his autobiography, *My Wicked, Wicked Ways,* from the sale of his yacht, the *Zaca,* and from the increased value of his plantation in Jamaica. His last wife, Pat Wymore, from whom he was separated at the time of his death, spends most of her time there. The divorce was not final when he died, and young Beverly Aadland, whom he was going to marry when he was free, got nothing at all.

Bill Spier and Kay Thompson were married the November before they came to live at the Garden in 1943. They stayed until the great exodus after the war. Bill was the first hippie of Hollywood. By accident. During 1943 he directed a *Suspense* show in two parts. This had never been done before in radio. It was *Donovan's Brain* with Orson Welles, who was famous then in Hollywood for having the courage to make *Citizen Kane,* which satirized William Randolph Hearst and Marion Davies. The strain was great and he believes this caused his heart attack. He collapsed during dinner at an Italian restaurant across the road from The Garden of Allah. When he came out of the hospital, six weeks later, he was told to do nothing but lie on his back, he was not even to shave, or he would have to return to the hospital. Kay tried to make their bedroom at the Garden as comfortable as possible because Bill would be in it for three months.

The first two days after he was home, Kay shaved him. "But it was too much for me, Kay coming at me with a razor. I forget now why, but I hated the barber who came to shave me, I think chiefly because he looked like Al Jolson. So I grew this beard," which he still has. "Very few people have the time to get away from society to grow a beard," Bill told me with satisfaction. It was the first beard, like King George's—which is what Robert Montgomery used to call him—and people used to come by to marvel at it.

Mrs. Spier, Kay Thompson, was a good friend of Judy Garland, and when Judy sometimes disappeared from MGM and they couldn't find her, she was usually with Kay and Bill in their spare bedroom.

"I did *The Harvey Girls* with her," Kay told me. "I also did a couple of numbers in *The Ziegfeld Follies* for Arthur Freed." More recently she played a role for Otto Preminger in *Tell Me that You Love Me, Junie Moon*. Apart from her visits to this country on "Eloise" business, Kay lives in Italy.

She enjoyed talking about her time at the Garden to me. As did Bill, from whom she is long since divorced. They both remembered vividly the great Garden robbery.

"Bill and I were in our villa," said Kay. "The Conover girls next door, Dusty and Susan, were sleeping. Everything was quiet. Bill was getting restless staying in bed because of his heart attack. 'If I have one more night in this bed in this room,' he exploded, 'I'll blow my brains out.'

"To look less of an invalid, Bill decided that he would not wear pajamas. He was an exciting man in the nude. It was all very quiet when I suddenly awakened and saw something flying through the air. A man was at the foot of Bill's bed. He had been reaching into the pockets of his pajama pants to find his wallet. Bill awakened, and the man threw the pants at him. Bill, in his confusion, threw them back at the man, who ran through the door, and Bill quite forgetting his heart attack got up and chased him to the patio. He was about to call for help when he realized he was stark naked. And besides, he wasn't supposed to get out of bed. I was yelling, and Bill was yelling, and in the morning the Conover girls told everyone, 'Bill and Kay had such a row.'

"Everyone was around the pool, and everyone had been robbed of something. Mostly money, but also all the radios had been taken from the cars in the parking lot. The police interviewed everyone; and Bill, to make it more interesting, told them, 'They took my gold cuff links.' I don't believe they did, but he always had a sense of the dramatic."

"They caught one of the thieves at the racetrack," Bill told me in

Connecticut, where he now lives with his wife, June Havoc. "He admitted the thefts and said wryly 'We'd never have been caught except for the man with the beard.'" The two thieves had robbed the villas very systematically, starting with bungalow 1, all down the line. "The next day you could hear everyone exclaiming, 'My watch . . . my money!' The police brought the man they captured to our bungalow for me to identify him."

Dusty Negulesco remembers the robbery because she slept through it. "I am a sound sleeper. I can sleep any time until noon, no matter how early I go to bed. I had been at the beach all day and was sleepy and went to bed at nine thirty. Something awakened me. I looked up from the covers and saw this shadow on the window. I thought, it's a thief, but if I scream he might hurt me. I had fifty dollars in cash and my watch, worth one hundred dollars. I thought I'd rather lose them than get hurt. I pretended to be asleep. But I actually went to sleep. In the morning my fifty dollars and the watch were gone, and everyone in the Garden had been robbed."

There were holdups at the front office from time to time. On June 25, 1941, at 3:30 A.M. William Everest, the night clerk, was bound and taped by two armed bandits who fled with one hundred fifty dollars from the cash register.

On February 21, 1942 the villa occupied by Mrs. Mary Stewart was robbed of a twenty-five-hundred-dollar mink coat, a ten-thousand-dollar ermine coat, a fifteen-hundred-dollar diamond ring, and other jewelry.

A night clerk, Carl Aldinger, was murdered on July 19, 1942. He was shot three times in the chest and twice in the back. The killer escaped with twenty-five dollars from the cash register. Nat Benchley had a twinge of worry. Was it his fault? Nat and his father had gone to the Farmer's Market where Nat had bought a cap pistol. When they returned to the Garden they went to the front office to complain about the lack of ice in their refrigerator. Nat pounded on the counter with his cap pistol. When the clerk was killed he thought, Maybe I got him used to the sight of a gun. Maybe he thought it was another joke.

It was fashionable during the war for film stars to pick up servicemen and take them home for a meal or a drink. When Red Skelton was at the Garden during the war, he picked up a marine on Sunset Boulevard and brought him home to his villa. They discussed firearms and

Red showed him a German luger that he owned. The marine examined it and asked, "Is it loaded?" "Yes," said Red, whereupon the marine pointed the gun at the comedian and robbed him of his watch and wallet and escaped, taking the revolver with him.

A waitress was arrested for peddling narcotics—they say she carried the stuff in her pompadour. A jealous husband broke into his wife's villa, put all her clothes in the bathtub, and set them on fire. Muriel King was there when it happened and the fire engines came clanging.

Toward the late forties, undesirables gathered in the bar every day at 4:00 P.M., and the regulars began to move out. When George Oppenheimer returned to the Garden after the war, Natalie Schafer sublet her bungalow to him until he could find a more permanent place to live. After settling into the bungalow, George bought a complete wardrobe of civilian clothes. He put his new clothes in the closet and went out for dinner. He returned to find the closets bare, his entire new wardrobe stolen. He called the front desk, but the clerk was drunk. No one else had been robbed and no one seemed to care, which made George even more miserable and frustrated. He hardly slept at all that night. The next morning, to cool off, he took a shower, and the bathroom ceiling fell on him. To make matters worse, he received a telegram the next day from Miss Schafer saying she was returning and that he must vacate her villa. George was saved by the comedy writer, Harry Kurnitz, who offered to share his villa with him. He was glad, he said, that they finally tore down The Garden of Allah.

Jim Andrews did not like the way his servant, Johnson, said, "There's a guy outside looking for ya."

"You must say, 'There's a gentleman to see you, sir,' " he admonished.

The next day Johnson said it right, "There's a gentleman to see you, sir." He led in the gentleman, who had a gun and said, "Stick 'em up!" and robbed Andrews of his wallet.

Kyle Crichton, in his book *Total Recoil*, claims to have been among the Garden's steadiest customers. "For fifteen years I went to Hollywood twice a year for *Colliers*, staying six weeks each trip. Robert Benchley, Gloria and Arthur Sheekman, and Eddie Mayer might have stayed in the institution longer continuously, but I'll give odds of three

Jackie Gleason, who lived at the Garden when he first went to Hollywood in the early forties. *Springer/Bettmann Archive*

to one that I stayed in more bungalows at The Garden of Allah than anybody else in history."

Jackie Gleason was at the Garden in 1945 when he was barely known and appearing for little money at Slapsie Maxie's in Hollywood. He was not a big drinker in those days, and he was sometimes aghast at the goings-on around him. He made up for it later, but at last report, Gleason was on the wagon.

Katharine Hepburn with Garson Kanin, the director, and Ring Lardner and Michael Kanin, the writers, locked themselves into a villa at The Garden of Allah for five days and nights to finish the script of *Woman of the Year,* her first film with Spencer Tracy, pictured here. *Springer/Bettmann Archive*

Ed Gardner, the star of *Duffy's Tavern,* lived at the Garden with his wife, Shirley Booth, near the end of the war. In his radio show, Ed was a tough barman. He was a quiet man in real life, but somewhat eccentric. When it was hot—and the Hollywood summers are always hot—Ed stood in the middle of the pool dictating his scripts. Out of the pool you saw him shuffling back and forth with a glass in his hand. He held it as though it were an extension of his hand.

Orson Welles was a slender young man when he lived at the Garden. He was always egotistical. He was working on a screenplay in his bungalow with two writers. They reached a sequence where Orson would recite the Lord's Prayer. Orson read it, mumbling and grumbling. Then he rewrote it. The two writers were outraged. "You can't rewrite the Lord's Prayer," they protested.

Orson replied, "But my version is so much better." His attitude was, You can't tell me about the Lord's Prayer because I am God. This was too much for the writers and they started to leave. Orson yielded, then tried to go back on his word.

"We can't allow you to change it," the writers insisted.

"Wait a minute, boys," said Orson. He opened the heavy Spanish door and looked up at the sky. "Forgive me," he said, went back to work without closing the door, and with the eye of the Lord upon him, he did it God's way.

Katharine Hepburn's first film with Spencer Tracy was *Woman of the Year* in 1942. The credits state that it was written by Ring Lardner and Michael Kanin, Garson Kanin's young brother. But the idea was Garson's. He had just been drafted and his time was short.

Miss Hepburn had won acclaim for her role in the film version of *The Philadelphia Story.* She needed something good as a follow-up. Garson, a devoted fan, had studied her plays and films, mostly because he wanted to have an affair with her. It was the height of his dreams. He also wanted to do something for Ring, and his brother. He came up with a fast formula for a film. But he had only five days left as a civilian.

He had just finished *Tom, Dick, and Harry* at RKO. The script of *Woman of the Year* had to be delivered to MGM before he left. Garson, Ring, Mike, Katharine, and two secretaries locked themselves into Garson's lavish villa at the Garden. They stayed there for five days and five nights, never setting foot outside. Chasen sent in the food. At the end of the five days, the script was finished.

MGM bought it for $111,000, the most money ever paid at that time for an original screenplay. It was Kate who figured out the price. One hundred thousand dollars for the script, ten thousand dollars for herself for putting the deal together, and one thousand dollars for the bill at The Garden of Allah. Not only was the film successful, but it was the start of the long association between Miss Hepburn and Mr. Tracy.

This was a happy experience for two young writers in Hollywood. It rarely went as well as this.

"We all felt guilty pulling down those salaries," said George Oppenheimer. "So most of us worked for various causes. We worked for Helen Gahagan against Nixon. We were that thing hated so much by Louis B. Mayer—liberals. We became involved mostly because we were unhappy with what we had to write in Hollywood."

During the Red witch hunt, some of them found their problems of guilt solved. At the "Waldorf Declaration" of 1947, all those suspected of being a Communist or of having Communist or leftist sympathies, were blacklisted. The producers agreed they would not hire anyone from this group. Some of the writers who were suspect sold their stories under different names. Others, including Carl Foreman and Jules Dassin, went to Europe and made new careers as producers and directors.

The whole system has changed. Writers are now hired by the script, not on a salary under contract. But it was more exciting in the days when you could walk down the corridor in the writers' building at MGM and see among the names on the doors of the cubicles Somerset Maugham, Thornton Wilder, Sinclair Lewis, Dorothy Parker, John O'Hara, Sid Perelman, Scott Fitzgerald, and William Faulkner.

[XIII]

going down

RUTH GOETZ, THE PLAYWRIGHT, came to Hollywood for the first time in 1948. She had been signed by Paramount with her husband, Augustus Goetz, to adapt *The Heiress,* for Olivia de Havilland and Montgomery Clift, from their play based on the Henry James novel *Washington Square.* Mrs. Goetz had read about the famed authors who stayed at The Garden of Allah, and wanting to do the right thing, she booked herself into a bungalow. It wasn't quite as easy to get in as it had been in the early days, but the pressure of the war years was off, and she was delighted that there was a villa for her. The disillusionment was swift.

"It was all so tatty," she complained to me. "The walls were dirty, the furniture was spotty, and there was a dead mouse in the pool floating upside down in a fetal position. I stayed a week and left. It was too much like the film *Sunset Boulevard.*"

You could always tell from Ben the bellboy when things were not good at the Garden. Toward the end of his reign, when the Garden was going down, he was no longer the polite man he had been. It became more and more *his* Garden of Allah. The new, sometimes questionable guests, were interlopers.

In the midfifties, Dr. Frank Nolan—who had treated the hangovers of the thirties and forties from his office above Schwab's—tried to buy the Garden for $180,000. He thought it would make a good hospital. He was outbid by Sonny Whitney, who bought the place in partnership with Dudley Murphy, who owned Holiday House, a fancy motel at Malibu. Dudley, a good trader, had persuaded Mr. Whitney

"Sonny" Cornelius Vanderbilt Whitney owned The Garden of Allah in the midfifties. Shown here with his wife, former Mrs. Mary Hosford, on their wedding day. *Wide World Photos*

to put up the money. Dudley would run the hotel in exchange for 25 percent of the property.

Dudley promptly sold 75 percent of his 25 percent to Lawrence Lee of the Lee Hotel chain. Sonny agreed that Lee could have a twenty-year lease with Dudley, who was to be responsible for certain repairs, including care of the roofs and bathrooms. Whitney was responsible for structural changes. Lee and Murphy did not get along, and they were soon looking for a buyer of their combined 25 percent.

"Dudley and his wife, Ginny," Mr. Whitney explained to me, "were good friends of mine. I met them in 1954 when I went to Hollywood to form the C. V. Whitney company. I was frequently at Holiday House to relax. It was then a modest beach hotel with a restaurant. Dudley wanted to make Holiday House an outstanding hotel with gourmet food, and he asked me if I would help him. I bought a 40 percent interest in Holiday House, which was refurbished, and a French chef was brought in." I remember the sudden blossoming.

There was talk that The Garden of Allah was to be torn down, that a group was interested in buying the site to erect an office building. This is when Dudley suggested to Whitney that Holiday House should acquire it.

Dudley was devoted to the Garden during the forties. On the rare occasions that I went through the main house, I saw him sitting at the bar in a dark shirt and sneakers, always alone. I often wondered what he was doing there all by himself. He seemed to be waiting for someone, anyone, to stop and have a drink with him. Now that he was part owner, he wanted it to be like the old, wild days of the parties. He asked Cobina Wright, Hollywood's prize eastern socialite, to hostess a soirée at the Garden. Cobina, who died recently, wrote a society column for the Los Angeles *Herald Express*. She chronicled the event as follows: "In spite of the downpour, throngs of people gathered for the preopening party at the new Garden of Allah recently bought by Cornelius Vanderbilt Whitney and Dudley Murphy. . . . It has been given a complete face-lift, is beautifully decorated in Moroccan-modern, and at last is a glamorous place of which Hollywood can be proud."

Joy Windsor, a starlet, was the most important name among the minor celebrities present.

The old days had gone, and it wasn't the same. But Dudley was sure he could turn the Garden into a money-making operation, which it had never been. If he made a go of it, he confided to Mr. Whitney, he would enlarge the Garden into a 250-room hotel. The plans did not materialize. Sonny was never sure why Dudley's dream went wrong.

Sonny and his cousin, Jock Whitney, had originally come to Hollywood in the thirties. They were interested in films, and at one time financed Selznick International, which made five films, starting with *Becky Sharp,* in color—the first feature-length film in the new three-color Technicolor, Jock Whitney told me at the time—*The Prisoner of Zenda, Rebecca,* Fredric March's *A Star Is Born,* and *Gone With the Wind.* Soon after the Margaret Mitchell epic was released, the rich cousins bought out David Selznick, who needed the cash. Later, Sonny bought out Jock. Now, every time *Gone With the Wind* is released, it brings more millions to the attractive multimillionaire and to MGM, which released the film.

Jock Whitney participated in the daily business of the company. I often saw him at the Selznicks' home, and more frequently in Bob Benchley's villa at the Garden. Sonny was a silent partner in the films at that time, as he was involved with other business ventures, including the Pan American Company and the Hudson Bay Mining and Smelting Company.

Merian Cooper, the director, was a partner in the original company with Jock and Sonny. He and Sonny had been in the same unit in World War II, and he wanted him to be more active in film production. At about the time Sonny was getting involved with the Garden, he approached him and said, "Why don't you have your own picture company; why don't we make some movies together?"

Through Cooper, Whitney became involved with *This Is Cinerama.* By this time he had a definite idea of what he wanted to do in Hollywood: make a series of six films about America, the final one to be called *The American,* which Sonny planned to write with Cooper. They made three of the films: *The Searchers,* with John Wayne; *Missouri Traveler,* with Lee Marvin, Gary Merrill, and Mary Hosford, who gave up her acting career to become Mrs. C. V. Whitney; and *The Young Hand,* with Pat Wayne. When Whitney married Mary, he dissolved the company. Perhaps he did not want her to act anymore.

Sonny lived at the Garden during the filming of *The Searchers,* but he did not stay there again. The place somehow looked even more run-down after it had been renovated by Murphy and Lee.

"I usually stayed at The Beverly Hills Hotel or The Bel Air Hotel, but I remember Dudley—" he kept calling him *Deadly* Murphy "—did a good job of running the place. It was his job to look after the swimming pool and the cottages around the pool. The main refurbishing was done in the dining-room section. And the cottages were refurnished. I thought we would do well. It was such a convenient location. And the swimming pool was marvelous, although it was always leaking or one thing or another. It had somewhat the same atmosphere," he added, "as the Bel Air Hotel did later."

Not to my knowledge. The Bel Air Hotel has always looked expensive, and high jinks would not be encouraged there. Also, there is a very respectable lobby you must navigate before going to your exquisitely furnished bungalow.

When Dudley took over the Garden, he decided to get rid of all the old Spanish furniture. He had it stacked up in the parking lot to await the removers. Denver Pile—who played the sheriff who killed Warren Beatty and Faye Dunaway in *Bonnie and Clyde*—was driving by with his friend Dick Dickson. They stopped at the sight of the massive pieces of furniture filling most of the parking lot. Dudley was supervising the operation. "How much do you want for the lot?" they asked. Dudley was anxious to sell to enable his customers to use the parking lot again. Looking from the men to all the junk, he said quickly, "Three hundred dollars."

The furniture had been there since the beginning of the Garden in 1927. The two men could save him the expense of carting it away. Denver wrote out a check for three hundred dollars. "It was all the money I had at the time," he told me recently when he was working in the "Doris Day Show." "Then Dick and I looked at the furniture and wondered why we had bought it. While we pondered, a man passed by and asked, 'What do you want for that chair?' We sold it to him for three dollars. Pretty soon dozens of people were converging on the old furniture. We set up a bar and did a roaring business.

"People came from all over and they called their friends. Sunset Boulevard looked like *The Grapes of Wrath,* with old mattresses and beds and chairs and tables loaded on top of old cars. We made the most money on the big double beds. I told them, 'Errol Flynn slept here.' And here, and here. Errol's beds went the fastest, since many of the buyers had never heard of Benchley or Butterworth."

Denver and Dickson made $2,000. They kept what was left of the furniture, and Denver still has a maple-framed mirror with a shoe box on the bottom.

Residents at the Garden under the Murphy regime included Burl Ives, Fernando Lamas, after the foundering of his marriage to Arlene Dahl, and Luise Rainer. Dudley hired a press agent, Ed Schofield. It was the first time in its history that the Garden had a press agent. Ed was also handling John Arcesi, a singer. To celebrate his Capitol recordings of "Lost in Your Love" and "Wild Honey" on the other side, Schofield gave a party at the Garden for the disc jockeys of Los Angeles. A tie-in was made with a honey distributor. Gallons of honey were stationed around the pool. Feather pillows were given to the disc jockeys. When Arcesi appeared in swimming trunks, the DJs covered him with honey, and then with feathers. The singer was the first person to be honeyed and feathered. The stunt received good newspaper space for the singer and the hotel.

There was a resident in the Garden at this time who gained fame and fortune from her facial-rejuvenation concoction. It reportedly contained carbolic acid and certain oils. Smoothed over the face and covered for three days, the lady claimed that it drove away all signs of approaching age—or even age that had already approached. Mr. Schofield and his mother tried it first, and it worked. The customers were housed in the main hotel in twenty-dollar-a-day rooms so that the rejuvenator could keep an eye on their faces. Several aging film actresses tried it, and I heard of one woman's cheek sagging into a corner of her chin.

The Federal authorities stepped in and the woman ducked out to Mexico, reportedly taking with her the one hundred thousand dollars she made from the venture.

In 1956, Murphy and Lee, discouraged with their losing proposition, decided to sell their interest in the Garden, with the permission and blessing of Sonny Whitney, who previously had sold some of his percentage to Mr. Lee. The transactions are too complicated for me to explain. The only clear fact is that when Frank Ehrhart bought it in 1956, it was deeply in the red.

The next time Whitney Tower—who had been a regular at the Garden during his uncle's ownership—went to Holiday House, he was amused to find most of the plates, towels, ashtrays and silverware had The Garden of Allah insignia. According to Mr. Ehrhart, Dudley also took as many of the appliances as were still in working order. I assumed he purloined these commodities to compensate for the lack of profit during his brief partnership in the Garden. But he bought many of the articles at the final auction before the wreckers took over.

I have known Mr. Ehrhart since the midforties. Until he bought the Garden, he was general manager, secretary, and treasurer for Charlie Morrison at the Mocambo. Frank, a genial everybody's-friend kind of man, decided to make the Garden into a paying proposition. And he might have if he had not sold 15 percent of the syndicate he set up to William Door, a maker of pornographic films who was later murdered.

Ehrhart tore down all the bungalows, making two units of each. Where there had been twenty-five there were now 50. He put a big entrance into the main house. He built a new restaurant, with an open kitchen all in brick. The rooms in the main house, so rarely used in previous years, now featured new paneling, new carpets, and new appliances. He threw out the Ping-Pong table. He put in new shrubs, cut down the barren banana trees, and installed seductive colored lights in the trees and bushes that surrounded the pool.

He also removed the small bar with its drab green paper and faded green stools, and enlarged the whole area with a big glass sliding window as wide as the pool. There were eighteen new bar stools, and the new wallpaper featured flamboyant candy stripes. The Garden of Allah is no more, but Frank's lavish bar still exists. It is at The Little Club in Beverly Hills. They bought it lock, stock, beer, and barrel when the Garden was demolished.

To lure the customers into the bar, Frank instituted the Clock Watchers Tower. You paid for your drink according to the clock in the bar. At 5:00 P.M. a drink cost fifty cents, at 6:00 P.M. sixty cents, at 7:00 P.M. seventy cents, up to seventy-five, the maximum. It worked. "In their best month, Murphy and Lee had taken in only $18,600. In July of my first year," Frank told me proudly, "we made $96,000. Of that, $42,800 came from the bar. I made a fun thing out of the Garden of Allah. In the afternoons I had a Starlets Pool Club. I gave the starlets membership cards which supposedly cost $300. Actually, they were free. I put a telephone box in the big oak tree in front of Errol Flynn's villa with a sign For Central Casting Only. It wasn't really a direct line, but as soon as a girl picked up the phone, the hotel operator immediately switched the call to Central Casting. The caller was not aware that she did not have a direct line."

Another of what Frank calls his "improvements" was paving the dirt parking lot on Crescent Heights and putting a fence around it. He dressed a girl in cowboy clothes, put her on a big white horse and stationed them both at the new entrance to the parking lot, to lead the cars inside. *"Life* took pictures," Ehrhart proudly remembers.

His proudest achievement at the Garden, the bar, signified its decline. From 4:00 P.M.—when the drinks were a cut-price bargain of forty cents—the bar was packed with bums and deviates, delighted with what Frank called The Happy Cocktail Hour.

Nat Benchley, who had found the Garden so bright, clean, and glamorous when he first went there in 1939, was shocked when he saw the changes during the regime of Mr. Ehrhart. "I didn't stay there. I was at the Chateau Marmont, but I went over to the Garden and took a lonesome sad walk around it, reviewing all those memories. There were drunks at the bar and no sign at all of the old joy."

"In the last years, The Garden of Allah was the kind of place

Pat Medina, the last resident of The Garden of Allah. *Springer/Bettmann Archive*

you'd go to alone," Whitney Tower remembers. "All the hookers in town were there. It had a steel combo band. The bloody noise was awful until three in the morning. It was the kind of place where you would not want to stay for more than one night. This was after Sonny Whitney had bailed out."

But Pat Medina, who became Mrs. Joseph Cotten while she lived there, loved her bungalow so much that when the time came to raze the place, she begged to buy the cottage that had been her home from 1951 until late August 1959.

"Sometimes you could hear the whisperings of all the great people who had stayed there," said Pat. "It was a wonderful place as far as I was concerned. When people heard I was living at The Garden of Allah, they said, 'How can you live in a place where there are robberies and prostitutes?' I'd tell them it was the safest place for a single wo-

Stravinsky. He lived next door to Pat Medina (Mrs. Joseph Cotten in the 1950s) at the Garden and swam with her. *Springer/Bettmann Archive*

Leopold Stokowski. The maestro found the Garden a convenient place to live and swim with his children from his marriage to Gloria Vanderbilt. *Springer/Bettmann Archive* man. The police had their eye on it constantly. If anything went wrong, you picked up the phone and the police were over in a minute. I was never afraid while I lived there."

Pat recalled some of the people who lived at the Garden during her time—Errol Flynn, Whitney Tower, and Grace Kelly. Stokowski played in the pool with his two small children. But mostly they were businessmen out for some fun. "Whitney came every year during the racing season. He wrote a column for *Sports Illustrated*. Bruce Cabot was always dropping in to see him. And Ethel Barrymore's son, Sammy Colt, used to hang around." Whitney attended an earlier party that lasted two days, given by Bogart for James Thurber. Pat remembers Grace Kelly sitting around the pool surrounded by the young bucks of the town. "Grace talked about the color of her nail polish and her lipstick, while the men hung on every word and were enthralled."

Everett Sloane, the fine character actor, stayed at the Garden during Mrs. Cotten's time. He committed suicide. Sammy Davis was in and out. Billy Eckstine, Harry Belafonte, Johnny Carson—who was in the bar when he was not in the pool—and Burgess Meredith were also there.

Hugh O'Brian, while he was trying to make it as an actor, washed windows and cars at the Garden. It was what he called exterior decorating. He could not afford to stay there but lived with several girls, including Linda Christian and Ruth Roman, who were under stock contract to various studios at what they called the House of the Seven Garbos nearby. At the House of Seven Garbos, Hugh slept on the pool table. At the Garden, while he washed windows, he could see Errol Flynn making time with the girls at the pool. "I wondered if I would ever be doing the same," he said. To take you out of your suspense, Hugh did.

Errol always had a stream of girls coming in and going from his villa. Except when his wife Pat Wymore came back. Pat had been staying on Errol's yacht, The Zaca, off the coast of Spain. When she returned to Hollywood, she decided they should buy a house with a swimming pool and a tennis court. As soon as she arrived, she had a tremendous fight with Errol that was heard all over the Garden. No matter how much they had renovated the place, the walls were still thin. After the fight, Pat again left Errol, and the girls swarmed back in.

She decided to divorce him. When the process servers came to the Garden with the papers, Beverly Aadland, fifteen when she met Errol,

Young Beverly Aadland whooped for joy when Pat Wymore served Errol Flynn with divorce papers at the Garden.

Wide World Photos

seventeen when he died, whooped for joy. Woodsey, as Errol called her, rushed outside and around the pool, wearing only a brief towel and doing an Indian war dance. She foresaw a bright future as Errol's next wife, but he died before he was free to marry her.

Frank Ehrhart remembers Errol at the Garden in 1956. "His villa was at the end, facing the pool, with the big oak tree in front of it. He used to sleep late. His secretary arrived at ten thirty to pick up the mail. At twelve thirty she usually emerged and placed a chaise longue by the pool. Also a bottle of champagne with two glasses on a table. At one o'clock Errol appeared, gorgeous in a blue blazer with white or gray pants and an ascot in place of a tie. The secretary had been ordered to place all the paraphernalia next to the prettiest girl around the pool. Flynn lay on his chaise and said to the girl, 'My child, do you mind if I sit next to you?' Mostly she said, 'Why, no.' Then he said, 'My child, will you have a glass of champagne?'

"They were peeping out of the villas and wondering how long it would take Errol to get the girl into his bungalow," said Frank. Which doesn't sound too different from the old days.

One Sunday morning, Errol called Ehrhart to his villa. "I have to go to New York," he told him. "Do you mind if my childen [from his marriage with Nora Eddington] use the pool while I'm gone?"

Frank asked, "Are you going back to do a play?"

"No," said Errol, "A television show."

"A series?" queried Frank.

"No, 'The $64,000 Question.' "

Frank and millions of others watched as Flynn pushed his total to thirty-two thousand dollars. Would he take a chance at the jackpot, the sixty-four thousand dollars? "No," he said, and bowed out with the thirty-two thousand dollars.

Back at The Garden of Allah, he had a drink with Frank Ehrhart in the new, gaudy bar. "Why didn't you go for the sixty-four thousand dollars?" Frank asked him.

Errol smiled broadly. "Frank," he explained, "they guaranteed me sixty-four thousand dollars. Thirty-two thousand dollars of it was under the table. It was all fixed. Although," he concluded modestly, "I knew all the answers." Errol may have been lying.

Shortly afterward, "The $64,000 Question" came to an end when the cheating on "21" was exposed.

Ehrhart had bought the Garden for $375,000. In 1957, he sold it to the final owner, Morris Markowitz, for $500,000. Markowitz sold it in 1959 to the Lytton Loan and Savings Company for $775,000. They bought it only to tear it down. The property, now owned by the Equitable Savings and Loan Association, is worth about 2 million dollars.

William Door, who had managed The Garden of Allah for the Ehrhart Syndicate, was forty-six when he was murdered in 1963. The Garden was no longer in existence, and he was living nearby on Fountain Avenue. His mistress, Mrs. Ernestine Ellen Criss, was found sprawled on her back, nude and suffocated with a pillow. Door's body, fully clothed, was face down, with his feet bound, on the dining room floor. He had been shot once in the back of his head and once in a hand. Two head-blows indicated that he had struggled with the killer. Police theorized he was the victim of a grudge killing by someone associated with him in the pornography racket. Robbery was ruled out as a motive as there was money in his wallet and in Mrs. Criss's purse. It was believed she was slain to prevent identification of the killer. Door was a six-footer weighing 230 pounds, and could have handled himself if the odds had been even.

Door had had a police record before working at the Garden. In 1952 he was convicted in Los Angeles of possessing lewd literature, and paid a fine of one hundred dollars. In 1957 he was convicted of income tax evasion—at the time Ehrhart was selling the Garden—and was fined twenty-five hundred dollars. The indictment identified him as "the proprietor" of The Garden of Allah, when in fact he had only been the manager, with a small percentage of stock. His estate was valued at three hundred thousand dollars. He left his FAX Record Company to his secretary, Mrs. Myrtle Swanson. Mrs. Ernestine Criss was bequeated one thousand dollars and the remainder left in trust for his six-year-old son. Neither of the killings was solved.

But this was still to come. When he joined Ehrhart's syndicate at the Garden, Door claimed to have been a football player, but he never was. Harrison Carroll, the columnist for the Los Angeles *Herald* knew a bad egg when he smelled one and warned Ehrhart, "You've got a rough partner." "After we broke up," Frank told me, "I never spoke to Door again."

When Ehrhart sold the Garden in 1957, he kept some of the old registers with the famous names inscribed through the decades. A year ago, his home in Beverly Hills was robbed, and the registers of The Garden of Allah were taken.

A few years before its demise, a former resident, Pamela Moore, wrote a book, *Chocolates for Breakfast*. It was the story of an adolescent girl who lived at The Garden of Allah with her actress mother in the early 1950s.

"The Garden shouted its identity to the passersby on Sunset Boulevard," she wrote, "by a glaring, blinking, shifting neon sign of generally neurotic behavior. The palm trees, of course, were lit by floodlights. The general impression given to the uninitiated by the sign and the bizarre name was one of a particularly brazen house of ill repute, but the prices of the villas were equal to those of the bungalows of the more sedate Beverly Hills, and any behavior of ill repute indulged in by the inhabitants was generally not on a professional basis."

This was only partly true, according to Pat Medina. When Pat rented an extra bedroom for her mother, who did not want the same room as her father, who snored, the noises of professional as well as amateur lovemaking from the surrounding bungalows kept Pat's mother awake. "It was less noisy with your father," she told Pat, and moved back.

"When I told Morris Markowitz that I wanted to buy my bungalow —it was the best one there—he said, 'It's too late. I've got the Cleveland Wrecking Company coming tomorrow.'"

Pat called the company in Los Angeles. "I told them I had a problem. I didn't have a place to take the bungalow. Perhaps to the beach. But I did not have a lot. There was another problem: to get it under the Sepulveda Bridge. The next day a lovely young man, William Fenning, came from the Cleveland Wrecking Company to see if we could figure out the problem. As we talked, every bungalow, all of them now empty of furniture, including mine, was being bulldozed to the ground. I realized there was nothing I could do, so I collected my clothes, put them over my arm, and walked across Sunset Boulevard to the Chateau Marmont."

"The last owner," Ehrhart told me, "could not decide what to do with the place, renovate or sell." When Markowitz's financial backer died, the decision was made for him: the widow, Mrs. Beatrice Rosenus, decided to accept the offer from Lytton.

The first news story that The Garden of Allah was to be sold by

Markowitz and Mrs. Rosenus appeared in the Los Angeles *Times,* April 12, 1959. In June, the same newspaper mourned, "The Garden of Allah, once an oasis, awaits Kismet. The day of its grandeur was awesome, but it will be razed in September to make way for Lytton."

Time joined the requiem, quoting one of the maids, "It's all run-down now, but it's still got a lot of what you'd call dignity. The same people kept coming back. Oh, they'd go away complaining, but they came back because there was nowhere else like this. Now where will they go?"

Time mentioned the last big-time spender, a drunk from Kansas City who made his fortune on kiddie horror films. "For months in 1958, all drinks served in the Garden were put on his bill. Eventually he broke the record set by Benchley and his pals but it was not enough to keep the place going."

Jerry Wald started filming *Beloved Infidel,* my autobiography, in June of 1959. The Garden of Allah was essential to the film because of its important association with Scott, played by Gregory Peck, and me, played by Deborah Kerr. Jerry would still be making the film in August when the Garden was due for extinction. He had a replica built on the back lot at 20th Century-Fox, complete with the pool and the bungalows and Benchley, played by Eddie Albert, cavorting around with a glass in his hand.

The Garden of Allah did not go out with a whimper. It had a last bang. It had opened with a party, and it ended with one. It was fitting. It had been a nonstop party from start to finish.

Mr. Markowitz asked his guests—three hundred and fifty were invited but about one thousand came—to impersonate the people who had been glamorous stars when the Garden had opened in 1927. The host was dressed as C. B. De Mille. His wife was Nazimova. Nazimova's *Salome* was shown to the assembled Valentinos, Clara Bows, Lon Chaneys, Chaplins, Coogans, and Mae Wests. Doodles Weaver was Dracula, his wife Gilda Gray. They drove to the Garden in a 1935 La Salle. Ben Lessey of vaudeville fame looked almost authentic as Ben Turpin until he became weary crossing his eyes. The lawyer Arthur Crowley and Jana Lund were dressed as Mickey and Minnie Mouse. Jack Lemmon danced with his wife, Jack as (?) and his wife as (?).

Only Francis X. Bushman and his wife, Iva, who had been at the original party, ignored the request to come in old-time star fancy dress.

The last party. August 1959. Old-time star Francis X. Bushman, who attended the first party in January 1924, with his wife. *Allan Grant,* Life *magazine © Time Inc.*

Bushman was seventy-six and he sighed, "I only wish there were more of us here." He and Betty Blythe were the sole celebrities from the Nazimova era.

Bart Lytton was dressed as a devil with a 5 percent interest sign on his back. William Fenning of the wrecking company drove into the parking lot at the wheel of a thirty-foot crane, symbolic of the impending destruction. Most of the other guests were shapely starlets, young male feature players, and middle-aged executives, along with the pretty hookers who regretted the death of their profitable playground.

I heard a man say to a group of girls, "You all look like prosti-

The last party. The end. A starlet is dunked for old time's sake while "Valentino," "Will Rogers," "Harold Lloyd," and "Clara Bow" look on. *Allan Grant,* Life *magazine © Time Inc.*

tutes the way you are dressed and made up." He thought this was their impersonation for the costume party. One of the young women replied, "We dress and make up this way because we *are,* but the yellow pages don't list us."

Someone tried to push Joi Lansing into the pool for old times' sake. An announcement was made that Tom Mix and Buck Jones were buying each other drinks at the bar, but it received only a hollow laugh. Most of the starlets were scantily dressed, hoping to catch a producer's roving eye.

The photographer who was hired to make a lasting record of the demise of the Garden was paid in advance and absconded with the money. Fortunately *Life* magazine sent a man with a camera.

By midnight, the pool was full of empty liquor bottles. The party had cost Markowitz and Lytton Loan and Savings Company seventy-five hundred dollars.

The day after the party, the fixtures and furnishings of the Garden were sold at public auction. And again, Errol Flynn's beds were the most sought after. "Did Errol really sleep here?" they asked, sitting or lying on the mattresses. Some of the former residents were among the bidders. A dozen policemen were present to prevent pilfering.

Today, where the pool and the villas stood so securely, where Benchley laughed and Scott weaved along the narrow paths, where the bamboo and banana trees hung in dusty decay, there is not even a whisper to remind you of the old days.

But you can still see what the stucco and the stones of The Garden of Allah looked like. There is a model on a stand in a glass case on the grass under the trees. The hippies rest there in the evening after strolling along the Strip. They barely glance at the replica of a little world that has vanished.

index